Through the Shatter, *She Became*

My wounds wrote this story.
Her strength finished it.

Andrea Panteli

HEMBURY
—BOOKS—

About the author

Andrea Panteli lives in Sydney, Australia, where family and faith are the centre of her life. Born in Padstow Heights to parents from Cyprus, she grew up closely connected to her relatives and cultural traditions, ties deepened by the day-to-day realities of her mother's long complex health journey. In a childhood marked by sterile hospital corridors and cold towel presses, Andrea learned about responsibility, resilience and the quiet strength it takes to persevere when life is uncertain.

Opening a fitness studio was never part of the plan yet it became a turning point – one that reshaped her confidence and sense of purpose. Now, Andrea is committed to supporting other women to become physically and emotionally strong. Following her mother's passing in 2024, Andrea has discovered a deeper strength within herself - one that allows her to honour her mother's legacy by choosing love, peace, and faith.

Being a wife and a mother shapes Andrea's perspective and inspires her to prioritise presence, compassion and steadiness. When she isn't writing or working, she is usually found on the sidelines of a soccer field, proudly cheering on her two boys. Even after years of watching, she still doesn't know the rules – but she is, without question, their biggest supporter.

Through the Shatter, She Became is Andrea's debut memoir.

A catalogue record for this book is available from the National Library of Australia

To my mum

You are the heartbeat of this story. Through every trial,
you stood tall with a strength that carried us all.
Your resilience gave me hope when mine was gone.
This book is because you showed me how to
keep going, even when it hurt.

To my family

Your love was my safe place. In the silence, in the chaos,
and in every small moment, you held me up.
Thank you for never letting me fall.

And to God

For being my light in the dark, my peace in the storm,
and my reason to believe that no struggle is ever wasted.
This is all for you. You are my inspiration, my strength,
and my saving grace.

Contents

CHAPTER 1

From the beginning

My childhood feels like a haze, a fog that lingers at the edges of my memory. Sometimes I wonder if that fog is a kind of shield protecting me from my past. The fragments that slip through are like open doorways, drawing me back into the same haunting question that's followed me for years: Why? How does a child go from basking in the warmth of the most radiant mother to watching her life crumble before their eyes, and then suddenly becoming her caretaker? My sister and I, still so young, became our mother's keepers before we even understood what that meant. How does that shift happen so fast?

Thirty-nine years later, those moments still grip me with the same force. The same questions whisper through me like echoes I can't silence. Why my mum? Why me? Why us?

I was only four. My sister, D, was eight. Our mother was thirty-two. She was vibrant, beautiful, and full of life when everything began to change. One moment she was laughing, her energy lighting up the house like sunlight streaming through open windows, and the next she was gone somewhere unreachable, punched down by her first stroke. She was in her prime, overflowing with love and possibility. It seemed impossible that her bright future could disappear in an instant. Yet it did.

Mum was pregnant with baby number three, a brother I was thrilled to meet, so I'm told. But there was a strange warning: her body couldn't carry boys. I couldn't grasp it then, and it still puzzles me. How could a body choose one sex over another? Her older sister, we later learned, faced the opposite problem; she couldn't carry girls. Pregnancy, to my childish mind, was a mystery wrapped in several whispers.

Mum shared her story again and again, her voice steady even though the pain still lived inside her. It was on a quiet Saturday afternoon during her first trimester in 1986. We had gone to the airport to see off my dad's brother, who was travelling overseas. The car ride home was silent. Mum's hands stayed wrapped around the seatbelt on the passenger side, gripping it so tightly her knuckles turned white. Her face grew pale, her breathing uneven. By the time we reached our home in Padstow Heights, she was already feeling sick. Dad later explained that her body had gone into shock. The left side had started to grow numb, as if a stroke or seizure was slowly pulling her away. She had miscarried, and toxins had spread through her bloodstream, reaching her brain. That moment became her first stroke.

Going from dreaming of a new baby to clinging to life was unimaginable. Yet the truth was even worse: medical negligence had caused it. The obstetrician had brushed off her concerns with a curt, 'You're pregnant, G. That's just morning sickness.' But what followed was nothing short of a nightmare.

The doctors, who were a married couple, soon faced intense scrutiny. Then came the shocking twist: both were later found dead.

His death was ruled a suicide; hers remained a mystery. The news chilled me to my core; it was like a thriller too dark to be real.

Their clinic still lingers in my memory; the roaming dogs, the strange warmth of the place, and the two of them – an elderly pair with white hair and thick glasses, he always in crisp suits, she with bold lipstick and a messy updo. They had brought my sister and me into the world, yet their negligence had nearly taken our mother from it.

My parents never sought revenge. They wanted only to survive; to focus on Mum's fight for life rather than on blame. Looking back, I realise that choice shaped my understanding of love.

♥

Large swathes of my childhood are blank, like a film reel with whole scenes cut away. Maybe my mind is protecting me from the pain. The sharpest memories, the hospital corridors and the cold towels pressed to Mum's necklace, are the ones that left the deepest marks.

We were passed from aunt to aunt, never knowing which bed we'd sleep in. Dad was a ghost, always at work or at the hospital. I clashed with cousins, envying their mothers and their sense of normalcy. Even now, the smell of grilled cheese toast for breakfast makes my stomach turn. We were never truly neglected. Food, shelter, love – our family's fragile network held us together, giving Dad the space and peace to care for Mum.

The stroke left Mum with left-side paralysis. This was the beginning of her battle. But faith became her anchor. She could've cursed God or the doctors, but she didn't. Instead, she held on to her belief that God had kept her alive for her girls, and that conviction gave her the strength to fight.

I watched her push through the pain at Royal South Sydney Hospital in Zetland, gripping resistance bands with her face tight with determination, then easing into the hydrotherapy pool where the sharp scent of chlorine filled the air. Each movement was small, but it meant everything. Slowly, she grew stronger. She regained the use of her left hand. She walked again, unaided. And in one of her proudest moments, she passed her driving test. That licence wasn't just a card; it was her freedom, her independence reclaimed. For a woman who hated relying on anyone it was nothing short of victory. Our mum was our miracle, our fighter.

Before the stroke stole so much, Mum was a vibrant force, a renowned dress designer in Sydney's Greek community. Everyone loved her legendary wedding gowns. She'd left school at fifteen, defying Pappou's wish for her to become a hairdresser. At college, she topped her class, then worked at Wella Fabrics, and even modelled on runways. Check her out: she's glamorous and confident, with short dark hair styled weekly at Richard's on Oxford Street. Her make-up was flawless, her outfits impeccable, always with matching shoes and handbag. She dressed D and me in identical Fredelle outfits, tiny gold studs glinting in our ears, D with her long ponytail and me with my boyish crop. *Ugh, why, Mum?*

By 1987, after her recovery, Mum dived back into life – work, family, and travel. Our days were filled with laughter, Cabbage Patch dolls, Glow Worms, and love. One afternoon while we were driving home, I sat in the back seat with the seatbelt practically choking me across the neck. Out of nowhere, some random man in the next car waved at my mum, signalling for her to roll down her window. Thinking maybe she had a flat tyre, she cracked the window open. Instead, he shouted, 'Hey lady, did you know your number plate is 666?'

She froze for a second, not expecting such a comment.

'Yes, I do,' she answered.

'Do you know that's the devil's number?' he pushed.

'Yeah, maybe it is,' she said, 'but it's been lucky for me.'

He stared at her, his face cold, and said, 'Not anymore.' Startled and pale, she swiftly rolled up her window. She drove off cautiously, uneasy yet focused. She made the sign of the cross and kept driving. But his words lingered, casting a faint shadow that never quite lifted.

Not long after that car incident, my Thio C (Thio means 'uncle' in Greek) noticed Mum was wearing a lot of peach-coloured blush on her cheeks. She loved make-up, but this time it was a little too much. When he asked about it, Mum tried to dismiss it. The truth was hard. She had a deep-blue vein running along the side of her face, and it had become quite prominent. She was trying to hide it, hoping no one would notice. But the vein only grew darker and more obvious, and around that same time, she started feeling unwell again. She went back and forth to her specialist and the tests revealed the kind of news that knocks the air out of a person – she had three aneurysms ready to explode and needed surgery immediately. Like, Wtf.

She didn't want to believe it. She searched for another answer, another doctor, and a different outcome. But every time she sat across from a new specialist, the words were the same: 'We need to operate. And soon.'

She even travelled all the way to Israel because she was desperate for help. She sat across from one specialist with my aunt beside her, and he had the nerve to say, 'Do you have money, madam? If so, I will send you to America.' It sounds even more shocking when my dad retells it in Greek, but the meaning is the same: the specialist cared more about the money than the patient, someone who had crossed an ocean searching for medical treatment.

One afternoon in August 1988 she picked up my sister and me from God knows where, probably school. We were heading home. She didn't look well. She didn't feel well. She drove slowly, doing everything she could to get us home safely. We lived, far from her family. She felt uneasy, like something was terribly wrong. When we turned into our street, Berima Avenue, she pulled up outside one of my dad's cousins' houses, just up the road. She beeped the horn a few times. When they came out, she asked them to follow her home because she felt unwell, and she asked them to call my dad and her sister-in-law, who lived not too far away. This was before mobile phones were everywhere.

She pulled slowly into our steep driveway. D and I opened the car doors, slammed them shut, and chased each other up the stairs like little kids do, huffing and puffing, yelling and laughing. We kept shouting, 'I'm going to win!' and 'No, I'm going to win!'

But down below, Mum stood still on the bottom step, silent, looking up at us. I remember her gripping the rail like she needed it to hold her together. She was trembling, sweat gathering across her forehead. She took one step at a time, each one heavier than the last. Her breathing grew louder and slower, as if every inhale demanded all her strength.

I can't remember if we ran back down to her or if we just stood there, watching. Everything felt quiet. Too quiet. It was a slow-motion scene unfolding right in front of us. When she finally reached the top step, she collapsed at our feet.

Did we scream? Did we cry? I don't know. It all turned into a blur. In a flash, people were everywhere. Noise filled the air; sharp, white noise mixed with murmurs and hushed voices. I still don't know how the neighbours knew to come outside, but they surrounded her within seconds.

We stood there, frozen like statues, watching people run in and out of the house. The front door kept opening and closing. Someone put a pillow under her head to make her comfortable. Cold water splashed against her face. Damp towels were pressed around her neck. She was vomiting. I remember that clearly.

Was it minutes? Was it within the hour? Time didn't make sense. Everything felt like it was happening all at once and yet far away.

The muffled sound in my ears slowly faded and sirens began to ring. They grew closer and closer, louder and louder, until the ambulance pulled into our driveway. Doors opened and slammed shut. Moments later, the paramedics rushed up the stairs.

Were they there for a while? I couldn't tell you. One moment they were checking her pulse; the next, they were taking her away. We just stood there, watching. Standing on the top step, looking down, we watched the ambulance drive off with our mum in the back.

Who was in the ambulance with her? Surely, she wasn't alone. Who did we stay with? Where did we go? Where did we end up? I have no memory of any of that. All I know is that our nightmare was happening all over again.

We were placed back in the care of family members while Mum was being prepared for surgery. I wondered if someone had created a care roster for us, or if everyone was just doing what they could.

The risks of this upcoming surgery were astronomical. She was given a five per cent chance of survival, with the possibility of being left paralysed again. After many discussions, Mum felt she had no choice but to take a leap of faith and do everything in her power to survive. She put her faith in God. She did it for us, her two little girls. She signed the consent forms and placed her life in the surgeon's hands.

I was told many years later that Mum was so distraught about her decision and the possible outcome of the surgery that she openly asked for a divorce, just so my dad could go on with his life without the burden of caring for a sick wife. She was even prepared to hand us over and walk away so our lives wouldn't be disrupted by her medical condition. This woman, practically on her deathbed, was so selfless.

My dad, completely shocked by such a thought, wouldn't even consider it. Anyone who knows him understands that he is a selfless man, full of love and support, a true family man. No wonder they found each other.

August 14th. Surgery day. It was also the eve of a very special day in the Orthodox Faith: the Dormition of Our Theotokos, the Falling Asleep and Assumption of the Virgin Mary. Of all days, Mum was scheduled for her surgery on one of the holiest days. What were the odds? It felt like a sign. Our Virgin Mary was going to look over her.

Surgery took 16 long hours, all under the hands of the incredible Professor I.J. How could anyone forget that name? The name of the man who saved my mum's life. In the operating theatre, they expected to do three clippings once they'd opened her up. To everyone's surprise, they ended up performing a total of eight. It was a complete catastrophe.

Dad told me not long ago that this surgery was so uncommon and so new to medical science that during the procedure the professor was on a conference call with his senior specialists in China, who were remotely assisting him through each step. Thinking about it now, that is totally insane.

She remained in a vegetative state after the operation. She was in the Intensive Care Unit. Man, I hate those words; they still give me chills. She stayed in the ICU for months. Her brain was severely inflamed, and they couldn't put her cranium back during the first surgery. She had to stay without it until the swelling went down and it was finally safe to operate and reattach it.

Our aunts often took my sister and me to visit her, but we were so young that I didn't fully understand what was happening. We played in the corridors, running around and making noise, thinking we were on some kind of adventure. How were we supposed to know? To be honest, the woman lying on the bed was, in my young eyes, just a sick woman. I didn't truly know who my mum was.

After being passed around from aunt to aunt, I eventually started calling one of my mum's sisters Mummy S, because I stayed with her for a long time. In my eyes, she became the mother figure I desperately needed. But my cousin T, her eldest son, hated it. He got jealous every time I said Mummy S. He would shout at me, 'She is NOT your mum; she is MY mum!' That never stopped me, though. Maybe I was a little shit-stirrer pushing boundaries, but even now he still says I've always stood my ground and never backed down. 'Feisty and rebellious Andrea, always backchatting.' Sometimes I look at my own kids and wonder where they get it from. Any chance he got, he would try to torture me, not in a cruel way, but playfully in his world. To me back then it felt horrible. I laugh about it now. I guess it was his way of marking his territory, being a typical teenager.

Foxy was their tiny Pomeranian-Chihuahua, and I was bloody petrified of that fluffy little thing on four legs. There was absolutely nothing scary about its yapping, yet I was shit-scared. The rule was that Foxy stayed outside when I was in the house, but not when T was around. Being the territorial big cousin he was, he would open the back door and 'accidentally' let Foxy in. I'd scream, climb onto the couch then up onto the window ledge, refusing to come down until someone dragged the dog back outside. Foxy would be yapping, I'd be screaming and crying, and T would be on the floor, laughing until he got in trouble. HA! Who's the real boss now?

Despite all of this, I formed real, deep bonds with my cousins. The bond I now have with T is unbreakable. He calls me *Mikri*, which means 'little one.' To him, I was – and still am – his little sister. I never had an older brother, but he stepped into that role and became my protector as I grew up. It's strange how a tragic event can pull a family together, but that's exactly what happened with us.

There are some funny moments I've captured and still laugh about, but there are also many horrible and heart-wrenching memories I don't ever want to relive. I remember being taken to the hospital to visit Mum, and I would scream, 'That's not my mum; my mum is dead.' My godmother smacked me gently on the hand and said, 'Don't ever say that again.'

Writing all this down, feeling it all over again, breaks my heart into pieces.

There was a day that still sits heavy on my chest. In a moment filled with both faith and desperation, my godmother clung to Mum's bedside, her tears falling like rain as she begged God to bring her sister back to us. She dug through her bag with shaking hands and pulled out the Holy Water from church, something she had been holding onto like a lifeline. She poured it gently over Mum's lips, her hands trembling, as if she were pouring her last hope. The nurses rushed in, alarm written all over their faces, but my godmother's pleas didn't stop. Her voice broke as she begged them, 'Please, just let God work His miracle.' And then, the impossible happened.

The next day Mum's eyes, once closed in silence, slowly flickered open, glowing like small beacons of hope in all our darkness. The nurses were stunned. Our grief turned into gasps of joy. We had witnessed a miracle that stayed with us forever.

Mum had awakened. Her fight for life had begun.

❤

We lived in Padstow Heights in a monstrosity of a house. Dad decided to sell it and move closer to Mum's family. Mum needed a single-storey home and wanted to be near the hospital.

We changed schools and began a new life. I started at St Joseph's in Rosebery in Year 1. Mrs G was my teacher. I remember her and her smile. Her favourite saying was, 'She goes, she goes, she just goes'. And of course, those spelling words. I recited the word 'because,' B-E-C-A-U-S-E, and to this day, whenever I write it I recite it like a song.

Oh, and I can't forget Miss O, a stylish woman with short blonde hair. She was my teacher in Year 3. I remember her denim knee-length skirt and bright pink lipstick. When she was angry, boy, did we know it! She would slam that classroom door, BOOM!

In the summer months when it was hot and steamy, the teachers would let us play in the playground. They would open the hose and we would run through it to cool off at the end of the day.

We moved in with Yiayia and Pappou (grandmother and grandfather) in Marrickville for a little while. I could say months or years, but honestly, it didn't matter; we had no real sense of time. Meanwhile, Dad was busy renovating our new home to make it comfortable for Mum. I have no idea where he got his decorating skills, but why he thought painting the walls peachy pink was a good idea is beyond me. Apparently, it was 'very fashionable.' I beg to differ.

Back in Marrickville, Yiayia became my personal hairdresser every morning before school. Oh, the trauma! Oh, the glamour! She would slick back my hair, create a precise side part and secure it in a low bun with hairpins – not an elastic because, apparently, that was just not classy. The result? I was basically a mini version of her. I love you, Yiayia, but you scared me for life. To this day, I have Side Part PTSD; the mere mention of it sends shivers down my spine. But, hey, at least I learned to rock a mean bun. Thanks, Yiayia...I think.

The trauma of Yiayia's side part still lingers. At my cousin's wedding in 2022, I was a matron of honour. When the hairdresser finished styling my hair, I froze. One glance in the mirror and I panicked. 'Please, pull it out! Go centre! No side part!' I begged, my anxiety spiking. The stylist looked taken aback, but I couldn't shake it. It's crazy how the memory of Yiayia's signature side part still gives me conniptions, making me ultra-particular about my hairstyle. Those childhood mornings left a mark, a testament to the lasting power of love, family...and hair trauma.

One cherished memory that stands out is learning the Greek Orthodox Creed, *To Pistevo*, in Year 5. My yiayia, a devout woman, saw this as an opportunity to pass on our faith and heritage. Every night she would sit with me, patiently guiding me through the prayer. Her dedication was unwavering, and I can still feel her love and enthusiasm. Even today, I know *To Pistevo* by heart, and reciting it brings a warm glow to my heart. It is a beautiful reminder that, even amidst difficult experiences, moments of love, connection, and tradition shape who we are. My yiayia's legacy lives on through this prayer and I am grateful for the time we shared, learning it together.

I also have a vivid flashback to smoke and something catching fire, but what the hell was it? It was me! It was a cold winter's day and I had sat too close to the heater while my yiayia watched *Wheel of Fortune*. Somehow, even without speaking a word of English, she followed the show like a pro. Suddenly I smelt something burning and yelled, thinking Yiayia was cooking in the kitchen. But it wasn't the food; it was me! My jumper was melting as I huddled near the heater to keep warm. What a moron!

When we finally settled into our renovated home, my sister and I took on the responsibilities of managing the household. For a while we had a live-in carer to support us, but when that arrangement didn't work out we were thrust into a new reality. Overnight, we had to learn how to cook, clean, and care for Mum, navigating the challenges of caregiving alongside domestic duties. It was a steep learning curve, but we rallied together, determined to create a loving and supportive home for our family.

Mum's paralysis left her with limited movement in her arm, no function in her hand, and a limp in her step. Every morning, my sister and I would argue over who was going to dress her. 'No, it's your turn.' 'I did it yesterday.' 'You do it today, and I'll do it for the rest of the week.' 'Hurry up, Mum, we have to get ready for school.'

This was our life every day, every morning...for years. We were her carers. We bathed her, dressed her, and gave her medication. We were her people. Despite losing her independence, she remained our mum, a strong, remarkable woman. Every Saturday we took her across the road to her weekly hairdressing appointment, a tradition she insisted on keeping. She prepared home-cooked meals every night and made sure to teach us how to cook as well.

To help her in the kitchen, Dad bought her a suction chopping board with special spikes on one side to hold vegetables steady while they were chopped. Thanks to that, we always had fresh, crisp salads for dinner. I admired her when she prepared her famous chicken pastitsio, a Greek chicken pasta bake, but on a whole other level. The taste is pure magic. After years of watching her make it, I inherited her skill without even realising it. Every time I make it now, I feel closer to her, and I am reminded of how extraordinary she truly was.

To stand on her feet, boil the pasta, shred the chicken, chop the tomatoes, parsley, and onions, make the sauce, and prepare the bechamel…I get tired doing all that with two functioning hands. How the heck did this woman do it? She was a freaking superstar. With only one hand functioning, Mum would have everything ready when we came home from school. We'd be greeted by the smell of a hot ham-and-cheese omelette, garnished with parsley, of course. That's my mum! She made the most delicious schnitzel from scratch, and those hot chips…to die for! But oh, the oil splatter everywhere! And of course, we had no choice but to clean it up afterwards. Thanks, Mum.

Can you believe she would wake up at 5.30 or 6 every morning just to make Dad's breakfast before he went to work? I rave about her all the time, calling her inspirational, courageous, and a fighter, because she absolutely deserves those words next to her name.

If we didn't do the housework on Saturday morning, we'd get in trouble. Mum, the ultimate boss lady of the house, would punish us by not allowing us to attend Greek dancing, the social highlight of our week. We looked forward to going to the Cyprus Community Club in Stanmore for a few hours. We'd dance, hang out with friends, and even walk up to 7-Eleven to grab a Coke Slurpee after class.

Meanwhile, Mum would sit upstairs in the cafeteria with the other mums, gasbagging over her usual cappuccino and her favourite piece of cake, *Kalo Prama*. If you translate it, it means 'The Good Thing,' but personally, I think it's gross. It's some semolina syrup cake with almonds. Yuk! Give me a *Galatoboureko*, Greek custard cake, any day.

Our mother was a strict disciplinarian who never let us get away with anything. She had migrated to Australia from Cyprus at the age of eleven and spoke English fluently, unlike my father, whose English remained limited. We couldn't pull the wool over her eyes. Highly intelligent and always one step ahead of us, she caught us every time we tried any mischief.

My sister, being cheeky, once got into trouble for something trivial and had the audacity to tease her, saying, 'Ha-ha, you can't catch me,' assuming Mum wouldn't bother chasing her as she slow-walked away. We were just innocent kids playing. But let me be clear, Mum caught her!

Watching our mother as we grew up revealed her resilience. She showed it not only to us, her family, but also to her colleagues at work. Her determination to persevere was clear in everything she did. Driven by her love for us, she refused to give up. Instead, she drew strength from her unshakable faith in God, trusting that He would protect our family and keep my sister and me safe.

Miracle stories are abundant, but when one unfolds in your own family, the impact is profound. One moment that still gives me goosebumps is when Mum woke up from her 16-hour surgery. Her first words, laced with an otherworldly serenity, left an indelible mark on my soul. She recounted a vivid experience: 'I climbed the stairs, knocked on the door three times, and it slightly opened. A radiant light appeared, and a deep, gentle voice from behind the door whispered, "Go back, it's not your time." Then the door closed.'

Call it a miracle, a testament to faith, or simply an unexplainable phenomenon; whatever the label, it's a reminder that life holds more than what we can see or touch.

Looking back and reliving these events has shattered my world. Now, as an adult in my forties, I feel as though I was robbed of a childhood. I was robbed of having sweet, innocent memories, the kind of memories filled with sunshine, fun, rainbows and butterflies that childhood is meant to hold. I don't have those. What I have are memories of hospitals, and the colour cold grey constantly appearing in my mind.

I never had the chance to experience simple, everyday moments with Mum. I never got to have her take me to school and feel the joy of being picked up, imagining her at the school gate with her big smile and arms wide open, waiting for me to run into her warm embrace. I wanted to play with her, do girly things together, have her style my hair for school, and tell her my deepest secrets.

What hurts the most is that I didn't really know Mum before she got sick. I don't truly know what kind of person she was. I can only piece together her essence from what others tell me. Don't get me wrong, I am forever grateful that Mum was by my side, because she could have died all those years ago, leaving only bitter memories. But the hard truth is I never got to experience a true mother–daughter relationship, and this stings in a way I cannot fully explain.

Growing up, I received something unique to replace those missing childhood memories. I had the privilege of knowing and respecting a different version of her. I was raised by a powerful, resilient woman, a fighter, an inspiration. This incredible woman taught me far more than love; she shaped me into the person I am today. She is the reason I am the way I am, simply because I don't know how to be any other way.

People often say I am a carbon copy of her – looks, character, the whole lot – though not her height. Mum was tall, and I'm, well…a short one. I share her stubbornness when we are passionate about something. I take on other people's problems as if they were my own and extend my hand to help anyone in need. I am my mum's daughter.

I wear my heart on my sleeve and rarely ask for help, but taking care of my loved ones is always at the top of my list. She has shown me patience, and because of her, I have become empathetic, sympathetic, and deeply caring. All of this is a reflection of the woman who raised me.

Seeing her faith in God has brought me so much closer to Him. I don't know any other way to live; this is all I know: love and survive. Deep down, I know my Mum loved us so fiercely that she fought to live for us. That, to me, is the ultimate meaning of the word *love*.

As a mother now, despite the immense love I have for my own children and my willingness to go to great lengths to protect them and ensure their safety, I often wonder if I'm a good parent. My unconventional upbringing leaves me unsure if I'm doing things right. Not having a traditional parental example to follow scares me, and I fear I might fail them in the future.

Now, I fully understand her fight and her choice to survive. This is why I choose to survive too. I choose family. I choose love. And I will continue to fight for my own path.

CHAPTER 2

Navigating youth

I n a flash, I completed primary school. The memories are faint now, yet the foundation was laid for a long journey of growth and discovery. Maybe those years were the hardest I ever lived through, which could be why I've subconsciously erased so much of them without ever meaning to from my memory.

I don't remember much of the good times or bad times, only a handful of moments that sit in place, leaving me oddly neutral. I can still hear the squeak of sneakers against the hot asphalt of the playground and see my sister D racing me to the swings, her ponytail snapping in the air as she outruns me. And I can feel that quiet ache deep inside, the one that came from wanting a hug from Dad that never came. A small, wordless void I couldn't name back then.

In our Greek household, my sister and I were encouraged to learn our mother tongue; it was a central part of our upbringing. I'm profoundly grateful for that support. I can speak, read, and write Greek with ease. How valuable is being bilingual? Extremely cool and highly useful. I certainly used it to my advantage while my kids were growing up. Whenever they acted up (which was often) and wanted to argue their case with their dad, we'd switch to Greek and discuss it between ourselves. Most of the time they had no idea what we were saying. Until, of course, they did.

Funny thing, though: as fluent as I am in Greek, the minute I land in Cyprus, my tongue seems to tie itself in knots. I sound like a foreigner for the first few days, and it takes about a week for my speech to loosen up. Stage fright, perhaps. Once I get going, though, especially with my heavy Cypriot dialect, hang the fuck on; I sound as if I've stepped straight out of the ghetto, a.k.a. the village. I absolutely love it now. Growing up, it was a different story.

D and I went to Greek school every Tuesday and Thursday after school, though we did it reluctantly. Kill me now! Watching grass grow would've been more entertaining. For a while, we even had Saturday school for three hours – yes, three freaking long-ass hours.

Still, we made the most of it, embracing the experience and finding moments of joy along the way. As much as we hated going, we always found ways to enjoy the ride. In every class there was at least one kid who acted up, and there were always consequences.

One extremely cold and gloomy afternoon, the rain was pouring down. Not a gentle pitter-patter, but a torrential downpour, blinding sheets of water that made everything outside look grey and miserable. Of all days, my sister decided this was her moment to muck up in class. She must've had a brain snap. The chalk dust stung my nose as I sat there, frozen, watching her. Why? Such an idiot.

Back in the early 1990s, strict discipline was normal. Being sent out of class, getting a ruler across the knuckles, even an ear-pull – none of it raised eyebrows. Can you imagine if a teacher did that now?

D misbehaved one day and our short-tempered, unimpressed teacher marched over, grabbed her by the ear, and hauled her out. Let me clarify one thing before anyone jumps up and down: no one got hurt. May I also add, among us Greeks, we have a Greek custom: if it's your Name Day (the day we celebrate your patron saint), or if you're getting in trouble, you might get your ear pulled.

Well, it wasn't her Name Day; D was in deep shit. Still, as the younger sister, I found it awful to watch. We always fought with each other, but I hated seeing her shamed. I've always been against any kind of violence. What could I do to help her? I sat at my desk, eyes glued to the door, not hearing a word of the lesson and already plotting how to sneak her back in. She was outside in the freezing rain while we sat warm inside, and I knew I'd cop the aftermath if she got sick. She was such a sook. I had to do something. One hundred per cent.

I took it upon myself (what a little sister, right?). I crept to the door and eased it open, praying it wouldn't squeak. D slipped back in like a thief and slid into her seat, flashing a cheeky grin that made my risk worth it. When our teacher turned from the chalkboard, there she was, still wearing that grin.

He lost his marbles. We Greeks – our temper can go from zero to a million in a millisecond. With his loud, screechy voice, he yelled out, 'Who opened the door?'

Of course, being me, I stood up innocently and confidently, then answered, 'I did.' I didn't think I'd done anything wrong...Or had I?

To make matters worse, everyone in the class burst into laughter. That must have pushed him over the edge, because after that I got into so much trouble. As punishment, I had to write 'I will not open the door' a thousand times. Oh my gosh, my poor little hand, though I can laugh about it now. My ear was pulled, my knuckles were smacked, and I was thrown outside for the rest of the class. I stood there in the freezing cold, shivering with a throbbing ear and an aching hand. To be fair, I didn't really mind being sent outside. I didn't want to be in class anyway.

We begged Dad to pull us out of Greek school. We complained endlessly, but he wouldn't be swayed. I even tried negotiating with him: could he move me out of my primary school and into the Greek Orthodox school instead? Very dramatic of me, I know. But I knew exactly what I was doing. I'd done my research and discovered that Greek lessons there were taught during regular school hours, so there would be no more after-school classes.

After all the nagging, I finally persuaded Dad. He moved me halfway through Year 4, and I couldn't have been happier. Cheering! After that rainy day, I was more than ready for a change, a chance to escape the monotony and maybe, just maybe, find a place where I truly belonged.

Starting at my new school was a rush of anticipation mixed with a touch of uncertainty. But I was ready to get on and face whatever came along. The uniform, the rules, the playground rituals – everything felt overwhelming at first. Coming midway through the year was daunting; everyone already had their friend groups and I was the new kid, sticking out like a sore thumb. I was paired with a buddy, a sweet girl named L. She was so angelic, with long dark hair tied up in a ponytail with a blue ribbon, big brown eyes, and the warmest smile. She took me under her wing, introduced me to her friends, and made me feel at ease. It's pretty amazing how kids can be totally shitty if they choose, yet when they decide to be kind, you feel safe and welcome.

One unforgettable lunchtime in the playground, while we were all playing and laughing, the asphalt scorching under my shoes, something happened. I'm not sure what exactly, but the words 'Oh sugar!' flew out of my mouth. (I didn't swear back then.) I remember those words loud and clear, as if I'd said them yesterday. My sweet buddy L suddenly exploded. 'How dare you use my mum's name in vain!' she yelled, then stormed off.

I stood there, dumbfounded and speechless. What on earth had just happened? She literally walked away and never spoke to me again, and I mean never. We finished Year 6, went through another year and a bit of school, and still never exchanged a word. We avoided each other completely. How awful.

I told you; kids can be real shitheads. All that because I said the word 'sugar'? Insane. Much later, I discovered that Sugar was her mum's name. Oh, right. I had no idea.

That loss made a small but lasting crack in my confidence, which lingered through those early school years.

During my time at the Greek Orthodox private school, our parish priest often visited our religion classes. One particular lesson stayed with me. With a warm smile, he told our year group that we were exceptionally special. I sometimes wonder if he said that to every class, but in that moment, it felt uniquely meant for us. He reminded us that we would be graduating in the year 2000, a milestone that, in 1994, felt light-years away. Six years of school stretched out before us, yet his words ignited a spark of excitement and anticipation within me. Was life even going to exist past the year 2000?

Our school day ran from 9 a.m. to 3 p.m., followed by after-school activities. It was showtime. Our afternoons were youthful and carefree. Our home's large backyard became a magnet for neighbourhood kids. They came over so Mum wouldn't be left alone. I loved how accepting our friends were; they chose to come to our house so we wouldn't miss out.

We made very good use of our long driveway. We fancied ourselves the super-cool kids on the block because we all had rollerblades. We'd race up and down, inventing our own games and rules. We coloured the pavement with bright chalk and played hopscotch. We played elastics, jumping up and down and singing, 'England, Ireland, Scotland, Wales, inside, outside, inside on.' As you passed each level, the elastic climbed higher. I never got above the waist. We tied skipping ropes together to make extra-long ropes, did single jumps, double jumps, and 180-degree turn jumps, and then we'd add a second rope and attempt the elite move of jumping through two ropes at once. We were mini athletes.

We even turned the backyard into a handball court, drawing squares and labelling them king, queen, and jack, then moving around the court like it was a human-sized chessboard. We let our imaginations run wild. We made up half the games, which was half the fun. And when we lost, we'd argue and carry on like sore losers. We would play from the afternoon into the evening. I'm surprised that any homework ever got done. No one wanted to go home. We'd be sweaty and huffing and puffing as if we'd just run a marathon. Mum would always set out drinks and snacks on the kitchen bench, her chair nearby, a quiet presence as we raced in and out as we pleased.

Even if none of my friends could come over, I'd still find a way to play. Poor Mum, I seemed to make her my victim, though she never complained. In truth, it was actually a lovely bonding time, away from the usual duties of caring for her. I'd tie one side of a skipping rope to something sturdy and fetch a chair for her to sit on. She'd swing the rope while I jumped, shouting, 'Faster!'

Those were the innocent, fun days. That's what I associate with childhood: fun, games, laughing, and playing, moments where I felt close to her, even if the words 'I love you' were never said.

Two doors up lived another Cypriot family. Over the years, our families grew incredibly close. We treated their grandparents like our own. That's how our lives became. It was normal to pop in and out of each other's homes as if they were extensions of our own.

One Friday night we were at their house for a movie night. The boys were set on watching *Candyman*; the alternative was Freddy Krueger. I had always loved Freddy Krueger films – horrible, warped, and thrilling. So, when I heard *Candyman*, I thought it would be brilliant. How wrong I was. *Candyman* was not brilliant. It was terrifying. Truly terrifying. Beware, do not watch it. I must have had my eyes covered for most of the film; it scared the living daylights out of me.

The boys lived just two doors down from our house, with only one house in between. It was late and dark. We were supposed to walk home, but I was petrified. There was no way I was walking home alone. Yet I had to get there somehow. I said my goodbyes, slipped out the front door, counted to three, and ran for my life. Anyone watching would have thought I was being chased by a serial killer, or even worse, Candyman.

After that movie, I developed a massive fear of going to the toilet. I truly believed that Candyman, this massive, terrifying bee creature, would rise from the toilet bowl and attack me. I had someone check the bathroom once or twice and wait outside until I was done. This routine went on for a long time. I don't have a clear memory of how I finally grew out of it.

In 1995 I embarked on an exciting new chapter: high school. Being the youngest in the school again felt like a fresh start. Most of our year group had remained the same. We were a Kindy-to-Year-12 school, but new friendships were waiting to be made. I suppose that's always how it works: interests shift, subjects change, and who ends up in your classes plays a big role. It was a welcoming new formation.

Four of us girls from primary school plus one newcomer became fast friends. I clicked instantly with her; she was Cypriot too, so we had a lot in common. The five of us became the Five Musketeers, stuck together like superglue, each of us bringing something different to the group and always having each other's backs, no matter what.

As primary school faded behind me, new challenges loomed: my body, my confidence, and my place in the world. Do not ask me to recount my high school experience; I simply cannot. It's as if I didn't exist. Whatever I do remember are tiny snippets. My high school years feel like a jigsaw with too many pieces missing.

Throughout my teens, I went through a massive developmental stage, and I mean major. Oh, the joys of being a girl. One day I was as flat as a pancake, and the next, I was a DD, at fourteen. To some people, that was super cool, but for me it was absolute torture. I cried every night, begging God to take them away. Each morning, they were still there. I'd stare into the mirror, hating the reflection staring back at me, feeling trapped in a body I didn't recognise, a stranger to myself.

Because of that, I absolutely hated summer. I was painfully body-conscious, and the beach was completely out of the question. Nothing fitted right. My hormones were raging, and I loathed school sports. I would've rather poked my eye out with a sharp pencil than run around in PE. I was paranoid about the bounce, imagining the teasing or, worse, two black eyes.

Sometimes, I wore two bras just to try to flatten my chest. My physical shape shattered my confidence. I hid in oversized clothes and hunched my shoulders, desperate to disappear. There was no way in hell I'd ever participate in a school athletics carnival, let alone wear a swimsuit and swim. Are you kidding me? No friken' way!

I made up any excuse under the sun not to take part in PE. If you pulled out my student file, it would be a small bible of excuses Mum had signed for me. She always had my back, understanding how deep this complex ran – her quiet nod a comfort, even without words of love. I didn't hate my body; I just felt so uncomfortable in it. Up until then I'd had no reason to be anxious. Then, seemingly overnight, I developed. Fully developed. And I spiralled out of control. My insecurities took hold, echoing that old outsider feeling from my Greek school days.

My struggles with body image fuelled persistent self-doubt and crushed my confidence. I felt unworthy. Once, someone close to me (not my parents) asked why I wasn't as skinny as a family friend's daughter. It hurt. It shattered me. I was compared to her again and again, which only cemented my lack of confidence. I was even told to go to Weight Watchers to lose weight. That's so fucked up. I was only a teenager.

To put icing on the cake and add to my long list of complexes, in Years 8 and 9 we were told we had to take part in a compulsory extracurricular sport. Get fucked! There was no way I was playing netball. All the 'fit' girls were in that team. I didn't fit in. I wasn't athletic; I wasn't lean. I was a tomboy with big boobs. I hated anything to do with sport and exercise, yet here I was with no choice but to join a team. Netball was a hard no-fucking-way, so my girlfriends and I chose softball instead. That could be fun. We had no idea how to play, but we learned the rules as we went, mostly winging it.

And honestly, we had the best time. Maybe not during the game itself, but the bus rides to and from were pure joy. I'd never laughed so much in my life, doubled over, tears streaming down my face. As we rode, we blasted Alanis Morissette's *Jagged Little Pill* on repeat. Because of that, I've grown to hate that song. If I hear her voice on the radio, watch how fast my fingers manoeuvre to change the station, or I'll lose my shit.

Our favourite part of softball clearly wasn't the match; it was the banter. That was next level. And the ride home? Always the brilliant finisher: McDonald's cheeseburgers and fries...mmm. What a well-deserved treat. See? Total athletes.

In high school I was fortunate to have a close-knit group of friends. Our bond felt unbreakable, and I cherish those memories deeply. With them, I could be my authentic, awkward, honest self. No superficial bullshit. We weren't into brands, we weren't into make-up, and we weren't infatuated with boys. We didn't care about the outside world; we were happy in our little circle. And if we ever needed help with anything, we knew we could count on each other.

One of my closest friends, H, didn't live far from me, but if she took public transport she needed two or three buses to get to school, which meant a crack-of-dawn start. So we hatched a plan: she'd come to my place before school, another reason or opportunity to spend more time together. She'd be dropped off early, we'd have breakfast, and we'd catch the bus together. In the afternoons, we'd take the 693 school bus to Kingsford and, depending on the weather and how heavy our bags were, we'd either jump on a second bus to my place or walk home. Imagine forty minutes of talking shit the whole time, laughter spilling between us like a secret language.

We'd push open the front door with our feet, dump our bags and, without fail, call out, 'Mum, we're home!' Mum always had a meal ready, anticipating our hunger; her quiet presence was a steady anchor in the rhythm of our days.

We loved food. We loved anything and everything Mum presented to us. Sometimes we did our homework, but more often, we watched video clips, sang, and danced. We went through a huge Cypress Hill phase, 'Insane in the membrane…insane in the brain!' Our own house party, with only two invited.

Twenty-five years after graduation, my bond with my girlfriends is still strong. Life pulled us in different directions for a while; some were working, others travelling the world, and a few were buried in books, chasing their dream careers. I took a different path, marrying young and welcoming my first baby. But when Facebook burst onto the scene we reconnected, and our friendship roared back to life. Even after long silences, family commitments, and life's chaos, we always pick up exactly where we left off, as if no time has passed. I love this uncomplicated friendship, filled with no judgements, no expectations, just pure, unfiltered fun. When we all catch up we're the same ridiculous schoolgirls, laughing over the silliest things. Honestly, you may not be able to cope with us if you're not one of us; we're *that* loud. I feel sorry for anyone sitting near us while we howl over old stories and harmless mischief. The teasing, the in-jokes, the laughter; it never stops.

I remember a conversation we once had. In that conversation, H asked, 'What were we like at school?'

I answered, confident as ever, 'We were good kids, well-behaved.'

She paused, frowned, and said, 'Which lifetime are you talking about?'

I was taken aback. Then she reminded me that we were relentless chatterboxes, always pushing boundaries and getting into trouble for it. *Umm, what? No way.* For a moment, I was in denial, and then the memories came flooding back. Those girls were (and still are) my safe place; their loyalty stitched me together in ways I didn't yet understand.

I remember being rebellious, experimenting with different hair colours every few weeks. Working at a hair salon had its perks; I could try any shade I fancied, much to our principal's dismay. She'd pull me aside, eyebrow raised, commenting on my 'natural red' with a hint of sarcasm. Natural? Hmm, sure, that's why it changed every month. Some memories are foggy, but others remain crystal clear, like the look on our principal's face each time she spotted my latest hair creation.

My friends kept sharing stories to jog my memory, but I stayed blocked and blank to these supposedly notorious incidents. They told me about the time we got in trouble in the girls' toilets, pushing and shoving, yelling and screaming. And then there was a classroom drama that they swore brought our maths teacher to tears and sent her running out of the room.

I crossed my heart, genuinely perplexed. I have no recollection whatsoever. It's as if my brain selectively edited out the madness. Shit, we were arseholes. Which parallel world was I living in? Which colour rose-tinted glasses was I wearing? Did I really block out most of my high school life? Was my protection mode stuck on 'on'?

These are the memories I want to keep; I want to keep all the dumb shit we used to do. Why can't I recall them, even though I'm certain I engaged in rebellious behaviour during my teenage years?

Was I retaliating for the childhood I never had, or simply hungry for attention? Or maybe, back then, forgetting was the only way I knew how to survive.

Dad's work ethic was remarkable. His hours were long, exhausting, and unpredictable, stretching from the early morning into late evenings. As a Greek father raising two daughters, he was fairly strict, adhering to a traditional, protective upbringing. If I wanted to go out, I had to give him a week's notice, just so he could sit with the idea. Through this I quickly learned the subtle art of negotiation and persuasion.

One rule was non-negotiable: no sleepovers at friends' houses. His reasoning was simple: 'You have a bed; come home.' Our friends were welcome to stay with us, but never the other way around. Looking back, I realise Mum's health influenced that rule as much as our culture did. I understand the reasoning now, though at the time, I craved his warmth, his words of love that hardly ever came.

After years of being the youngest in school, suddenly, we were in Year 10. See what I mean? One minute it's Year 8, and the next, there's barely anything in between connecting the dots. The girls were buzzing with excitement over the planning and preparation for our Year 10 formal. Their excitement made sense, but I felt left out. Old insecurities from my younger years flared up again, reminding me that I was always the outsider.

In the end, I set a trend out of necessity. With my heavy chest, I couldn't find a dress that fit, so I wore pants. The other girls looked exquisite, and I envied them. I wanted a pretty dress too, but nothing looked right on me. A top and pants were all I could manage. I was gutted, truly, but there wasn't much I could do. Still, I dragged myself to the formal. Everyone was surprised to see me in pants, but instead of feeling out of place, I felt...fine. Different, in a good way. The scene

I'd imagined in my head, everyone laughing at me, never happened. We partied, we laughed, and the night turned out to be brilliant. So brilliant, in fact, that one of the girls invited practically the whole year group back to hers.

Dad had no idea what time I'd be home or how I'd get there. The less he knew, the better, I thought to myself. Remember, it was 1998; at this time there were minimal mobile phones in circulation, so I didn't have one. At the last minute, I cheekily arranged for my cousin to pick me up. We drove through neon-lit Kings Cross, demolishing juicy Whoppers from Hungry Jack's, exactly what the doctor ordered for a late-night feed. Instead of going home, I crashed at his place, not thinking about the repercussions waiting for me later.

Totally dead to the world, the next morning I was startled when the phone rang. My cousin walked into the TV room and found me sprawled across the sofa. 'It's for you,' he said. Still half-asleep, I stumbled to the phone and answered, 'Yeah?'

Dad didn't bother with a hello. Just 'Wait till you get home.' He was pissed, I could tell, his grey eyes turning icy blue through the phone. Too tired to care at that moment, I fell back to sleep, knowing I'd have to deal with it later.

Eventually, I made my way home. I was late but I was safe; that's what counted, right? Mum stayed quiet, her silence a heavy weight louder than words. That alone told me I was in deep shit. To be honest, I was shitting myself. And D didn't help the situation, throwing petrol on the fire with her two cents' worth: 'Oh, you're going to cop it when Dad gets home.' *Oh, piss off, will ya.*

The night played out in slow motion as I waited for Dad. The sound of his car pulling into the driveway sent a cold rush through my body. My heart thudded; my mind ticked over: Do I pretend to be asleep? Do I look busy? What can I do to soften the blow? I held my breath as the engine cut and the front door slammed. I swear, for a moment, even the walls held their breath. FUCK. I'm dead.

Dad has grey eyes. When he's angry, they go crystal blue. If you see that change, you better run, because you're going to cop it. He ignored me. I mean, he really ignored me; it was as if I didn't exist. He didn't even turn to look my way. He refused to speak to me for an entire week.

I was confused. What had just happened? Where was the yelling? Why the silence? That caught me off guard. Although I appreciated his restraint, I would have preferred a proper direct confrontation. My dad's silence was, in its own brutal way, devastating. What had made him react like that?

Ah, reverse psychology – that's how he got me to reflect on my behaviour. Yes, yes, I get it now. For the first time, I realised Dad wasn't about shouting or punishment. He was strategic, and remarkably good at it. His silence cut deeper than any yelling ever could, a quiet ache for his approval that I couldn't name.

I had a habit of challenging authority, testing my parents' patience at every turn. I was quick with backchat and refused to back down. I always had a comment ready to spit out. My aunts would joke that I must have swallowed a radio as a child. I was self-sufficient, Little Miss Independent. Life circumstances meant I got little practical help from my parents: Mum's health often kept her from providing support, and Dad's long, unpredictable hours kept him away.

Yet despite all that, I navigated the commute to and from school on my own, juggled housework with homework, helped care for Mum, and even held down a job. I craved freedom, a chance to step beyond our front door and figure out who I was in the world. I'm certain now that my difficult childhood forged the person I am today.

Throughout my school years, my parents took a relaxed approach. They wanted my best, not just perfect grades. I was an average student, although my parents knew I was full of potential but with little motivation for subjects I hated. Science was my nemesis; I couldn't stand it. Staying engaged felt impossible, so I'd often retreat to the back of the classroom, playing hangman or counting down the minutes to freedom. I couldn't wait to drop that subject in the final two years of school.

I wasn't academically gifted, but in Year 12, something remarkable happened. I decided to knuckle down and focus on subjects I genuinely enjoyed. And, surprise, I did well. It's amazing what genuine interest can do for your effort. I loved my subjects: English, Maths in Society (though I used to jokingly call it Maths in Space), 3 Unit Business, 3 Unit Greek, and 1 Unit General Studies. I started with 2 Unit Maths, but knowing I didn't want to go to university, I dropped it. I was lucky to have standout teachers who saw my potential and brought out the best in me.

Even so, Year 12 was a mix of grounding and rebellion. I turned eighteen and got my driver's licence, a recipe for disaster. Between school, home, and my constant craving for freedom, I felt like I was balancing on a tightrope. And, of course, just when I should've been laser-focused on my HSC, I did the most 'me' thing ever: I ditched studying for Ricky Martin.

The night before my first HSC exam, you'd think I'd be stressed out, buried in notes, studying like a maniac. Nope. I was out. I went to Ricky Martin's concert at the Hordern Pavilion. And because Dad's English was limited, I could get away with pretty much anything, mostly because I didn't tell him...whoops. What a little shit. So instead of being at home preparing for my final exams, I had loud music pulsing through my veins, dancing and singing the night away. Who would've thought I had my first exam the very next morning?

Wednesday 11 October 2000 was Dad's birthday. Happy birthday, Dad! My alarm went off. I hit snooze. I woke up late and dragged myself to school. Boy, did I get into trouble for being late to my first exam. Clearly, my head was still in the clouds, singing 'She bangs, she bangs.' One night, music was pounding through my veins as I danced to Ricky Martin; the next, caffeine was surging through me as I knocked back cup after cup of coffee, eyes burning as I skimmed and reread pages, cramming in all the study I could. Really, I should've been preparing weeks earlier. Talk about flipping a switch.

There was one exam I stayed up all night to study for. Dad heard footsteps, the kettle, and the clink of a spoon stirring and got up to check the noise in the middle of the night. To his surprise, he found me at the table, notes scattered everywhere. He was speechless, maybe a little proud. Instead of going back to bed, he made tea, sat on the lounge and kept me company till dawn, his tea steaming, untouched, his eyes on me. He didn't say a word. He couldn't sleep knowing I was awake studying. It remains one of the kindest things he's ever done for me. Behind those strict grey eyes was something softer, a tenderness he rarely showed. That night, when I really needed it, he did. Sitting there in silence, keeping me company, was his way of saying *I see you*. And in that quiet, I felt held. I felt a grace in these small hours shared.

Beautiful moments need to be captured – screenshots for future reference. My life, in fact, was exactly like that quote from *Forrest Gump*: 'Life is like a box of chocolates; you never know what you're going to get.' That was me; my life, every twist and turn, down to a T.

I must have eaten that weird chocolate again, because I was with my rebellious acts just in time for our Year 12 formal. Finding an outfit had been a nightmare back in Year 10, but by now I'd grown into my body; I no longer looked or felt disproportionate. Yes, I was still very top-heavy, but it wasn't nearly as brutal as in those early teen years. Excited, I found a black two-piece corset-style dress that actually fit me. Boom!

Being a girl, I felt more comfortable telling Mum my plans, so she'd know where I was. I never wanted her to worry. I told her we were going to an after-party after the formal, but I said nothing to Dad. I knew one hundred per cent he'd say no. All dolled up and ready to go, I packed a bag with a change of clothes and set off. Our formal was in Double Bay, and we finished the night in the city. Nothing too crazy, but I did rock the boat by returning home at 5 am in jeans and a T-shirt.

I tried to open the front door quietly, careful not to wake anyone, but Dad somehow sensed me and got up. *Oh no, here we go again.* As I passed his bedroom, he was already out of bed, peeking. He yelled something daft at me: 'What time is this? You're only just getting home, and I'm about to go to work.'

I tried to walk away, but he continued, 'And you took other clothes too, bravo.' I dropped my head and left without a word. For once, I wasn't in the mood to make things worse – probably the smartest thing I'd ever done in my life. To top it all off, 20 minutes later my phone began ringing. I'd completely forgotten I'd left my bag in his room while he was ranting. That set him off again. I told my boyfriend to call me when he got home. Safety first, right? That rattled Dad even more. 'Who the fuck is calling you at this time of the morning?!' Oh man, I just wanted the earth to open and swallow me.

In a nutshell, my school life and teenage years were always sprinkled with mischief or rebellion. This time I thought it would be pretty cool to get my belly button pierced. *Here I go again.* I casually mentioned it to Mum. I always seemed to tell her about the dumb shit I was planning. What did I expect her to do? I knew she couldn't punish me, the poor thing. She never told Dad about the things I got up to and always covered for me. Fuck, I love this woman! I remember her nodding her head and saying, 'Don't you dare.' I dared.

That night, I came home after getting the piercing, after she had said, 'Don't you dare.' While we were chatting, me helping her get ready for bed, I turned to her. 'Remember when I said I wanted my belly button pierced? Look, isn't it cool?' I lifted my top to show her. She stared, eyes wide, utterly disappointed, her quiet sigh a heavier rebuke than words.

'Your dad's going to kill you,' she said.

Ignorant and stubborn as I was, I totally ignored her feelings. I begged her not to say anything to Dad. And she didn't. She never stitched me up.

♥

Despite all my rebellious streaks and teenage years of self-discovery, I was given the most extraordinary opportunity: I flew overseas for my cousin's wedding in my first year of uni – yes, I ended up deciding to go. It was the sort of adventure everyone dreams of. I felt blessed and deeply grateful, and my passport already carried a fair few stamps. With grandparents living abroad, our family had travelled quite a bit, but this time I was lucky enough to fly solo.

After years of feeling trapped by Dad's rules and Mum's watchful eyes, Cyprus was my escape, a chance to finally spread my wings.

It was the summer of 2001. Young and free. Parent-free. Life was good. Family celebrations, laughter with Yiayia, and the mouthwatering souvlakia and chips from the taverna, its lights glowing softly against the night sky – these were the simple joys I soaked up. I partied the summer nights away, beach by day, clubs by night. That's what you do when you've just finished school. In Cyprus, I felt the shackles around my ankles loosen, and my guard slowly came down.

One scorching hot afternoon, my cousin and I were taking our midday siestas when her dad, my thio, Dad's brother, walked into the room and spotted my bellybutton piercing. All my dad's siblings are firecrackers. He didn't ask; he yelled in Greek, *'Fer mou tin persa!'* Bring me the pliers! I woke up fast, let me tell you. I panicked, begging him not to tell my dad. He stormed out, slamming the door behind him, but his wife's kind glance softened the moment. The last thing I wanted was to be sent straight back on the first flight home with my tail between my legs.

I thought I'd gotten away with it for a while. I actually forgot I had the piercing and started to get a bit reckless again. One night I was sitting at my aunt's house, my top rising up right under the spotlight, when my Dad noticed a sparkle. It was like God had planned it. Payback, bitch. Without hesitation, he yelled, 'What is that?' Me, the idiot, said, 'What, this?' and pulled my top up. Full exposure. I ripped the bandaid off; might as well cop it all at once.

He went off, on and on, lecturing about how I could go overseas and disrespect the family by showing off my belly button with a piercing (a bit extreme), and what would everyone think? Blah, blah, blah.

'OMG, who cares? Get with the times, Dad.'

He was stuck in the 1950s, unwilling to move on. I saw things differently; maybe that's why I always challenged him. I don't think that's entirely a bad thing. I completely understand that Dad faced many hardships himself, arriving in a foreign country at a young age. But what I couldn't understand was why he stayed so rooted in the past. Imagine being a bird trapped in a cage, flapping its wings, desperate to break out but unable to. I was that bird. I wanted to spread my wings and show the colours of my feathers, but it felt as though my wings had been clipped to keep me restrained. The more that bird thrashed, the more it tried to break free. That was me, craving freedom and independence, yet weighed down by so many responsibilities that I couldn't be a normal teenager.

Was I a normal teenager, or was I just a shit? Maybe I simply wanted to explore life. I was curious. Between my sister and me, I always felt like the bad one. I was the one who had to break the ice for everything; the one who always argued. You'd think being the second-born would make it easier for me to go out and have some freedom, but it was the opposite.

My sister was quieter; she went along with things. I was the loud one. I was the one who wanted to go out with my friends, the one who constantly tested my parents' patience. Honestly, it was remarkable how they put up with all my shit.

I often wonder why my teenage years were filled with rebellion and mischief. Looking back now, I can see that my character was only a mask, a way of hiding a personal crisis I didn't yet have the words to describe. I was missing something in my life, something I couldn't quite identify, so I kept searching for anything that could fill that void. Affection, I guess, was the key. That hollowness, that quiet ache that began in childhood, followed me. It drove me to act out, to chase after what I couldn't seem to find at home.

We were undeniably loved, but we were rarely shown affection. Our parents' actions spoke louder than words: Mum was fighting for her life, while Dad was working tirelessly to provide for us, yet the simple phrase 'I love you' was seldom heard. I believe this came from their own upbringings, shaped by the hard edges of war and migration. Maybe they just didn't know how to express love with words. But the question of whether this cycle will continue stayed in my heart. Umm, no.

Not on my watch. I refuse to let my children grow up feeling unloved, even if they're cared for. I'm determined to show them what love looks like, not just through sacrifice, but through affection and words. Now, sometimes, I doubt myself, having never fully received that kind of love from my parents. How can I be sure I'm giving the right kind of love to my children? Still, I try. Every single day. I love them fiercely. I pour into them the warmth and security I once longed for. My heart beats for them. And every day, I tell them I love you; words I craved but rarely heard growing up.

❤

Growing up, I often felt an overwhelming hollowness, an emotional numbness I couldn't quite name. I've made it my life's mission to ensure my children never feel that same emptiness. Over the years, through self-discovery and painful reflection, I realised that void came from a desperate search for something I craved but rarely received. I longed to hear those three simple words: 'I love you.' But they were almost never spoken by my parents.

Our family life was a delicate balancing act. Dad had his own way of showing love, one that didn't always include words. I don't judge him for that; it's just how he was taught to express affection. Still, a part of me always wondered what it would have felt like to hear him say those words out loud, even just once.

The bond I share with my children now is everything I once wished for. It's rooted in love, laughter, and playful banter. Without these, I'd feel so incomplete. I make sure our home is filled with affection, and I never miss a chance to tell them I love you. When my kids respond with a cheerful, 'Love you more,' I can't help but grin and shoot back, 'Impossible,' keeping our exchange warm, tender, and full of humour.

Since Dad lives with us, I sometimes catch him watching me, silent and thoughtful as I tell my children, 'I love you.' And in those moments, I can't help but wonder what's going through his mind. Does he ever think about how rarely he said those words to me? Does he realise how much I needed to hear them back then? Or is he quietly questioning why he never raised me this way?

♥

I've come to realise that much of my teenage rebellion wasn't just about attitude; it came from a place of unmet needs. I can see that now. I'm learning from those mistakes, trying to correct my behaviour, and using my past as a set of lessons rather than regrets. My goal is to take everything I've learned, from the pain and the confusion to the small victories, and turn them into something good. I want to create a loving, supportive space for my children, one that helps reduce the chances of them falling into the same patterns of self-destruction I once did.

Having lived through chaos, I know my kids will still make mistakes; they'll do dumb shit, just like I did. And that's okay. It's part of growing up. What matters most to me now is being the kind of parent who uses those experiences, both mine and theirs, to guide, nurture, and encourage growth instead of judgement.

I understand now how much our upbringing shapes who we become. The influence of our parents runs deep; it's like a mirror we can't help but reflect. People often say we mimic what we see, and for the most part, that's true. But I've also learned something powerful: we can rewrite that story. We can choose what to carry forward and what to leave behind. By holding on to the good and letting go of what no longer serves us, we can build a new narrative, one that feels whole, healed, and intentional.

❤

I've always had a deep appreciation for our family traditions, values, and morals. As the daughter of a well-respected family in our community, I take pride in where I come from and in being my parents' daughter. I've always admired their work ethic. Mum and Dad worked diligently to provide for us.

I once vowed to carve my own path and to do things differently. But the truth is, I'm more like them than I ever imagined. Since I was sixteen I've been eager to work, to earn a living and to stand on my own two feet. Financial stability has always mattered to me, but what truly drives me is the desire to keep learning, studying, and growing. There's something fulfilling about constantly expanding my mind and my skills. It makes me feel alive. I love our cultural heritage and the traditions that shaped us. Ironically, I now hear my own children making the same complaints I once made, and

I can't help but laugh. Life has such a funny way of coming full circle. Still, I'm genuinely happy with who I've become and who I'm still becoming, thanks to the wide range of experiences that have shaped me.

Mum's perseverance has always been a guiding force in my life. I'm forever grateful to have been raised by two remarkable people I proudly call my parents. And if I could go back, I'd offer my sincerest apologies for the trouble I caused in my younger years.

Sometimes, though, I wonder, is karma really a bitch? As I stepped into adulthood, it felt as though the cage door finally cracked open. But even then, I couldn't help pondering if I would ever feel truly free.

CHAPTER 3

Love rewritten

It's pretty much every girl's dream to have a bedazzling, fairytale wedding, to be swept off her feet and live happily ever after. I wanted that too.

As a child, some nights I'd just lie awake, picturing myself in a flowing white dress, standing beside a man who would hold my hand the way Dad held Mum's through her illness. I dreamed of meeting someone who would accept me for who I am, love me despite every flaw, be compassionate about my unusual circumstances, and stay when life turned unpredictable. A love that felt safe, steady, and true. Someone who would understand my moods, and someone who would still choose me every single day. A partner who would not only love me but also respect me. I don't think that's asking for too much, is it?

I was fortunate to be raised by a man who embodied everything I believed a true gentleman should be. My childhood wasn't easy. I faced things no child should ever have to face and carried emotions far too heavy for my little shoulders. Yet, even in those moments, I had Dad. Dad was strong, grounded, and loyal. I watched his unwavering devotion to Mum as her health declined. No matter how hard life hit, he stood tall, unshaken by the storm around him. That image of him, that steadiness of love and the fierceness in loyalty, etched itself deeply in me. It became my silent definition of what love should look like. I wanted a partner who would stand beside me just like that. Someone who is supportive, dependable, and present.

Growing up under Dad's firm rules and Mum's quiet grace, I learned discipline and endurance. But somewhere in between, I also longed for something lighter. I longed for a love that felt free yet grounding. It was a balance I rarely saw at home, but one my heart never stopped craving it.

♥

Then I was reunited with my childhood crush. This really felt like a blessing, a real chance to see where things could go. My happily-ever-after seemed to arrive after eight long years of ignoring him. And trust me, when I hold a grudge, I hold it with an unrelenting grip. After 20 years navigating life's game of snakes and ladders, I had convinced myself that a conventional life wasn't meant for me, and by extension, it seemed unlikely that my romantic life would follow a different path.

Back when I was a young teen, I had a major crush on a boy from my Greek dancing school. He was charming in that effortless way that made hearts skip a beat. Every time I saw him, mine would flutter uncontrollably, and I'd suddenly turn shy, unsure of what to say or how to act. Who was I, anyway? We were family friends, both from Cyprus, even from the same village.

My grandparents lived in Cyprus in the 1990s, so it was normal for us to travel there to visit them. On one particular trip the stars aligned and my crush happened to be visiting his family too. Magical, right? Sparks somehow flew across the ocean and found us in this small village. Our friendship blossomed effortlessly. We spent hours together, went to the local cinema, feeling ridiculously cool because we understood the English-speaking films and didn't have to squint at the Greek subtitles, and lingered in cafes with our friends, learning little things about each other day by day. As a young girl, I was utterly smitten. I even saved my pocket money to surprise him with a small gift: a football pendant for the chain he always wore around his neck.

It was an icy winter Christmas, a far cry from the warmth we knew in Australia. Most social life happened indoors, wrapped in cosy vibes, warm fireplaces, dim lights, and that welcoming snugness. The air was thick with the smell of coffee and cigarette smoke.

Socialising overseas felt completely normal. Teenagers in Cyprus had so much more freedom than we did back in Australia. It made sense: small country, small village, everyone knew everyone, and it all felt safe. That's why I loved visiting my grandparents. We could wander freely and explore and our parents didn't have to worry. Back home, our town sprawled endlessly and our neighbours were almost strangers. Two very distinct worlds. In Cyprus, I felt unshackled, far from Dad's rules and Mum's care, chasing a spark I hoped was love.

During that trip, I was over the moon to be invited to the village's biggest winter party. Practically everyone would be there. I felt a little like the cool kid in town, labelled Charlou, a slang term for foreigners. The thought of going thrilled me even more because my crush was going too. Honestly, these were shaping up to be the best school holidays ever.

Like any young girl caught up in butterflies, I fussed endlessly over my hair and pieced together an outfit that would turn heads. And then came the familiar dilemma: how to make a good impression on him without looking desperate. We planned our arrival times, hearts pounding, waiting anxiously for the night to finally come.

❤

The party was getting closer and nerves were already kicking in. By eight o'clock, we were dressed and ready, buzzing with anticipation for what was supposed to be the best night ever. The cafe venue was packed; virtually every teenager in town seemed to be there. I stood, trying to stay calm, patiently waiting for Master M to arrive.

Time slowed. The music blared, thumping through my chest, but I couldn't hear a thing. From where we were dancing we could see everyone coming in and going out. Every time the door opened, my heart leapt. Every time it closed, I caught my breath, hoping. Waiting.

And then it hit me. He wasn't coming. I was being stood up.

Swallowing my pride and burning with embarrassment, I had no choice but to force on a brave poker face. I danced, but my heart wasn't in it. Humiliation wrapped itself around me like a cloak. Why didn't he come? Had he been leading me on all along? All my insecurities bubbled up at once, suffocating me. I wanted to leave the party, but that wasn't an option. My presence wasn't just for him; my friends were there too. Although, sharing this night with him would have been...fun. Different. Special. I wanted answers, but there were none – no phones back then to call, no texts to send, nothing. Just me, my friends, the music, the crowd, and the hollow ache in me. I was on the verge of tears; I felt so humiliated.

Days passed in utter disappointment. I was shocked that there was still no contact. I couldn't find him anywhere in the village; it was as if he'd vanished off the face of the earth. Part of me wanted to march up to his thia's (aunt's) door and demand answers, but I couldn't stoop that low. I didn't want to look desperate. I just wanted to know why he never showed up and still had made no contact. How could he do that to me?

❤

Another outing was up and this time, I was with my cousins. They dragged me to the dance floor, refusing to let me sulk. Their laughter became a kind of lifeline, pulling me out of my hurt even when I tried to stay buried in it.

I hated boys. They sucked. No wonder I didn't want a boyfriend. Feeling let down was the worst. I didn't want to feel shit. Still, I tried to put it all behind me. I swallowed what pride I had left and decided to enjoy the trip. It's not every day you fly halfway across the world to make new memories. I wasn't going to let one humiliating moment ruin everything. My cousins knew I was hurting and they comforted me with real empathy. They kept me laughing, refusing to let me stew in silence, not even over some random boy.

We spent the season hanging out at the local cafe, went into the city with our older cousins, and did what teenagers do best: sweet fuck all. No worries, no responsibilities, just freedom. And honestly, that was the best feeling ever.

A few nights later, we ran into Master M's cousin. Small-town life – you're bound to bump into someone you know. Being friends, we chatted about the party, laughed, played cards, and argued over the snooker table. Then I pulled her aside and asked where he'd disappeared to. To my shock, she said he'd flown back to Australia.

Just like that? Gone? No message, no goodbye, not even a hint. The questions crowded in: did he dislike me that much? Couldn't he at least have had the courtesy to have a conversation? Rude doesn't even begin to cover it. That was a big strike in my book. Cross me once and I move on. And that's exactly what I planned to do.

♥

Several weeks later I returned to Australia, my heart heavy but determined to forget him. My life quietly slipped back into its familiar rhythm. Summer ended and a new school year began. I reconnected with friends and kept moving forward. But there was one snag: Greek dancing. If I went back, I'd probably run into him. And that thought alone made my stomach twist. What was I supposed to do? I wasn't about to put myself in the path of fresh embarrassment. *No friken' way.* So, I quit dancing.

I loved those classes, especially the music, the laughter, and the early afternoon walks from 7-Eleven for an icy cold Coke Slurpee. But still, I quit. I refused to go back. I never wanted to see him again. Better to protect my peace than feed false hope. Call it stubborn if you like; I called it a boundary.

My teen years were full of adventures that kept me busy and entertained. Five years flew by before I even realised it. I threw myself into school and work, doing everything I could to forget the sting of being rejected and build a life where I finally felt like I was enough. When you're busy living, time really does fly, especially when you're having fun. I was having the best fun of my life. I barely thought of him at all. As far as I was concerned, he didn't exist. Master M, who?

Until he reappeared. After all those years, we were invited to his brother's wedding. *Why, God? Why would you do this to me?* Karma must have been catching up with me just as I was starting to straighten things out. My rebellious streak had finally settled, and now life was handing me a proper reminder. Our parents had been long-time friends, and since my dad and his family were from the same village, it was only natural they'd invite us. Yayyy! (Eye roll.) #EndSarcasm.

♥

Having my driver's licence meant there was no escape from it. I was summoned to go to church with Mum and my sister. Dad was working, lucky him. I had to swallow my pride and actually show up in person after so many years. Honestly, the fact that I stood in that church without throwing up felt like a miracle. The ceremony dragged on and on. I kept glancing at the clock, silently begging it to end already. Every hymn and every prayer felt like an eternity. The only saving grace was that we didn't have to stay for the reception. We had another family event that evening, which gave us a valid excuse to slip out early. Still, we couldn't just walk away. We had to personally congratulate the bride and groom.

When the ceremony finally ended, everyone lined up to congratulate the newlyweds. Mum nudged me forward to hurry, but I was rooted to the spot. My nightmare of facing him was right there, staring me in the face.

Our tradition has the entire bridal party standing at the altar beside the bride and groom, not just the newlyweds. Which meant everyone, every single person, would have to pass by and offer their good wishes. And of course, Master M was a groomsman. *Oh, dear God, you're killing me here.*

Mum took my arm as we made our way towards the loved-up couple. She had no idea what was going on inside me. Congratulations, congratulations, kiss, kiss, kiss, everyone chorused.

I shuffled along, trying to blend in with the crowd. Thank the Lord there were so many people ahead of us. Somehow, I weaved between them, practically invisible, like a ghost.

Then Mum came face-to-face with Master M. She smiled politely and said, *'Kai sta dika sou,'* which means 'all the best for your future.' I almost rolled my eyes, but I was reminded I was standing in the house of God. I had to show some level of respect.

There he was, standing next to his girlfriend. How nice. A definite eye-roll moment. I tugged Mum's arm, pretending there was a long line behind us, and hurried past without making eye contact. Bullet dodged. My heart was pounding so loudly it echoed in my ears. My breath came in shallow bursts and my palms were slick with sweat. Once we stepped outside, my heartbeat finally began to slow. The sunshine felt like a small mercy, a glimmer of hope that maybe, just maybe, I wouldn't have to see him again. Hopefully, that was the end of it.

Laugh now? Yeah. Apparently not.

We Cypriots are a small but big community. Somehow, everyone knows everyone, through family, friends, or a friend of a friend. So of course, I was bound to bump into him sooner or later. And bump into him I did. How lucky am I, right? I had already given up on love, or at least that's what I kept telling myself. But deep down, a quiet part of me still wondered if I'd ever find someone who truly saw me for me.

A year went by, filled with the usual stream of weddings, christenings, and engagements. Our family calendar was endless. On this particular evening, we had gathered to celebrate my cousin's son's christening. I remember exactly what I wore because, for once, I felt confident and good about myself: an asymmetrical black skirt paired with a denim-style halter-neck top. My shoulder-length hair had just been cut, highlighted with blonde and red tones, and straightened to perfection. The room buzzed with laughter and chatter as I mingled with my cousins. But then, suddenly, the air shifted, as if the atmosphere had grown heavier. While I was still smiling and talking, my gaze drifted across the room. And there he was.

Master M.

He sat with his siblings and their partners, directly across from our table. My heart dropped. *What the actual fuck?* This was my family's event. Why was he here? He looked uneasy, his eyes flicking towards me, his fingers tapping nervously on the table. My heart started racing again and my breathing went shallow. Why was this happening to me? Why was I so affected? I didn't even like him. If anything, I couldn't stand him. I scanned the room for his girlfriend, but she wasn't there. Weird. I wondered why she wasn't.

I did everything I could to ignore the shit out of him. I avoided crossing paths, making sure there was no reason for us to exchange a single word. If I'd had a magic wand, I would've waved it around like fairy dust and made him disappear. But no such luck.

As I danced with my cousins, I could feel his eyes on me. It made my skin crawl. Please, look away. I weaved my way through the bodies on the dance floor, trying to lose myself in the music so he couldn't find me. I stood my ground. This was my family, my moment, and I wasn't going to let anyone dim my sunshine. From that stubbornness came a strange surge of confidence, like something inside me finally snapped into place. I didn't care about him anymore. Be gone. *Ha-ha-ha! Okay, settle down, woman.*

The celebrations were finally over, and I couldn't hide my relief. I was thrilled, almost giddy, that I'd managed to get through it all without any contact with him. That was the second close encounter, and honestly, I couldn't help wondering how lucky I was – twice.

♥

A few days later, I was hanging out with my cousin when she mentioned her car was acting up and we needed to stop by the mechanics. With nothing better to do, I went along for the ride. We pulled up outside the workshop, and the moment I saw where we were, I yelled, 'WHAT THE FUCK?' Where the hell had she brought me? I turned my head and there he was. Standing right there at the entrance. The smell of oil thick in the air hit me like a slap. *What the actual fuck is going on? Am I reliving a nightmare?*

Master M and his brothers owned the workshop. My cousin somehow forgot to mention that tiny little detail. I hate being blindsided, just saying. 'Just breathe,' I told myself. But no. I refused to get out of the car. Not happening. I didn't care how rude it looked; I wasn't stepping out to say hi. I sat there like a statue, arms folded, jaw tight, not moving an inch. My cousin burst out laughing, clearly entertained by my reaction, but I was too stubborn to give in.

Those next 10 minutes felt like an eternity. The sun blazed through the window, and soon sweat started trickling down my neck. Great. Not only did I look rude, but now I smelt like it too. *Oh gee, thanks!*

My cousin opened the car door, jumped in, and drove off. Just like that. I must have cussed her out about something silly. You all know by now how colourful my mouth is. But to be fair, she had no idea why I hated him so much. So, I went on and spilled my guts. She laughed, because she found it amusing. She even said it was cute.

Cute my ass. Being the nosey bitch I am, I asked her why his girlfriend didn't join him at the christening. She told me they had broken up and that he'd been single for a while. Ohhh! Then she added that he told her to say hi to me. I rolled my eyes, of course.

That weekend, Saturday night to be exact, I was enjoying a relaxing dinner with my parents. I remember exactly where we were: Rockdale Tennis Club. Dad, being a butcher, supplied meat there and liked supporting his customers, so it was normal for us to go there for dinner on a Saturday night.

We were enjoying our meal, wrapped in our usual family conversations when my phone started ringing. I wasn't going to answer it; I didn't want to look rude. I figured if it was important, they'd call again. But the phone kept ringing and ringing. That famous Nokia ringtone echoed through my bag until I finally gave in and answered.

'Hello?' I said, not recognising the number.

'Hi Andrea, how are you?'

I held my breath the moment I recognised the voice. My heart jumped, but I forced myself to play dumb. 'Who is this?' I asked, pretending not to know.

'It's M. I got your number from your cousin. I hope that's okay. How are you?'

'I'm great,' I said, trying to sound calm.

'I was wondering if you'd like to go out for a coffee tonight?'

I started fidgeting, my fingers trembling as I answered. 'Um…I'm at dinner with my parents right now. Maybe I can meet you after.' *OMG, what on earth was I saying?*

My nerves were everywhere. After all these years of quietly passing each other, he suddenly had my number, and now we were going to sit face-to-face over a coffee. I offered to meet him at the cafe, thinking it would make things easier, but he insisted on picking me up. What a gentleman.

'I'll come out when you call me. Just ring when you're outside,' I told him.

'No problem. See you soon.'

After the call, I went silent. Not a single word left my lips during dinner. My appetite vanished; a rare thing for me. My breathing grew heavier as I tried to steady myself. I could hear my parents talking, but their words didn't reach me. It all sounded like slow, slurred echoes floating around the room. My mind kept racing. *Should I go? Shouldn't I? Why am I even going? What does he want after all these years? I should just cancel.*

But then another voice in me pushed back. *Oh, stop it. It's Saturday night. You're single. You might as well go. You've got nothing to lose.*

Fine then. I'll go.

The whole ride home after dinner with my parents was silent, painfully so. My voice stayed trapped in my throat. It felt like all of us were nervous, even though my parents had no idea who I was about to meet. On a normal night, the radio would be playing and Mum would tap her hand against the door, humming like she always did. But this night felt different: heavy, quiet, and tense. The music was off, and honestly, so was my calm.

When we finally pulled into the driveway, it felt like the stillness right before a storm broke. My stomach twisted so tight I could barely breathe. I was practically shitting myself. Dad turned off the ignition and I jumped out before he could even pull out the keys. The engine purred softly, but in my ears, it sounded like a roar. My hands were shaking as I fumbled with my own keys. I rushed inside as if the house could protect me from the weight of everything building in my chest. After that, everything turned into a blur. My phone could ring at any moment, and even the thought of it made my skin heat with nerves.

Quick spray of perfume: check. Lip balm: check. Hair in place: check. I took one last look at myself in the mirror, trying to calm the pounding in my heart. Yep. I was as ready as I could be. I sat in my room with my phone in my hand, waiting, my heart racing just like it did at that Cyprus party years ago.

❤

Then the doorbell rang. Wtf. No, this couldn't be him. I told him to call me when he got outside, not ring my doorbell. My heart skipped as I walked to the front door; my palms suddenly sweaty against the golden knob. I turned it slowly and opened the door.

My jaw dropped at the sight of him. Instead of greeting him with a warm hello, the first thing that flew out of my mouth was, 'What are you doing here? I told you to call me when you were outside.' The words came out sharper than I meant to. *God...how rude was that?*

But he didn't flinch. He just smiled that calm, confident smile and said, 'I couldn't come pick you up without saying hi to your parents. I know them; they'd think it rude if I didn't at least come in and say a quick hello.' And just like that, I softened. Well, didn't I pipe down fast? What a thoughtful gesture. I liked that more than I wanted to admit.

I opened the door wider and welcomed him in. Together, we walked down the hallway. Dad was outside watering the garden; it was his pride and joy. He loved tending to his tomatoes, avocados, and mangoes, caring for each plant as if it were a piece of himself.

As we passed through the kitchen, he went over to Mum.

'Hi, Thia, how are you?'

'I'm good, M. How are you? How are your parents? Make sure you say hi to them for me,' she replied warmly.

Oh great, I thought. *Now everyone would know we were going out for coffee.*

We continued walking towards the backyard. I slid open the glass door and called out, 'Papa!'

'Ti?' 'What?' he answered.

We walked over, and I had no idea how Dad would react. My stomach tightened as I held my breath.

'*Ooo, M, ti kamnis, pos apo dw?*' he said in his familiar, friendly tone, a way of greeting that meant, 'Oh M, how are you? What brings you here?'.

I was caught off guard by how calm, confident, respectful, and even engaging he was.

'I'm good, Thio,' M replied with a gentle smile. 'I wanted to take Andrea out for a coffee and thought it would be nice to stop in and say hi. It's been years since I've seen you all.'

Dad nodded, his eyes softening. '*Kala ekanes,*' he said, meaning, 'I'm glad you did.'

It was the first time I ever saw Dad smile at me. That smile undid years of wondering if I was enough. And just like that, something softened inside me right there. With just one smile, I got the ultimate tick of approval.

Dad's eyes remained the same grey the whole time, with no change in colour and no sudden mood change. He wasn't angry. He was calm, even happy. And when he spoke, his voice changed too. He simply said, 'Have fun,' as we walked off.

That moment became a quiet milestone in my life. For the first time, I didn't feel like a child chasing validation. I felt seen. I felt responsible. I felt grown. It warmed my heart in ways words couldn't capture, because for years I had been chasing his approval. Though I'm still not sure what for, exactly. Was it his love I wanted? His pride? Or simply to know that I was worthy of being his child? That smile didn't give me all the answers, but it gave me something: peace.

As we left the house, a thought hit me like a punch: *Oh my God, I'm trapped now. My parents knew who I was going out with, and they liked him. Shit. What if I didn't like him? What if I ended up disappointing them again?* That was exactly why I hadn't wanted him in the house until I was sure. But why did I feel like such a failure? Why did I feel I didn't deserve good things? It wasn't that they'd ever said anything; maybe I was just punishing myself for all the stupid mistakes I'd made in the past.

We drove out of the driveway into the empty street. Normally it was busy, but not that night. It was just me and M in his sleek red BMW, 1980s funk music pulsing through the speakers, windows rolled down, fresh air filling my lungs. For the first time in a long time, I felt calm. I felt...comfortable. I was okay.

The conversation started lightly, a little awkward at first, given how long it had been since we'd last spoken, yet I felt completely natural. But still, considering everything, I found myself curious, even excited, to see how the night would unfold.

We pulled up outside my favourite cafe in Maroubra, Tradewinds. Their waffles were unbeatable, seriously the bomb. He stepped out of the car, and before I could even unclip my seatbelt, my door swung open. *Oh wow, what a gentleman,* I thought.

I stepped out with casual flair, staying true to myself; there was no need for some staged, dramatic exit just to impress him. The car's low profile made my step a little awkward, but he waited patiently, hand on the door, smiling. Once I was out, he closed the door with a flourish, and we walked towards the cafe, the hum of conversation and clinking cups wrapping around us like a soft background melody. My heart started to race, a hot flush prickling my skin. The voices in my head refused to be quiet: *What are you going to talk about? Be polite. Don't say anything stupid.* I shushed them. *I've got this,* I told myself.

We sat down opposite each other. Great. Just me, just him, face-to-face. Okay...just breathe. He broke the ice.

'So, what's good here?' he asked.

Without missing a beat, I launched into a full-on tribute to the strawberry waffles: three warm, fluffy waffles, a scoop of cold vanilla ice cream, a perfectly made berry compote, and fresh strawberries piled on top. Oh, yumm. My favourite. Heaven on a plate.

'We have to try them,' he said, eyes lighting up.

When the waitress came over, he grinned. 'I heard the waffles are good here. We should try them, and two Cokes, please.' You can't drink coffee with waffles. You need something cold and refreshing to wash them down with.

The initial awkwardness melted away and we slid into conversation like familiar friends. The back and forth felt effortless. Light banter and laughter replaced the nervous static in my head, and I could tell he was caught up in the moment too. When the waffles arrived, we attacked them without shame, forks first, straight in. He chewed, then looked up.

'These waffles are unreal.'

'Told you,' I said, feeling smug.

We sank back into our seats, letting the conversation drift. I asked him about work, his family, and the usual small talk. But beneath the surface, something churned inside me. There was this weight on my chest, something I needed to say, but I kept stalling.

A quiet pause settled between us, and then my inner voice nudged me: *Ask him.* Oh, do I? Should I bring up the past, or let it lie? I would have let it go. However, those persistent whispers grew louder, screaming, *Ask him now.* So, I did.

'Can I ask you something?' I blurted, my voice tinged with nerves.

'Yeah, of course,' he said, leaning in slightly.

'So…What stopped you from showing up to that party all those years ago?'

He laughed. *Oh God, why did I even open my mouth? What an idiot.*

'Honestly, I wanted to come,' he said, straightening in his seat. 'I was so sick with gastro. I knew you'd be waiting, and I was even hoping to make it for just an hour. But I was too sick to even take a step out.'

'And you didn't think to tell me afterwards?' I asked, keeping my voice steady. No sugar-coating. I needed the truth. I needed answers.

'The next day, the doctor came to our house and gave me an injection so I'd be okay for the flight back,' he explained, his voice calm, almost casual. 'I tried to tell you afterwards, but then you quit dance classes.'

'Yeah, I quit because I didn't want to see you. I hated you for what you did,' I said bluntly.

'Fair call,' he shrugged. 'Then I saw you at the christening and wanted to talk, but you ignored me. I couldn't even get you to look my way. So, I spoke with your cousin a few days later and got your number. I hope that was okay.'

I had nothing to say. For the first time, I was truly speechless. Me, speechless? That never happened. I stared down at my plate, trying to avoid his eyes, and mumbled, 'Want the last waffle?'

He smiled faintly. 'No, I'm full,' he said.

After all those years of wondering why he hadn't shown up, I finally had my answer. He hadn't stood me up because he didn't like me, but because he was sick. Suddenly, a pang of guilt hit me for calling him an arsehole.

'Well, we're here now, I suppose,' I said, shovelling the last waffle into my mouth. Couldn't let that go to waste. Getting that off my chest felt like a release. My body melted into the seat, and for the first time in a long while, I felt light. There we were, two people sitting across from each other trying to rediscover something that once was. It was simple, unforced, and oddly comforting.

One night turned into a few nights a week. We texted and called, hung out, and introduced each other to friends. It was effortlessly easy and without judgement. It just felt right, whatever it was.

The funniest moments always came at Yiayia's. Every time we stopped by for coffee, she'd start on me, just as grandmothers do. In rapid Greek. 'What is this?' she'd scold. 'You've been dating for months. Isn't it time you got married?'

'YIAYIA!' I yelled. 'WTF, Yiayia, shut up, don't scare him off!' He laughed.

That comment must have stayed in his head, because not long after Yiayia's digs, he turned to me casually and asked, 'Well, what do you think?'

I looked at him, a little thrown off. 'Think about what, exactly?'

'What your yiayia said.'

Was he really asking me to marry him? Was that his way of proposing? My heart skipped a beat, but I played it cool, shrugged, and said, 'Yeah, eventually,' then left it at that.

He surprised me after that with sudden little dates and long, aimless drives. We would just cruise around with the music low, the windows down, and the warm air brushing against our faces. We started spending time with friends, laughing more, and falling into an easy rhythm. Our lives began to intertwine. For the first time in my life, I felt truly seen and appreciated. This was a different kind of affection. It was genuine, warm, and new. I had always longed for love, and for once it felt like maybe I had found it.

One afternoon, he took me for a picnic at Observatory Hill. The sun was slowly painting the sky in golds and pinks as it set. We spread out a blanket and he pulled out strawberries and a bottle of chilled Verdi. Cringeworthy now, but back then, I thought it was the best lolly water ever. I remember the sweetness of the strawberries, how it lingered as he talked.

But something about the way he was acting made me pause. Why was he being so extra nice? What was brewing beneath that calm smile? Sure enough, before I could piece it together, he reached into his pocket, pulled out a ring, and with a grin that stretched wide across his face, asked, 'Will you marry me?'

Of course, me being me, I couldn't help myself. I let out a soft giggle, pretending to play it cool, and asked, 'Can I think about it?'

Without missing a beat, he looked at me with that mischievous grin and said, 'Can I push you down the hill?'

That did it. We both burst out laughing so hard that my stomach began to hurt. And right there, caught between laughter and love, half-joking yet half-swooning, I threw my hands up and shouted, 'Yes, yes, I'll marry you!'

♥

Our journey as husband and wife began on Saturday 19 February 2005. It was a fairytale wedding, one of the best days of my life. The weather was scorching, around 40°C, but nothing could steal the magic of that day, from being surprised with a horse and carriage to the moment Dad walked me down the aisle. Everything felt beautifully surreal.

The sun blazed through the church windows, washing the room in a warm, golden light. Dad took my hand, holding me firmly, and said, 'I got you.' Those three simple words of reassurance eased so much tension inside me. Mum sat in the front row, her eyes glistening with pride, arrayed in her emerald green outfit, a quiet strength radiating from her that spoke of her own life's journey.

During the photo session I accidentally spilled Scotch and Coke over my dress. I laughed it off; there was nothing I could do about it. It was my wedding day, and perfection wasn't the goal; joy was. Then, as if the heavens wanted to join the celebration, a storm rolled in. Lightning cracked across the sky, thunder roared, and the rain came pouring down. We ran for cover into the car. It took five umbrellas just to get me out again because my dress was so enormous.

My absolute favourite part of our wedding aside from the ceremony itself was our reception entrance. It was mind-blowing. The doorway was filled with dry ice, and the smoke machine hissed as the *Bongo Song* blared through the speakers. We waited at the back, dancing, anticipating the exact moment to make our grand entrance. When the doors finally opened, 480 guests rose to their feet, cheering and welcoming us as we danced in. I'd never had so many eyes on me at once. *Oh, my goodness!* What a feeling.

I had just married. I was now Mrs P. While I'll always be my dad's little girl, I had just become someone's wife. *When did I grow up? When did all my fears disappear?* It was at that moment that I realised he loved me for who I truly am, not just for my appearance.

But let me rewind a bit. Long before we were engaged, or even married, when we were just starting to date, I still felt uneasy in my own body. I hid behind my clothes, covering up what I thought were my flaws. After numerous consultations with surgeons, I made the biggest decision of my life: I had a breast reduction.

And he didn't bat an eyelid. He knew how much I struggled with my self-image and the inner demons I faced each day, and he stood by me through it all, supporting me. It was in that moment that I truly realised he was a good man with sincere intentions.

For years, I chased happiness, the kind of happiness that is heartfelt. For years, I was rebellious and bitter, carrying the weight of sadness and brokenness. I felt trapped by my worries and fears, burdened by the unspoken love I never received in childhood. I spent so much time trying to fill that void with anything I thought might make me whole. But then, after all those years of running, the chase finally found me. Master M wove his way back into my life, bringing with him everything I had longed for. For the first time, I felt the strength to lower my guard. Through his compassion and understanding, he earned my trust, and with it, I embraced his commitment.

Yes, the journey of my life started off rocky, and it took many unexpected turns. But I've come to realise that fairy tales aren't just for girls in sparkly dresses. They're for stubborn, guarded women who learn to let love in. Women like me. As I stepped into marriage, I found myself wondering: would this love be the one to rewrite the hollowness I'd carried for so long?

CHAPTER 4

Seeds of hope

Fairytales belong to magical characters in storybooks and films. They don't exactly show up in Sydney, Australia. I'm no magical character. I'm just a normal gal trying to live my life, like everyone else in this big world.

On our first night in our new home, Master M and I stood in the empty living room, holding hands and dreaming about the life we'd build together. There was a mix of excitement and fear in our hearts. It was a huge adjustment. In the span of a single day, I went from living with my parents to becoming a wife. A whole new chapter unfolded as we began turning a house into a home. And with that came the weight of adult responsibilities: mortgage repayments, bills, putting food on the table, working, and juggling that elusive work–life balance.

Doing it all for yourself is hard enough. But doing it while learning to love someone...well, that's a whole other challenge. Your choices must make room for them. It's scary. It's overwhelming. It's stressful, not a fairy tale. This is reality.

I'd worked my way into a position in the accounts department at a car dealership in Warwick Farm, but the road there hadn't been a straight line. I had bounced between jobs, unsure of what I truly wanted. Unlike those students who finish school with a clear vision of their future, I was still searching, burdened by the weight of my teenage rebellion, hoping to find my place in the world.

I started a Bachelor of Social Work at the University of Sydney, but dropped out after just one semester. A lecture built around confronting case studies pushed me to my limit. I was left deeply traumatised and had to defer. That experience made me realise something important: I wasn't emotionally equipped for social work, especially not when it involved minors. I needed something else; something that would align better with who I was becoming.

Retail had drained me. The constant push to sell, to smile even when I didn't feel like it, left me exhausted. So, I enrolled in a Bachelor of Human Resources at the University of New South Wales, hoping it would be the right fit. But that, too, left me cold, so I withdrew, feeling like I was chasing something that just wasn't there. Directionless and unsure, I worried I was letting my parents down. While I tried to figure things out, I continued to work in retail, hoping clarity would eventually come.

The next year, I enrolled in a Diploma of Front Office Management at TAFE. I managed to finish the year, but it didn't bring me the sense of purpose I had hoped for. So, I took a hotel job. The hours were brutal, filled with odd shifts and my day had no rhythm to it. The hotel's chaos drained me, and my body clock was completely wrecked.

♥

I'd dreamed of being a flight attendant since I was young. The thought of travelling, seeing new places and meeting new people lit me up. But as time went on I started to second-guess myself. I questioned my height, my looks, and whether I was enough to pursue this dream. Then, one day, as I was scrolling through employment site SEEK, I saw flight attendant roles posted. A rush of excitement hit me, followed quickly by doubt. The dilemma hit hard: *Should I chase this dream now, or should I wait, especially with Master M now in the picture? Could I build a career that allowed me to travel and still honour my commitment to him? Should I take the leap?*

In the end, I decided I would. I applied for the job, and after several nerve-wracking rounds of interviews, I made it through. I sat there, heart pounding, hoping my passion came through in every word. I was so close. Just a few more stages to go and the dream would finally be mine. But then, during one of the interviews, I started to feel uneasy.

My gut was rarely wrong, and it was telling me something wasn't quite right. Then came the question: 'Do you have a criminal record?'

I paused. 'I'm not a criminal,' I said, my voice steady, though my heart raced. 'But technically, I do have a record. It's a technical distinction.'

♥

Tensions with my sister had been building for months, ever since her new boyfriend started pulling her further away from us. A few months earlier, she'd gotten involved with a total loser. Not going to lie, I couldn't stand the asshole. He consistently showed a lack of respect towards my parents, me, and Master M. He refused to eat with us at the dinner table, opting instead to stay in the bedroom and hide food there, as if to keep the rest of us from touching it. And the worst part? He never contributed a cent. My dad paid for everything.

As time passed, we all noticed a shift in my sister. Her behaviour started to change in ways that were so unlike her. It was like she wasn't herself anymore. I've always been fiercely protective of my parents, and seeing how she was drifting away from us, I hit my breaking point. I just couldn't sit back and watch it anymore. That frustration exploded one night in a heated argument with my sister. Raised voices, pushing, shoving...It was a full-blown clash and something that was bound to happen.

She packed her bags and left. Honestly, I couldn't have cared less about where she went. But then, less than 24 hours later, two uniformed police officers showed up at my door. I was blindsided. They asked for Andrea, and I told them it was me. Without missing a beat, they handed me an apprehended violence order (AVO) and informed me that I wasn't allowed to come within 250 metres of my sister.

I was stunned, unable to make sense of what was happening. Why would she do this? Why would she go to such lengths to act against me? My first reaction was to laugh, though it wasn't out of amusement; more like disbelief. How could an order like this even make sense when we were living in the same house? The officers patiently explained the terms and told me I had to appear in court.

I fucken lost my shit. I called Dad, who was at work, and within the hour he came home. The person who was supposed to be my sister looked like she was completely under the thumb of her boyfriend. Fucken scum. And honestly, I couldn't stand it. It felt like betrayal.

I showed up in court like I was told to, with Master M, Dad, and my cousin by my side for support. The air in that courtroom was freezing, cutting right through me. My sister was there too, but she wouldn't look me in the eye. She was avoiding me, full of shame. She kept her gaze down, refusing to meet our eyes. It was like she didn't even see me anymore.

Despite her being labelled the 'victim', honestly, it wasn't one-sided. We were both hurt. We'd both screamed, fought, and said things we didn't mean. It wasn't just me. But she chose to file charges against me, and that hit harder than anything. I walked out of that courtroom feeling betrayed, but strangely, there was a sense of relief too.

A few days later I got an email. My airline application has been rejected. Denied. All because of my record. That was it. My dream job? Gone. My sister had unknowingly just sabotaged everything I'd worked for. I was crushed. Furious.

I called Dad again, my voice shaking with anger. 'Your daughter has fucked up my life. I can't even get a job now because of what she's done to me.'

That evening, I overheard Dad on the phone. His voice grew louder, sterner, and shook with fierce love. 'You better revoke the AVO against your sister. You're ruining her life. You're both at fault. How could you do this to her?' he said. It was the first time I'd ever heard him defend me. The golden child, the one who had always been seen as faultless, was finally being held accountable. Within days, I received a letter confirming the AVO had been withdrawn. I hadn't expected that.

My sister, my own flesh and blood, had shattered my heart. She betrayed me. No job could fix that. The damage was done. It was the ultimate betrayal.

❤

For a while I worked in retail, but eventually I landed a job at a car dealership. The hum of engines filled the office, a steady rhythm that grounded me. It felt like a fresh start, an opportunity for some job security. I began in the service department and after some time I moved into accounts. It couldn't have come at a better moment, especially now that I was newly married.

Master M had just started his own business. A spray painter by trade, he opened a workshop and began spray painting kitchens for joiners. He started small, gradually building his clientele. Money was tight. My income was low, and there were weeks when Master M didn't get paid – just the harsh realities of self-employment.

Then, my body began to betray me. Out of nowhere, sharp, excruciating abdominal pain hit, episodes that would come and go, returning every month. I found myself in and out of hospital, enduring treatments for ruptured cysts, IV drips, and heavy doses of painkillers to ease the persistent ache.

During one hospital stay, a doctor pulled me aside, his voice gentle. He told me that my condition could affect my ability to have children. He suggested I consider starting a family sooner rather than later, as it might take a long time for me to get pregnant, if at all. The weight of his words hit me like a freight train. I couldn't shake the fear that my mother's history of loss might be repeating itself in me.

There was nothing but silence. My world came to a complete stop. The clock seemed to stop ticking. I guess all we could do was put our faith in a higher power. The power of God. If it's meant to be, it's meant to be. Sounds logical, doesn't it? But deep down, I felt anything but hopeful. Yeah, I felt inadequate. I felt shattered. I had always dreamt of having my own family, and just a few months into marriage, here I was. This should have been the happiest time of our lives, yet instead, we were staring into the uncertainty of it all.

Master M and I kept going through the motions, trying to survive adulthood. It was bloody hard. Living week to week on a tight budget, each day feeling like we were barely holding on, was daunting.

❤

My birthday was coming up, and my girlfriends had organised a low-key dinner and drinks at our local pub. I was looking forward to it, but something didn't feel right. I couldn't shake the discomfort. Was it just a cyst about to rupture, or was it something else entirely? Pregnancy seemed like the least likely possibility, given the medical prognosis that conceiving would take plenty of time. Still, I decided to pop into the chemist and grab a pregnancy test – two of them, just to be sure. Sensible, right?

On the Friday afternoon before the celebrations, I decided to take the test. I had just got home from work and Master M hadn't arrived yet. Perfect. I wanted to do this alone. I went straight into the bathroom, the cold tiles biting against my feet, and took the test.

My heart raced as I waited. Before I could even pull my gaze away, the second line appeared. My jaw dropped. No. I grabbed the second test from the box and tried again. The same thing happened. That unmistakable second line, appeared instantly.

OMG. I was pregnant! A current of shock ran through me, and I could barely catch my breath.

Just then, I heard Master M's car roar up the driveway, followed by the sound of the front door slamming shut. 'I'm home!' he called.

'I'm upstairs,' I answered, my voice trembling. He came up and when he found me in the ensuite, I held the test up and said, 'I'm pregnant.' He froze.

Without a word, he pulled out his wallet, then snapped it shut and bolted. I heard his footsteps pounding down the stairs and the front door slamming behind him.

I sat there, stunned, and then I burst into tears. *Did he not want the baby? What was I going to do? This was what we'd always wanted...wasn't it?* I lay on the bed, drowning in tears, the weight of uncertainty pressing down on me. The tiny life growing inside me suddenly felt like the biggest responsibility in the world, and I couldn't stop the panic rising in me. *What if he didn't feel the same way? What if I had to do this alone?*

My mind raced, jumping to the worst possible conclusions about being left alone to raise this child. I could barely take care of myself, let alone a helpless little human. The thought alone sent me spiralling deeper into fear.

Moments later, I heard the door open softly. I hadn't even realised he'd come back. My body went still, numb, almost lifeless as I braced myself for whatever was coming next. He walked quietly into the room, sat beside me and wrapped me in the warmest hug, followed with a soft kiss, and the tension inside me began to melt away. His soft eyes met mine as he kept kissing my forehead.

'I'm so sorry I reacted like that,' he whispered. 'You just caught me off guard.'

I remember my voice trembling as I asked, 'Do you want the baby?'

Without hesitation, he said, 'YES, YES, YES! This is the best birthday present ever. This is our baby.'

And just like that, the fear faded. We sat there holding each other, tears streaming down our faces. We were going to be parents. Oh my!

The irony wasn't lost on me. I had just found out I was pregnant, and that very night happened to be my birthday celebration with drinks and all kinds of things. How was I supposed to keep such life-changing news to myself? The thought of pretending to sip cocktails while secretly carrying a tiny human inside me felt overwhelming. I had to play it cool, at least for now.

We all arrived at my birthday bash. The crowd was excited, loud, and ready to make memories. The music was loud, the laughter infectious, the smell of grilled steak overwhelming the air. There were free-flowing drinks, endless chatter, and in the middle of it all, there was me, with a secret growing quietly in my tummy. When the girls offered to get me a drink, I lifted the glass I'd been nursing all evening, just Coke. 'I'm good. Next one,' I said with a smile. To everyone else, it looked like bourbon and Coke. But the act was harder than it seemed. My heart raced as I caught my best friend's eye. I grabbed her by the wrist and practically dragged her into the bathroom.

Short side note, which is pretty hilarious. Remember my Year 4 buddy, angel-faced L? The one who stopped talking to me after the whole 'Oh Sugar' incident? Well, fast forward to adulthood, we bumped into each other, patched things up, exchanged numbers, and just like that, we were inseparable again.

So, there I was, shoving sweet L into the cubicle. 'Do not react. Don't say a word. Just stay quiet,' I hissed, my voice low and serious. She nodded, completely confused. I took a deep breath and whispered, 'I'm pregnant.'

Her eyes widened, and before I could blink, she let out a squeal of excitement. I clapped my hand over her mouth, trying not to laugh as she bounced on the spot like a kid in a lolly shop. Then, just as quickly, she straightened up when the cubicle door creaked open.

'You're the only one who knows,' I whispered. 'Help me keep it under wraps. I'm drinking Coke, but everyone thinks it's bourbon and Coke. Please have my back.'

We reapplied our lip balm, fixed our faces, and walked back into the party as if nothing had happened. Without anyone suspecting our shenanigans.

♥

My first trimester was awful; riddled with morning sickness that lasted all bloody day. I was constantly running to the loo. It was getting harder to hide.

One day at the office, while I was sitting at my computer desk, my supervisor called me into her office and closed the door. Oh shit, this is serious. I'm getting into trouble. What have I done?

'Andrea, I've noticed you've been away from your desk a lot recently. Your productivity has also dropped compared with other weeks. Can you explain yourself?' She pulled her glasses off and fixed her eyes on me with such a suspicious but caring look. She was a damn scary woman, though.

I thought I was going to vomit. I sat in her office and stared at her. No words would come. I burst into tears. She was taken aback by my reaction. 'What's wrong? What's happened?' she asked.

Between sobs I blurted, 'I'm pregnant. I'm so sorry, I can't help that I've been so sick, I can't stop going to the loo.' She jumped up from her chair, wrapped me in a sudden hug and congratulated me. She apologised if she had come across harsh and told me that if I needed to go to any doctor's appointments, I could make them in the afternoon and leave early. She wasn't so scary after all.

❤

Throughout my first trimester, I wrestled with a constant sense of fear, especially the fear of miscarriage because of Mum's history, and fear of having a stroke. The anxiety lingered like a shadow. I had nightmares, cried virtually every day, and carried a gnawing worry about how we'd raise a child when there was so little money coming in. Still, we showed unwavering commitment. Master M pulled all-nighters, determined to make things work. We were meticulous about saving, creating budgets, and planning for our future. We genuinely did the best we could with what we had.

As my pregnancy progressed and the baby grew stronger and healthier, the morning sickness finally began to ease during the second trimester. But that's when the cravings kicked in; an odd kind of ritual that took over my afternoons. Every day at precisely two o'clock, I needed a Boost chocolate bar, a can of Coke, and a packet of Smith's Cheese & Onion chips. It had to be Cheese & Onion, nothing else could satisfy me. By the time I reached the third trimester, my cravings changed yet again from Cheese & Onion to Salt & Vinegar. Pregnancy does strange things to you.

One sweltering Saturday morning, I woke up feeling terribly unwell. It couldn't have come at a worse time. Our next-door neighbour was getting married and we'd been invited to the celebration. But as soon as I sat up I knew something wasn't right. My head spun, my body felt heavy, and a strange faintness washed over me. The heat only made it worse. There was no way I could make it to the wedding.

Still, I didn't want to seem rude. I moved slowly, forcing myself to get dressed, grabbed the envelope and my keys, and made my way next door. When the bride opened the door, her eyes widened in concern, I must've looked ghostly pale. I quickly urged her not to worry, telling her to focus on enjoying her big day. She hesitated, but I smiled, hugged her gently, handed her the envelope, and apologised for not being able to attend the celebration. She understood right away. I could see the excitement and nervousness dancing across her face. It was her wedding day after all, and I didn't want to hold her up any longer. So, I said goodbye and turned to leave. Usually we'd wait for each other to get safely inside before parting ways, but not today.

As I stepped down her front steps, gripping the railing, my body grew weaker with every step. By the time I reached our driveway, everything around me began to darken. The heat rising from the pavement seeped through my clothes as I struggled towards the front door. I barely made it to the step before everything went black, and I collapsed forward, landing hard on my stomach. I lay there, face down, the world silent and distant. I must've been out for a while, though I had no idea how long. Even though it was still daylight, everything felt heavy and dim, as if the light itself had vanished.

Then I heard the door creak open. Master M had come out to toss something into the bin. I could tell from the gasp in his throat that he hadn't expected to find me lying there, motionless.

'Andrea!' he shouted, panic rippling through his voice. I could hear the fear in it, the raw, trembling kind that makes your chest tighten. He knelt beside me, his hands shaking as he tried to lift me up. Then, in a flash, he ran back inside and came out again with a pillow, some water, and a few tea towels. Cold water splashed over my face. My eyes fluttered open, the world swimming in and out of focus. I could feel grit scraping against my cheek, the rough ground beneath me, and the pounding of my heartbeat echoing in my ears. *What had just happened? Why was I on the floor?*

Then it hit me, *oh God, the baby*. A wave of panic surged through me, and I started to cry loudly. He crouched beside me, hands trembling, and gently helped me to my feet. His face was pale with worry. He checked me for cuts, pressed a bottle of water into my hand, then bundled me carefully into the car. We drove straight to the doctor.

A deep, bone-deep panic gripped me. My whole body trembled uncontrollably. The fear of losing my baby felt terrifyingly real. I whispered a prayer under my breath, pleading silently to God. I couldn't shake the fear that my mum's fate might become mine.

While we waited for the ultrasound, my emotions spun out of control. Tears streamed down my cheeks. I couldn't even breathe properly. I felt so unsettled. My heart was racing, caught between dread and hope. I just needed to know.

When the sonographer came in, she spread the cool gel across my stomach and began to scan. Sensing my distress, she moved quickly but spoke gently.

'There's your healthy, happy baby,' she said softly, a gentle smile on her face. 'It's heartbeat is strong...steady.'

The tears kept coming, but this time they flew from relief. All was well. Our baby was safe.

As I edged towards the end of my pregnancy, the fear slowly gave way to excitement. Apart from the morning sickness and that one terrifying blackout, it turned out to be a strangely breezy season. I savoured every moment. The baby's tiny flutters sent ripples of joy through me; the midnight kicks made me smile even when sleep escaped me. Even the sharp foot cramps that made me yelp in the middle of the night and scared the life out of Master M, who thought I was going into labour, became part of our story. I loved it all, every single bit of it.

I was desperate to meet this child, ready to offer it a loving home and unwavering devotion. At that point, I didn't understand the depth of the bond forming between us, nor how much strength this unborn child was already giving me just to keep going. My will to survive had somehow anchored itself to this tiny life growing inside me.

Each night, as I sat on the couch feeling every kick and every tightening from those Braxton Hicks contractions, my thoughts drifted to Mum, her courage, her quiet determination. She had faced her storms with grace, and thinking of that filled me with resolve. I made a promise to myself to be a dedicated, nurturing mother, to give everything I had to raise a kind soul, and to lead by example. If she could make it through what she had, then I could bloody well do this too. After all, I am my mother's daughter.

When I first told her about the pregnancy, she squeezed my hand, no words, just pride shining through her silence. Her eyes said everything, holding both her battles and her blessings in one long look.

I was thirty-eight weeks along, heavily pregnant in how I felt, if not quite in how I looked. From behind, you might not have guessed; I was all belly, like I'd swallowed a watermelon.

At first, I thought it would be a girl. Maybe that was my fear of Mum losing a boy speaking through me, or maybe I just wanted everything to be okay this time. Either way, all that truly mattered was having a healthy child.

My obstetrician was about to go on holiday, so he suggested we induce since the baby was ready. The induction was set for the Sunday of Orthodox Easter, a date that somehow felt both symbolic and strange.

The midwives applied the gel and told me to let nature take its course. I even managed to get some sleep that night, which felt like a small miracle. But by six in the morning, the cramps began. They were planning to reapply a second round of gel, but since I was already progressing, they said it wouldn't be necessary. The nurse handed me a Panadol to take the edge off and suggested we head down to the delivery suite. They'd planned to wheel me to the delivery room, but I insisted on walking; apparently, it helps. What should have been a quick five-minute stroll stretched into thirty minutes as I stopped and started with every contraction. There was no denying it anymore: I was well and truly in labour.

When I finally clambered onto the bed, feeling like a beached whale, they ruptured my waters. And then the contractions hit with a vengeance, one crashing into the next. I was only a few centimetres dilated; there was still a long way to go. I needed relief.

Please, epidural, now. They started me on gas first, but it made my eyes roll back uncontrollably and they quickly pulled it away. I wanted the pain to stop somehow, anyhow. Just as the anaesthetist arrived to insert the epidural, another contraction began building. He paused, waiting for it to ease.

'Hold still,' he instructed. But the timing was cruel: a contraction came right as he was inserting the needle. Master M held me steady, his hand gripping mine, calm and unwavering. I gritted my teeth through that one, then the next rolled through, relentless. Gradually, the epidural began to work its quiet magic.

I gasped for breath and told the midwife, 'I need to go to the toilet.' She shot me a quick look, then hurriedly pulled back the covers. After checking how far I was dilated, she dashed out of the room, phone in hand. I heard her call the obstetrician, her voice urgent: 'Where are you? This baby's coming, it's not waiting for anyone!'

She rushed back in and said, 'You have two choices: we wait five minutes for your doctor, or you start pushing.' Before she'd even finished speaking my body took over. I began pushing instinctively, as if my body had a mind of its own.

Two pushes. *O-U-C-H.* A burning sensation shot through me; the epidural had not quite taken full effect. The baby's head crowned and the midwife told me to stop for a moment. She checked to make sure the cord wasn't wrapped around the baby's neck, then looked at me and asked, 'Do you want to see?'

I was crying, shaking my head. 'No, no, I don't want to see. I can feel everything. That's more than enough.'

She gently draped a towel over the baby's head, then lifted my hand and placed it on my baby's head.

Oh Lord, that was my baby.

Just as I felt my strength waning, a surge of energy rushed through me. Suddenly, I was fired up, desperate to meet this child. With the next contraction, I pushed with everything I had. One big, clean push. And then, I felt it: the miraculous slippery slide as the baby emerged.

For a moment, there was silence, everyone frozen in anticipation. Then, the sweetest sound I'd ever heard filled the room: a loud, wailing cry. 'Waaaaaa.'

'What is it? Is it a boy? Is it a girl?' Voices murmured around me, but no one dared to speak. The midwife carefully wrapped the baby and placed him on my chest. Its tiny hand curled around my finger as I held him close. I kept asking, 'What is it?'

Master M, standing beside me with the proudest grin, simply said, 'Check.'

I slowly unwrapped the tiny bundle in my arms. This was ours.

'It's a boy. We have a son,' I sobbed, tears of joy streaming down my face. Our sweet baby boy, A, was born.

♥

We welcomed him into the world at 9.01 a.m. on 24 April 2006. I was blessed with the gift of motherhood, and all the fears that had haunted me throughout my pregnancy suddenly faded. That tiny bundle in my arms brought a depth of love and joy I never knew existed. His warmth against my chest melted away every trace of fear.

I was completely wrapped up in him, utterly smitten with my newborn. Ten little fingers, 10 little toes, a button nose, and a set of lungs that could make the world stop and listen. Everything outside of that room felt miles away. My world had narrowed to this perfect little creature in my arms. All my worries dissolved and he was my only focus.

Visitors flooded in, eager to meet the newest member of our family. The attention was overwhelming, so much warmth, so much love. Mum and Dad were utterly smitten with their first grandchild. Every time they entered the room, their eyes immediately found him, hardly noticing me. Who was I, after all? Just their daughter, the one who had given birth to their grandson. Watching them admire him so much was both fascinating and surreal. I had never seen them this way before. This level of devotion was something new. They say a grandparent's love is different, and I could feel the truth of that in every glance and touch. It was pure, not just the result of postnatal hormones running wild.

Was my bliss a kind of blessed ignorance, or was there a quiet anxiety lingering, knowing that reality would soon come crashing down? Adulthood had arrived with full force – sleepless nights, nappies, feeding schedules, and the overwhelming weight of finances. Raising a child was no small task. Yikes! But we would get through it. After all, others had done it before us, right? But still, how did they manage to make ends meet?

The birth of A was a moment of immense excitement for us, a day we'd been dreaming of. We were overjoyed, floating in a bubble of happiness. That afternoon, Master M slipped out to freshen up, and when he came back, he had a bouquet of flowers in his hand. Such a sweet gesture, though unnecessary, because I already had my perfect gift: our baby, wrapped up in a striped blanket, right there in my arms.

He'd also bought chocolates for our visitors. It was thoughtful, but, in hindsight, I could hardly focus on anything except the miracle I was holding. On his way to pay for fuel at the service station, he'd run into a mate behind the counter. They celebrated for a moment, the joy of the day still lingering between them. When he tried to pay for the fuel, though, something strange happened. The card terminal flashed a big red cross, Declined.

He tried again. Declined. And again. Declined. Then Insufficient Funds.

'Oh, fuck,' he muttered, his face drained of colour, panic creeping into every feature. His mind raced: *Do I have any cash stashed away at home? No. We'd just paid the obstetrician. Maybe I could call my mum? No, too embarrassing.* He paused, thinking hard. Then it hit him. One of my aunts had just visited and slipped an envelope with a little money into the baby's greeting card. He dashed back to the car, tore open the envelope, grabbed the notes, and used them to pay for petrol. We'd just spent the baby's welcome money on petrol. How embarrassing.

When he came back to the hospital he looked even paler, like the weight of the world had settled on his shoulders. I could tell something was wrong the second he walked in, even before he said a word. He tried to brush it off, but I wouldn't let it slide.

'Tell me, now, or I'll scream,' I said, playing the drama queen to a T.

He finally told me the truth. We were flat broke. Not a cent left in the account.

Great. Just great.

I inhaled deeply through my nose, holding the breath for a moment before exhaling slowly, trying to steady myself. 'We'll be okay. We will. We've just had a baby; this is the biggest blessing. We'll be okay,' I whispered, gently cradling A in my arms.

I could see the strain etched across Master M's face. He was usually the calm one, the steady presence, so when I saw him looking shaken, I knew that the ground beneath us had shifted. I kept reassuring him everything would turn out fine. If I had to return to work sooner than planned then so be it. His work had slowed down, but it wasn't his fault. Some clients still owed him money for jobs he'd completed. We had resources to fall back on; we weren't completely without. And if it came down to it, we could always move back in with my parents. There was no shame in that.

That night, I sent Master M home, hoping he could get some rest. But how do you sleep when the weight of financial worry presses down on you? How do you rest when the load of responsibility doubles overnight?

I didn't sleep a wink. All through the night, I lay there, watching A, tears silently streaming down my face. I whispered apologies to him over and over, regretting that I had brought him into a world where we were already failing even before we'd begun. We hadn't even started and I already felt like I'd let him down.

I tried to breastfeed him, but he refused to latch. I didn't give up; I kept trying, but each time, he screamed louder. I tried again, and his cries grew even more frantic. Soon we were both crying. I was holding him close, my arms aching with effort. I wondered if he could feel my anxiety, my fear. Eventually, after what seemed like an eternity of rocking and softly singing to him, he finally settled against my chest. In the stillness of the room, I whispered into the darkness, *Everything will work out. It has to.*

By dawn, sunlight crept through the hospital blinds. A new day. A fresh start. Baby A slept peacefully in my arms, and for a moment, hope found its way back to me, fragile but real.

Just then, my phone buzzed, shattering the calm. It was Master M. I answered quietly, careful not to disturb the peace that had settled over the room.

'Hey, babe, did you get some sleep? Is A okay?' he asked.

'Yeah...nah, no sleep,' I admitted. 'We're both good, though. Did you sleep? What time are you coming?'

Instead of answering, he dropped a bombshell. 'About that...I'm not sure when I'll be there. I just got a call that I landed a massive contract. They want me to start right away.'

He was elated. I was stunned. Tears pricked my eyes, but this time, they were tears of joy.

'Oh my God, babe, that's amazing! Congratulations!' I managed to say, my voice was trembling.

Then came the words I'll never forget.

'Our little boy is our miracle. He's blessed our family. This was all God's work. From no jobs to being flat-out busy. He's the reason. Our son brought us luck.'

I was a blubbering mess, speechless. Two miracles in two days? That wasn't coincidence. That was divine intervention.

As I looked at our tiny family, I held A's little hand, his tiny fingers gripping mine, and in that moment, I realised that no matter what life threw our way, we would face it together. Money would come and go, but the love and bond we shared were unshakable. I made the sign of the cross, whispering a quiet, trembling 'Thank you God' for entrusting me with this precious family.

How would motherhood shape me, I wondered, as I stepped into this unknown chapter of my life? I didn't have a clear plan. I didn't have financial security, or even the faintest idea of what tomorrow might bring. But I had something far more precious: love. And that, I knew, was enough to give me the courage to step into this new journey. I held onto the hope that, somehow, everything would work out for the good of our little family.

CHAPTER 5

Heart of shield

I have always believed that everyone is born with a purpose, though what that purpose is often remains a mystery. At times, I wonder if mine is simply to protect and support the people I love, just like the night I held my son A close, his tiny breaths grounding me in my role as protector. In darker moments, I question whether this world is meant to be a place of constant hardship; a harsh reality designed to test our resolve. When pain and heartache strike, I find myself turning to God with questions I know may never be answered. *Why the suffering? Why the loss? Why the silence?* Yet even as I wrestle with these doubts, my faith in Him is also the very thing that sustains me. It becomes my anchor, a quiet reservoir of strength that allows me to persevere. That paradox – seeking answers, yet surviving through the very faith that feels shaken – is a delicate balance I continue to hold.

Growing up in a household with just one sibling, it often felt like I was an only child. The loneliness of that reality weighed heavily on me. I would look at sisters who shared a bond so strong it seemed unbreakable and feel a sharp pang of envy. I often asked myself: *Why not us?* My father's two sisters, for example, are inseparable. Watching them as I grew up was beautiful yet bittersweet; a reminder of what my sister and I lacked. We were (and still are) two very different people. Different in personality, appearance, behaviour, values, morals, everything. How could two people raised under the same roof, sharing the same parents and the same blood, turn out so extraordinarily different?

Her choices in relationships were another reason we couldn't really blend; it only widened the gulf between us. She made unwise choices, some of which I don't want to begin describing. I've already written about the first one, which thankfully was short-lived. I should have cut her off completely after what she did to me. But I didn't. Somehow, I found the strength to forgive her. That forgiveness wasn't for her; not really. It was for the sake of peace, for my parents, and for the fragile harmony of our home. Still, I cannot understand where she finds these men. It must be in some hidden corner where only the dodgy lurk, because she has been spectacularly unlucky in finding true love right from the start of her adulthood.

Learning from past mistakes clearly wasn't a priority for her. One relationship in particular was hellish for all of us. From the moment I met him, my stomach turned. His presence chilled my bones. He was a performer of the highest order, truly worthy of an Oscar. With carefully constructed charm, his smile hid a cold edge. He convinced everyone around him that he was gentle, kind, and trustworthy. He even won over my parents. But I wasn't swayed. Not for a second. My instincts were sharp, and I chose to keep my distance.

When my sister announced plans to marry him, my heart sank. Every fibre of my being wanted to step in and pull her away. But I knew it wasn't my place. I was just the little sister. All I could do was voice my concerns carefully, measuring my words so as not to sound bitter or overbearing. Do you know how hard that was? Cross my heart, my only motive was to protect her. I could see the storm ahead; I could feel it in my bones. My instincts had never been wrong before. He was not genuine. He never was.

The wedding preparations remain etched in my memory, the smell of lamb souvlakia filling the house as we set up for guests. Bring me a bucket! She was overflowing with excitement which, in fairness, I understood. She believed she was in love. Or perhaps she was simply infatuated with the idea of being in love, her eyes bright with hope but shadowed by fear. Who can say? Either way, I did what was expected of me: I offered support. Refusing wasn't really an option. I went along for the nightmare ride because that's what family does.

The night before the wedding, she went to bed early. Preparing for a Greek wedding is no small task. From rearranging the house to welcoming guests long before the church ceremony, from the endless last-minute touch-ups to making sure every corner looked perfect, the work seemed to multiply with each step. Setting up the grazing food tables alone had drained what little strength she had left. By the time her head touched the pillow, she was gone, fast asleep, lost to the world.

I, on the other hand, lay awake in the dark. I turned from side to side, unable to quiet the weight pressing against my chest. Thirty minutes passed. An hour passed. My mind was racing at a million miles an hour. I felt sick with dread. Bad omens. Bad juju vibes. I couldn't shake the sense that this was the worst decision of her life. I knew I had to try one last time to stop it. Better late than never!

I remember tiptoeing down the hallway towards her room at the back of the house, my heart thudding so loudly I could hear it in my ears. I eased her door open, flicked on the light and sat beside her as she lay peacefully asleep. I whispered her name, gently at first, urging her to wake. Nothing. She didn't stir. Louder now: 'Wake up, I need to talk to you.' Still nothing.

Frustration rising, I shook her shoulder. 'Wake up! I need to talk to you.' Finally, she blinked herself awake. Lucky for her, because the next step might have been a bucket of water on her if she didn't wake up.

'What do you want?' she mumbled, half-asleep, her voice heavy with irritation. She sat up and before I could overthink it, the words spilled out: 'Don't marry him. It's not too late to call it off. He isn't right for you. Please, don't do it.'

She just stared at me blankly, her eyes darting with a flicker of shame, rolled back down the bed and muttered, 'Turn the light off,' then went straight back to sleep.

I must have prayed all night for the wedding to be stopped. But morning came and the day went ahead exactly as planned. Nothing I said, nothing I begged, had made the slightest difference. The hardest part was plastering on the fakest smile of my life and congratulating the newlyweds when, deep down, every fibre of me wanted to scream. It was her happiest day, yet I could not share her joy. Instead, I carried the weight of dread.

The groom's speech at the reception was utter wankery, his smug grin fuelling my words. I saw red, like a bull let loose. With every lie that spilled from his mouth, I was half expecting lightning to strike. And the Oscar goes to… When he sat down and the formalities rolled on, I was sitting on burning coal. The cutting of the cake was next; this was my only chance to stand up and give an impromptu speech. Surprise! I couldn't help myself, what, I'm allowed? I was her bridesmaid and, at the end of the day, her sister. It felt like my duty to say something.

I rose, took the microphone in my shaky hand and smiled at everyone, outwardly calm. I welcomed the guests, offered the usual niceties, then aimed my real line at him. Smiling, I looked his way. The sight of him made me want to vomit, and said, 'Congratulations on marrying my sister. Make sure you look after her, because you've just married a butcher's daughter.'

He laughed and thought it cute. *No, you dick, it was a warning wrapped up as a joke.* I sat down. My cousins were mortified; they thought I'd lost the plot. But they knew exactly what I meant.

Months passed, but her marriage cast a shadow. Her visits grew tense, her smiles forced. Then things started to go missing; random items from around the house. Cash taken from Mum's purse after she'd visited. My parents were either oblivious or in denial. I watched her closely, sensing trouble. I knew something was brewing but had no hard proof. It happened a few times before Dad began to believe me. It wasn't just in my head; it wasn't coincidence. How could things vanish every time she came over? Her worse half never showed his ugly face; it was just her. Always her.

After a few recurring incidents, Dad had to see for himself. As much as he didn't want to believe it, he needed to be certain before confronting her. As shit as it sounds, he felt he had to set a trap. No parent wants to do that to their child.

He left some money in a drawer and set up a small security camera. We were all on high alert. She came over, polite as ever, helping Mum around the house, then vanished for a while. She slipped into Mum and Dad's room, a place she had no business being, and started rifling through drawers. That's when she found the money Dad had left as bait. She glanced over her shoulder to check no one was watching, then slipped the notes into her pocket.

Dad walked in. She froze, her eyes darting, full of shame. He confronted her, his hands trembling, torn between love and anger, and in front of his disheartened eyes the truth fell out of her pocket. She still denied it. He gave her a chance to come clean, to tell him what was going on, but she refused. Dad was mortified. With a heavy heart and to protect Mum above all, he told her to leave the house and never come back. Betrayal stung worse than anger.

We didn't hear from her for months; not a peep. I didn't know whether she was alive or dead, where she was or if she was safe. She had chosen to stick by him; that was her decision. We offered her chances to come clean, to get help, but she refused. That's on her. Dad's choice was to protect the sick woman in his house. He could not have someone coming and going and leaving destruction in their wake.

♥

One bright Sunday afternoon, Master M and I were driving along the M5, enjoying the last few hours of the weekend, relaxed and chilled, when my phone started ringing. The bright sky seemed to be dim. I glanced down and saw her name flash on my Samsung. I rolled my eyes and ignored it. The phone kept ringing. I shoved it in my bag. Master M said, 'Answer it.' I replied bluntly, 'No, she can go fuck herself.' He gave me a look and said, 'Answer the fricken phone. For her to ring you, something's wrong.' I stubbornly said, 'I don't give a flying fuck, let her call someone else.'

The phone kept vibrating, each buzz making my stomach flip. I finally gave in, rifled through my bag, and answered. 'What?' I said.

There were no words at first, only hyperventilating. Then the sobs, the bone-chilling screams: 'Help me, please help me, sister, I'm going to die.'

The world split in two.

Master M heard her voice and didn't need me to say a thing. His fists tightened and his voice trembled as he pressed his foot hard on the pedal. The car shot forward along the M5 like he was driven by something fierce and unseen. We flew past every light. I still don't know how the police didn't catch us.

When we reached her unit, he pulled over so fast the tyres cried out. We threw the doors open and ran for the stairs. I had no expectations. I felt numb, but adrenaline surged through me. I was paralysed with a kind of mortified horror; the world seemed to stop. Her front door stood wide open. My eyes scanned the apartment. Broken glass crunched underfoot as I heard her gasp, 'Sister, please help me.' She was lying on the floor, head down, sobbing. Drawers and cupboards were flung open; everything was scattered across the floor. She was covered in blood and bruises.

My heart split open. In that moment, I would have burned the world down to protect her. Rage consumed me, ready to fight. I was let out of my cage, roaring, 'Where the fuck is that cunt? I'm going to kill him!'

She cried hysterically, choking on her words. 'I don't know, I don't know...I had no more money to give him. He thought I was lying, so he tore the house apart. I begged him to stop, but then he started hitting me.'

My heart shattered into a million pieces. I couldn't breathe, couldn't breathe for her. We called the police, who arrived within minutes. As she gave her statement, reliving the nightmare blow by blow, she broke down, showing her cuts and bruises, wiping the blood from her face. Watching her was like being pierced with a sharp-edged dagger.

But there was a glimmer of hope. For the first time, she came to her senses. She requested a restraining order against this low-life. She was terrified he'd come back for more. Oh no he wouldn't, not if I had anything to do with it!

At last, my prayers were answered. There is a God. Through the tears and torture, a silver lining began to shine.

We attended court with her and not long after, she filed for divorce. Alleluia! That piece of shit didn't even bother to show up, which was probably for the best. If he had, between Dad and me, one of us would have ended up behind bars.

It turned out he had been using hardcore drugs. Didn't I tell you I smelled something rotten? He had forced my sister to do his dirty work, stealing from our family home, from our parents, threatening to kill her if she refused. She obeyed because she was petrified. Stuck between a rock and a hard place, she thought if she kept him supplied, he'd stay calm and she'd be safe.

I can't say I understand it. I don't get it. But then, I've never been in that position. Still, why not come to us? Why not seek protection from the people who love you most? We are your family; we have your back.

Years later, word went around that someone had seen him in a wheelchair. Apparently, he'd taken a bad hit of some concoction and suffered brain damage. As unorthodox as this sounds, forgive me Lord, but I can't help but think what goes around comes around. He touched my sister and now he suffers the consequences.

The past has left its scars, but when my family is threatened, my protective instincts awaken. I transform into a lioness. No one hurts my cubs. No one touches my loved ones without consequences. Having known heartbreak, I've tapped into a deep well of unconditional love; love that drives me to defend and support those I hold dearest.

I've always had everyone's back. I stand up for people. I protect. But too often, I feel like I'm fighting this battle alone. And sometimes I wonder, who really has *my* back?

❤

When my son A was just two years old, doctors discovered my pituitary gland was enlarged. After several medical issues, scans revealed a benign tumour. It needed close monitoring and surgery was a possibility. I was advised against having another baby in case the condition worsened. I worried how A would cope if I got sick.

I prayed and prayed, clutching A's toy, praying for strength. I stayed true to my faith. There wasn't a single saint I didn't call upon. I made a vow to Our Virgin Mary: if my results came back clear and no surgery was needed, I would make a pilgrimage to her church in Tinos, Greece.

The longest 365 days of my life finally passed, and I found myself back at the hospital, bracing for scans and a dreaded specialist appointment. The waiting room's fluorescent lights buzzed as anticipation gnawed at me; my nerves were raw. I practised deep breathing, trying to calm my racing heart. When my name was called, I trembled; my palms became sweaty, body flustered, my hands shaking as he spoke. I sat down, elbows on the desk, head heavy. The room spun; I feared I might faint. The specialist's lips moved, but his words were a distant hum. All I could think was: *Surgery or not? Just tell me!* My mind had already spiralled into worst-case scenarios.

Then the specialist's demeanour changed. He leaned back, composed and gentle, peering over his glasses with a warm, genuine smile. 'Andrea, positive news,' he began. 'The pituitary gland has returned to normal size.'

Time stopped. Relief washed over me like rain after a drought. I felt the weight lift from my shoulders. I had been given a second chance, and I knew exactly what I had to do. I had made a promise, a vow to Our Virgin Mary.

Before I got the results, my parents had mentioned a long-overdue family trip to Cyprus. Tensions simmered among relatives, and I'd been hesitant, my health worries consuming me. Then everything fell into place. It felt like my miracle was waiting. This trip wasn't just a holiday; it was my pilgrimage, a chance to honour the blessing I'd been given.

I had felt completely forsaken in the chaos, yet looking back, I now see that God had been my rock the entire time. My faith was the quiet strength that carried me when nothing else made sense. My mind had painted the darkest picture, the unbearable thought of dying on the operating table and leaving my child alone. But that fear was only a story written by my anxiety, not the truth of what God planned for us. In reality, He was watching over us.

The miraculous news prompted my parents to take us all to Cyprus. Dad was newly retired and longed to return to his motherland, perfect timing to fulfil my promise to Our Virgin Mary.

I travelled with my son A and the rest of the family. Master M stayed behind for a few weeks to wrap up work as things finally picked up for him, praise the Lord.

Travelling with an over-enthusiastic three-year-old is intense. Lil A was a menace to society. Amen to Phenergan; that stuff was a lifesaver. He crashed out before the plane took off; if he hadn't slept, I'm convinced he would have found a way to open the plane door and fly out.

We travelled in a large group of family members, voices shouting in Greek around us. As the designated point of contact, I organised passports, dealt with customs, and arranged wheelchair assistance. Having a rascal running riot was not on the menu.

After a gruelling 23-hour journey, we finally arrived in Larnaca, exhausted but intact. My nerves were frayed and I had no patience for nonsense. Managing a tired three-year-old, wheelchairs, and suitcases pushed me to the edge. Then someone's thoughtless words and actions, a blatant display of disrespect towards my parents, made me see red. Normally I bite my tongue, but on that day, I let them have it.

What happened next shocked me: the person grabbed me by the neck and choked me, right there in the airport. I froze, stunned that no one stepped in. The whole ordeal was over in seconds, but it left me shaken and speechless, my son's cries echoing in my heart.

I'm not sure if Dad saw the altercation; he was busy helping Mum into her wheelchair. By the time he looked up, I was already in tears, the hand marks on my neck proof of what had just happened. Lil A had seen the whole thing and burst into tears, screaming, 'Leave my Mummy alone!' His tiny arms clung to me as he bravely kicked out at the attacker. I pulled him aside to protect him from becoming the next target, whispering that he must stay quiet, fearing that if his father found out things would escalate even more. The situation felt volatile; I knew to expect the unexpected.

I kept the incident from Master M for two weeks, which still surprises me. He sensed something was wrong, though. When I finally broke down and told him, his reaction was explosive, exactly what I'd expected. His fists clenched, voice shaking. He was livid that I'd allowed someone to assault me and get away with it. Where was the accountability? In that chaotic moment, I had fallen back on pure instinct: fight or flight. I chose silence, not because I agreed, but because I didn't want to create a scene in front of my parents or frighten my son. I kept hoping the tension would ease on its own, yet Master M's sudden outrage made me see how my silence could be mistaken for acceptance.

And I was right. Master M was on the next flight.

❤

In life, you're lucky if you have a few people you can truly count on. I'm no different. My inner circle is small, and that's by choice. I've been hurt more times than I can admit, and every wound taught me to protect myself. So I built walls; high, solid walls, and I guard them with everything in me.

It's not that I don't want real connections. I do. I crave them more than I'll ever say out loud. But letting someone in comes at a cost, and I've paid that price before. The fear of going through that pain again keeps me careful, slower, and more intentional. So I stay guarded, choosing only a few people I trust enough to stay close.

I could have unleashed a storm in that airport, yelled, thrown a tantrum, made a scene. Instead, I swallowed it. For my son's sake I chose composure. I bottled the hurt and carried on. Or I thought

I had. The truth is harsher: I'm still in that moment, a scar on my heart. Their words are meaningless, yet they've cut deep; nothing seems able to soften the way I feel. 'Time heals all wounds' doesn't apply to me. Time has been kindling, feeding the fire rather than putting it out. Forgive and forget? Not for me. I can move on, yes, but I'll carry the loathing like a scar, a reminder and a warning.

I hope karma finds this piece of shit. After years of prioritising everyone else's safety, I'm finally learning to protect my own peace. If the past has to smoulder a little, let it; its embers light the lessons I've learned. How will these scars shape my role as a mother, I wonder, as I step into the unknown?

CHAPTER 6

Between chaos and candlelight

Feeling disconnected from my birthplace is an odd, unsettling sensation. I've always had the sense of being an outsider, like I don't quite fit in. I remember watching my parents laugh over coffee in Cyprus with such genuine joy, and I wondered if I'd ever feel like I truly belonged.

Australia has so much to offer, and yet there are days when it feels more like a place I simply live in rather than somewhere I truly belong. It's disheartening, especially when I look at the world around me – politics, conflict, suffering – and find myself living in this bubble of safety. It makes me question my parents' choices. Why did my dad leave everything behind at eighteen to start fresh? Why did my mum cross the ocean as a child? What were they searching for, or perhaps trying to escape from?

They came here seeking a better life, a life filled with safety and opportunities they couldn't have back home. Their sacrifices paved the way for us, allowing us to build a future they could only dream of. As one of the children born into this life of relative privilege, I'm deeply grateful. Yet there are times when I feel like I'm just going through the motions, living in a country that doesn't quite feel like mine. I often wonder: did they feel this disconnection at first? Or did belonging come with time? Maybe I need to find my own reasons for being here, my own path to belonging.

And yet I raise my hand in gratitude. I'm thankful for the medical care we can access, the education available to us, the job opportunities, the roof over our heads, and the food on our table. We're blessed to live in this peaceful country we call home. I would never deny that. But alongside that gratitude, there lingers this persistent feeling that something's missing, like there must be more to life than just being here. Maybe it's a deeper connection I crave. A sense of purpose, of belonging, something beyond the blessings of a good country and the security it offers, something like a faith that anchors me in both worlds.

For as long as I can remember, something inside me has felt incomplete. I've tried filling that void with friends, hobbies, and interests, but nothing has ever truly settled. I think I've been searching for roots I never quite developed. My parents came here seeking a better life, but what does that mean for me? Am I meant to be content with what I have, or is it okay to admit that I'm still searching for something more?

Going back to my parents' homeland always gave me peace I never found anywhere else. The smells, the food, the language, the people, everything felt like comfort. The scent of olive oil drifting through family dinners, the soft chatter around the table, the familiar rhythm of voices I grew up hearing, it all wrapped around me like something I had known long before I was born.

It is strange. Even though I was born in Australia, Cyprus somehow felt more like home. Maybe it was because I watched my parents come alive in their own culture, surrounded by people who understood them without effort. Or maybe it was because something deep inside me recognised where I came from, like a memory passed down through blood. Whatever it was, it stayed with me. Sometimes I wonder what it would feel like to live in a place that gives that sense of belonging every single day, instead of in brief visits that end too quickly.

Our first family trip there, taking our three-year-old son on a culturally rich adventure, only deepened that connection. It wasn't surprising. The local children enjoyed a freedom I could only admire, in a safe and welcoming environment, especially in the smaller towns and villages. And when I say village, don't picture a scene from the 1940s with horses and huts. This was a thriving town of more than 5,000 people, with schools, supermarkets, a hospital, police and fire stations, football fields, tavernas, cafes, and more churches than you could count.

My dad's village, Athienou, is my favourite place on earth. There's a Cypriot saying: *I Kypros einai paradisos, je I Athienou mes tin mesi,* which translates to: 'Cyprus is paradise, and Athienou is at its very centre.' Most of our extended family lives there, and the community is wonderfully tight-knit. Everyone is always ready to help, no matter how small the need is. The only downside? Everyone knows everyone else's business. If you burp or sneeze, the whole village will hear about it before you take your next breath. Yet even with that, the place feels alive in a way that's hard to describe. The energy there is electric. And even when a soft whiff from the nearby cattle farms drifts across the air, it somehow becomes part of its charm.

We spent eight weeks there, with Master M and our little boy, and it gave us a true glimpse of what life could be like. Lil A settled in beautifully. His tiny voice sang Greek songs as he picked up the language quickly, and he played happily with his cousins and the neighbourhood children. It was like he slotted effortlessly into village life. When he saw the other kids heading off to childcare, he felt left out, so I reluctantly enrolled him three days a week. He absolutely loved it. With his tiny backpack slung over his shoulder, he'd wave and call out, *'Yia sou, Mumma!'* as he toddled off. OMG. It was so goddam cute. It melted my heart every single time.

Master M had always been eager to help his cousins with their work or join them in their building and landscaping projects; areas where he naturally excelled. I, on the other hand, took a softer, more relaxed route. I slipped comfortably into the Lady of Leisure lifestyle, moving with the flow and keeping my heart light, without complaints or resistance.

Our time with family abroad became something sacred, especially for Lil A. Watching my child soaked in that rich cultural experience felt like witnessing education in its purest form. It was something no classroom could offer, an experience that shaped both memory and character. It was a gift I knew would last a lifetime. But as our departure drew closer, a quiet sadness began to settle around us. What had been warm, lively days started to take on a bittersweet glow. Each moment felt precious, as if time itself knew it was running out. And in those final days, the weight of leaving pressed softly on our hearts.

Packing our bags was an emotional ordeal. We were reluctant to leave, yet we knew it was inevitable, because our lives were waiting for us back home in Australia. Saying goodbye was brutal, and the tears came without warning. Lil A's heartbreaking whisper, 'I don't want to go, Mummy,' cut straight through me. Even after we'd passed through customs, the ache stayed. But it was the aeroplane's take-off that broke whatever strength I had left. My body reacted before my mind could catch up: uncontrollable sobs, a runny nose, and grief so raw it felt like something had been torn from me. To anyone watching, it probably looked like we were mourning a loss, and in many ways, we were. I was leaving behind a place that had given me peace in ways I hadn't felt in years. I cried through the entire three-hour flight to Dubai, unable to stop even when I wanted to.

Landing in Dubai came with its own story, thanks to a nine-hour layover. Thankfully, the airline arranged a hotel transfer, which saved us from what could have been a long, chaotic stretch inside the airport with a fiery, restless three-year-old. The idea of being trapped in that crowd with a tiny, determined ball of energy was enough to make my heart race.

As we approached customs, I buckled Lil A into a courtesy stroller, gently soothing him through a tantrum brought on by exhaustion and hunger. When he finally settled, I took a quiet moment to speak to my husband. I stepped closer, lowered my voice, and gave him a calm but firm pep talk. I reminded him to stay composed and avoid any unnecessary back and forth with the officers. With our history of random checks, I needed him to stay steady, focused, and out of any avoidable trouble. 'Yes, I know...alright, alright,' he muttered.

I wasn't trying to lecture him; just trying to prevent any avoidable trouble. With Lil A already falling apart, I couldn't handle another round of unexpected shenanigans. I pushed the stroller towards the bag check and went through first, keeping Master M within sight. Everything seemed normal as I struggled with the wobbly, half-broken stroller that kept pulling in every direction. It was already testing my patience, and I was trying to stay focused. Then I looked up. The officer was standing in front of Master M, his expression unreadable as he instructed, 'Empty your pockets.' My heart sank. *What now?* I moved towards them, keeping my face calm even though unease was already threading through me.

Kill me now. Of all the things he could have carried, he had a lighter in his pocket – not just any lighter, but one with an image of a topless woman on it, thanks to his cousin's questionable taste in gifts. And here we were, standing in the middle of a conservative Arab country where anything even close to sexual imagery was forbidden. My heart dropped. I was certain we were headed for real trouble. The idea of being dragged into a jail cell didn't even feel far-fetched.

The officers were shouting at Master M, each word louder and harsher than the last. We had no common language, which only made everything more confusing. We kept our voices calm, repeating, 'We don't understand. Please translate to English,' hoping someone would slow down long enough to help. Instead, I was waved off with sharp, impatient 'go away' gestures – rude and dismissive enough to make my stomach twist.

Just when the tension felt like it might snap, another security officer stepped in. He didn't raise his voice. He didn't scold us. He simply explained, in clear English, that the lighter wasn't allowed. No shock there. After all that drama, they tossed the lighter into a bin without a second thought and motioned for us to open our carry-on bags.

Master M had insisted there were no lighters in the bags, but the officers weren't buying it. 'Open up,' they demanded, suddenly switching to perfect English. My heart dropped the moment one of them pointed at my luggage, the one with the pink ribbon that made it unmistakably mine.

I quickly intervened. 'No, that's my bag. It's not to be touched.'

But the obnoxious officer didn't even look at me. He just repeated himself, flat and disrespectful: 'Go away.'

That was it. The last strike. He had just knocked over all ten pins and scored a strike. I was exhausted, overwhelmed, and completely DONE.

When he said 'go away' again and waved his hand at me like I was some kind of nuisance, something in me snapped. The audacity stunned me. I could feel the heat rising in my chest, but I held myself together. I walked towards him with all the calm I could gather. 'Excuse me, sir. That's my bag. I'm not the one being searched, so there's no reason to open it.'

Instead of listening, he stood up and turned the situation on me. 'Why don't you want us to open your bag? Are you hiding something?'

I actually let out a small laugh at the absurdity of it all. 'Sir, I'm travelling with a three-year-old. What could I possibly be hiding? Baby wipes? Snacks? A change of clothes for when he spills juice?'

He didn't react. He didn't even pretend to hear me. Instead, he reached for my bag as if my words were nothing but air. That was the moment my patience officially left the room.

'Get your hands off my bag, sir,' I said firmly. 'If you want to search it, ask me nicely. And a female officer should do it. You don't have the right to touch my belongings without my permission.'

He knew he had crossed a line. Thankfully, a female officer stepped in, her tone calm and respectful as she asked me to open the bag myself. I agreed immediately, relieved that someone had finally chosen professionalism over intimidation. But just when I thought things were finally settling, the stroller's wheels jammed and Lil A jerked forward. That was it, the final straw. My nerves were stretching thin, and before I could catch myself, I snapped.

I unclipped Lil A, pulled him into my arms, and shoved the stroller towards the officer with more force than I intended.

'Shove this up your ass,' I said, my voice low and shaking with anger. Then I stormed off, holding Lil A tight, leaving all that chaos behind me. Honestly, I'm still shocked no one ran after me with handcuffs.

Master M stood frozen, his mouth hanging open, while the officer stared, as if he couldn't grasp what had just happened. I kept walking, but I still heard Master M mumble to the officer, 'You made the wrong person upset.' He said it under his breath; the kind of warning someone gives when they know they've picked the wrong fight. Then he turned away, suddenly unsure of himself. When he finally caught up with me he sat beside me at the courtesy bus stop, quiet, trying to act like nothing had happened as we waited.

'Wtf was that?' he asked, calm as ever.

'What?' I replied, acting cool and collected, as if nothing had just exploded behind us.

'That entire fiasco,' he said. 'You gave me that calming pep talk earlier and you ended up being the firecracker.'

'Oh well. He deserved it. He pissed me off,' I said, trying to sound innocent. 'You think?' he laughed.

Looking back now, I can laugh too, but at the time, it was a miracle I didn't end up in a holding cell. I'm still surprised I managed to keep any form of composure, although clearly not much. And let's be honest, I wasn't even the one being searched.

The real lesson? Don't accuse me of hiding anything. Don't use your position or authority to intimidate me. And don't disrespect me because I'm a woman. *Simple!*

After that chaotic customs experience, we finally stumbled into the hotel, desperate for refuge from the sweltering heat.

The humidity was suffocating; every breath felt like a chore. We quickened our pace, eager to escape into the air-conditioned lobby. And then, bliss! The automatic doors slid open and a wave of icy air enveloped us, instantly soothing our sweat-drenched skin.

'I call dibs on the shower first!' I exclaimed, already imagining the heavenly relief.

We collapsed into our hotel room, Lil A completely spent. After a quick shower to freshen him up, I got him ready for bed. By the time I had gathered my own clothes for a shower, he was already fast asleep. His little face, bronzed from the sun, seemed to glow in the soft lamplight, golden-brown curls framing his cheeks. My heart melted. My little angel. I just wanted to squeeze him tight and cover him with kisses.

After our refreshing showers we settled into a moment of quiet relaxation. We ate, chatted, and let the world slow down around us. Yet a subtle tension lingered, a familiar, comical awkwardness. We both had something on our minds but didn't know how to say it. You know that feeling, when words catch in your throat and the silence grows heavier with every passing second?

Come on...spit it out.

'Okay, I'll go first,' I said, finally breaking the fragile barrier between thought and speech. 'So, how would you feel about moving to Cyprus?' I ventured, unsure how Master M would react.

His response was immediate, almost electric: 'I was thinking the same thing! Let's look into it and get the ball rolling.'

Did we just decide to move overseas in two sentences? I think we just did. Perhaps this village awakened something deep within me, reminding me of who I truly am. Maybe that's why we both instinctively knew this was where we were meant to be – it felt like home.

The decision to relocate wasn't made lightly. Uprooting our entire lives, reshaping our family's world, it was monumental. Yet the pull of my parents' homeland was undeniable. I'd always felt drawn to a simpler, more peaceful way of life. Stepping onto Cypriot soil brought a sense of calm I hadn't realised I was craving. The community's focus on culture, relationships, and what truly matters resonated with me on a profound level. I was done with the rat race, the endless cycle of stress, deadlines, and debt. Every place has its pros and cons, of course, but what I longed for was a fresh start. We both yearned for a life filled with serenity, rich cultural experiences, and meaningful connections; a life that felt like it belonged to us.

The remaining leg of our return journey no longer felt disheartening. Knowing we were putting distance between ourselves and Cyprus brought a surprising sense of relief. In fact, I was genuinely excited to be heading home. Excited to start planning for our big move.

After a gruelling 32 hours of travel, we finally arrived home safely. Exhaustion weighed on us, but it didn't dampen our sense of purpose. I was all systems go. I researched, made inquiries, booked flights, and even arranged a cargo container to ship all our belongings. This was really happening! We were planning to move everything within a few short months. Holy shit!

♥

Breaking the news to our parents was harder than I expected. Neither set of parents was overly enthusiastic, but they supported our decision nonetheless. Their cautious encouragement made the move feel all the more real.

We listed our house with an agent to rent it out and, to my surprise, a tenant appeared within a week. I hadn't expected it to happen so fast. Suddenly I had only seven days to pack up our entire home. Seven days to make everything fall into place, to box up years of memories, and to somehow get it all done.

Every night I carefully labelled, listed, and stacked our belongings into one of my parents' bedrooms until our home was finally bare. Master M and I took one room while Lil A had another. What had once been a quiet house, peaceful with just my parents in it, was now lively again. Lil A brought noise, mischief, and chaos, but in the most delightful way. I'm certain my parents cherished every moment of their cheerful grandchild's presence.

Master M tried to sell his business, but it quickly became a daunting task. One month passed, then three, and eventually six. The process was turning into a nightmare. What was meant to be a short stay with my parents stretched longer; not that they complained. Our travel plans were delayed, giving us more time at home, but the business remained unsold.

My frustrations grew with each passing day, The dream of relocating abroad, once within reach, felt stubbornly out of grasp. I began to resent Master M, even though I knew it wasn't his fault. He was making every genuine effort to sell the business, yet my emotions kept deteriorating.

A year had passed in the blink of an eye, and before we knew it, M and I were faced with a tough decision: we had to pull the plug and stay put. It felt as though the universe, or perhaps the gods themselves, were nudging us not to leave. Though the business was still running, a buyer appeared out of nowhere, and we finally sold it. Yay!

Even after the sale, we stood by our choice to stay, and for the first time in a long while we felt truly at peace. There was no lingering bitterness, no second-guessing. We were content, genuinely content, with the lives we had built. We carefully weighed the pros and cons of returning to our home, but the truth was simple: I loved being back in the family home. Lil A thrived with his grandparents nearby, settling seamlessly into childcare. I had adjusted my work and travel schedule to fit this new rhythm and it was working beautifully. But more than anything, what truly mattered was being there for Mum. With me around, Dad got the relief he so desperately needed. Having an extra pair of hands made a world of difference.

Months later, during a family dinner, Mum's pasta and chicken with haloumi had me devouring every bite as if it were gourmet cuisine. 'Hmm, yumm!' I savoured each mouthful, even sucking the chicken bones clean. Mum's curious glances didn't faze me. I was too caught up in the feast. Little did I know my insatiable appetite was more than a craving. A week or two later, I discovered I was pregnant with baby #2.

My stomach seemed bottomless. I craved everything from steak to cheeseburgers. Thankfully, my pregnancy progressed smoothly. Routine blood tests showed rising levels of the pregnancy hormone HCG, and I felt a deep sense of gratitude for the new life growing inside me; another blessing. No morning sickness, no exhaustion; just energy, vitality, and joy. I kept working, managing Lil A's endless energy and feeling truly blessed.

By eight weeks, my tiny baby bump was impossible to hide. Even if I had tried, it announced itself proudly. I chose loose-fitting clothes to stay comfortable and discreet, still hesitant to share the news before the 12-week scan. But that didn't stop me from strutting to work in my stilettos. Woo hoo!

❤

One hectic morning, I was racing to drop Lil A off at preschool and then battling traffic on the M5 to make it to Greenacre on time for work. I arrived with only minutes to spare. Hitting every red light hadn't helped my punctuality, a trait I take pride in. I like starting my day calmly, with a cup of coffee and a few quiet moments to ease into work. As I turned on my computer and began sorting through paperwork, my phone buzzed loudly on my desk. I glanced at the screen. 'Dad' was flashing. Strange. He rarely calls me at work unless it's urgent.

I answered immediately. 'Papa, *ela*...what's wrong? Are you okay?'

His voice trembled. 'Andrea...your mum had a fall and hit her head.'

My heart stopped. I grabbed the edge of the desk for support, feeling my knees weaken, and somehow sat down. 'Is she okay? Is she bleeding? Is she breathing? Did she break anything?' I fired off questions in rapid succession.

'She's responding...seems okay. We have a neurologist appointment this morning; I'll get the doctor to check her,' he replied quickly.

'Call me when you see him. I'm packing up and coming,' I told him, my voice shaking.

Just as my computer finally decided to load, I grabbed the mouse and shut it down. *Shut down, dammit.* I grabbed my bags and walked straight into my boss's office. He had overheard the conversation. Without a word from me, he walked over, placed his hand on my shoulder and said, 'Go. Go to your mum. You don't need to explain anything.'

I sped through the back streets, only to hit every single red light again, seriously, was it National Red Light Day? My phone rang through the speaker. I snatched it up. 'Papa, I'm coming. I'm on my way. What's happening? Is Mum okay?'

'We were with the neurosurgeon...and she was disoriented,' he replied. 'She went pale and started vomiting. They're taking her to the emergency department.'

'I'm nearly there,' I said, my voice tight, before hanging up.

The drive from Greenacre to St George Hospital felt endless. My hands trembled on the wheel. What happened? How did she fall? Was she going to be okay? My palms were slick with sweat and every few seconds I wiped them on my pants, desperate for a grip that wouldn't slip. I made a quick call to Master M, gave him an update, and promised to keep him in the loop. He was already on his way to the hospital, God bless him.

I rushed to Mum's side, tears streaming down my face. The antiseptic smell of the hospital hit me like a punch to the gut as I whispered, 'Mum, I'm here. Everything will be okay,' gently stroking her short black hair. Its softness was a small, fragile comfort amid the chaos.

The nurses' gentle voices brought updates I barely heard: 'We've done a brain scan and taken bloods; we're waiting for the results.' I paced the floor, heels clicking against the cold tiles, queasy with worry. Dad sat beside Mum, holding her hand, his head bowing, eyes red rimmed and tired. When the doctor arrived, his words hit me like a sledgehammer: 'The scan shows a massive bleed in her brain; a pool of blood.' My mind reeled.

'Does she need surgery?' I asked, my voice barely steady.

'Not yet,' he said. 'We need to induce a coma to let her brain settle. Once the clot solidifies, we can operate.'

The words swirled together, a blur of fear and helplessness. Then the world altered. My stomach twisted violently and the floor rushed up to meet me. Nurses were at my side instantly. 'Andrea, wake up! Are you okay?' Their voices sounded distant, muffled, as if underwater. I struggled to catch my breath, managing a shaky whisper: 'I'm...pregnant...eight weeks.' My voice cracked under the weight of it all. They helped me up, checked my blood pressure, and advised me to see my obstetrician, who luckily was just around the corner. But the world spun. My chest tightened, my heart raced, and I felt as though I was drowning in a sea of uncertainty.

As the nurses tended to me, the medical team prepped Mum for transfer to ICU. Meanwhile, I faced the dreaded calls to her sisters, the task of delivering devastating news. One by one I dialled their numbers, my voice cracking as I shared the details. They began arriving at the hospital before I could even process my own emotions, their faces etched with worry and concern. It was as if they'd sensed the urgency. Now, all of them stood in front of me, their presence both comforting and overwhelming.

I stayed by Mum's side all morning, all afternoon, all night. I didn't move; I couldn't leave her. I couldn't leave her alone. But where was my sister? Sitting there, I turned to my Dad and asked, 'Have you told your daughter?' He brushed me off. 'No,' he said. I felt the heat of fury rising in me.

The next day, Mum lay there, eyes closed; a sight I never wanted to see again. Leaning against the window, I asked again, my voice tight, 'Where is your daughter? Why isn't she here?'

'I haven't told her yet,' he said sharply, raising his guard.

'Why? Why the fuck not? She needs to be here. This is her mother, where the fuck is she?' I snapped.

'She is pregnant. She doesn't need to be stressed out,' he said bluntly.

Out of nowhere, Master M's voice cut through the tension. 'This daughter,' he said, pointing at me, 'is also pregnant. So, it's okay for her to be stressed out, but not her?'

The room went silent. Only the heart monitors beeped in the background. Beep. Beep. Beep.

Master M, usually respectful and calm around Dad, finally spoke up, his frustration spilling over. Dad realised his mistake and went quiet, his lips sealed. He knew he'd crossed a line. Then, in a quick, sneaky move, I watched him pull out his phone and slip out of the room to call his golden child; a sharp contrast to the tension and real concern we were carrying for Mum.

I was angry. Furious. Seething. My blood boiled and guilt weighed heavy on me. We had argued while Mum lay helpless in an ICU bed, fighting for her life. Yet, I couldn't stay silent, it didn't feel right. Why was it okay for me, I, who was also pregnant, exhausted, drowning in stress, to shoulder everything alone, while she lived her life freely, untouched by a single burden? It wasn't fair. It still isn't.

Mum remained in the ICU longer than expected, waiting for the swelling in her brain to settle. During that time, I moved back and forth between home and the hospital, spending almost every waking hour by her side. Work was incredibly understanding, which eased the pressure a little, because I had no choice but to take extended unpaid leave until I knew she was stable. With Dad's language barrier and my own fierce protectiveness, I knew I needed to be right there with her. Every day. Every moment.

After a few weeks, Mum came out of ICU, a tremendous sign of progress. She was still bedbound, as expected, but her speech remained intact. Every time a nurse walked in, she would thank them sincerely, always ending with a heartfelt, 'God bless you.' Her humility and gratitude for the care she received were palpable, touching everyone around her.

We turned Mum's hospital room into our second home, weeks blending seamlessly into months. As her condition stabilised, I returned to part-time work, arranging a schedule that allowed me to work mornings from 9 to 12, so I could be back in time for the doctors' afternoon rounds. My bosses were incredibly understanding, showing genuine kindness during such a stressful period.

Juggling a four-year-old, a hospitalised mother, and a growing pregnancy was chaotic, yet necessity forged my strength. I had to be strong for Mum, Dad, my son, and my unborn child. That mantra echoed constantly in my mind: *I just had to be strong.*

♥

During times of stress and sadness, a glimmer of hope or a fleeting ray of happiness can shine through the cracks. When a wedding invitation arrived, my first instinct was to refuse. No, I'm not going. I can't celebrate while Mum's in the hospital. It didn't feel right. But Dad's gentle insistence made me pause. 'Please, you have to go and represent the family. I'll stay with Mum.' I stared at him, torn between loyalty to Mum and the weight of family duty. Celebrations felt hollow without her presence, yet I understood his perspective. With a heavy heart I accepted the invitation, feeling the weight of responsibility settle onto my shoulders. We always choose the right thing to do, I reminded myself, repeating the familiar mantra, though this decision tasted bittersweet.

Mum was stable. There were no signs of decline. She was comfortable, settled, alert; peace of mind that allowed me to step away, if only for a few hours. But the condition was clear: I had to be contacted immediately if anything happened. Overprotectiveness at its best, yet a small comfort, too.

The wedding reception was a breathtaking spectacle; the lovestruck couple, the soft glow of dimmed lights, the elegant decor. Yet, as I looked around, guilt gnawed at me. How could I celebrate when Mum lay in a hospital bed? I tried to relax, to let the joy of the evening wash over me, but my mind kept drifting back to her. The weight of worry and responsibility pressed on me, a constant reminder that I was meant to be by her side, not here, surrounded by laughter and music.

I stayed on high alert, my phone on loud, vibrating beside me. I glanced at the screen every few seconds, expecting news about Mum. Nothing came. After a couple of hours, I began to ease up, telling myself that everything would be okay.

But a brief trip to the bathroom turned into a nightmare. I realised I'd left my phone behind. Panic surged through me as I dashed back, my heart hammering. The atmosphere seemed to thicken, the space around me closing in. And then I saw it, Master M's stressed expression on the screen. My pace quickened, a strange pull dragging me backward, anxiety spiking with every step. My fingers trembled as I grabbed my phone, its screen lighting up the darkening reality: eight missed calls from Dad, six from Mum's surgeon. Panic tightened around my chest as I hurried to call Dad back. 'Papa, what's going on?' My voice was already shaking.

His sobs met me first, raw and heavy, hitting me like a blow. I rushed outside, the music behind me turning from celebration to a dull, frightening noise. 'It's Mum…she's not well,' he managed, his voice breaking apart. Hearing my father, my rock, fall apart, made the ground beneath me shift.

I dialled the surgeon next, my fingers moving on their own. 'Andrea, I've been trying to reach you. Mum's condition has worsened. We're inducing a coma and operating tomorrow to remove the blood clot.' His words hit me like a wave I couldn't escape – cold, unrelenting, and crushing. My phone slipped from my hand and hit the ground with a soft thud, a small sound that somehow echoed everything collapsing inside me. A scream ripped from my mouth before I could stop it, sharp enough to tear through the night air. Wedding guests turned towards me, their faces blurred by shock and worry, and my family rushed to my side. Their arms wrapped around me, keeping me from sinking to the ground. Aunts hurried over, trying to comfort me, their words gentle but distant, as though my grief had placed a wall between us. Tears streamed down my face, falling fast and heavy, each one a reminder of how helpless I felt.

'Hold it together,' they whispered, soft but firm. 'For your son, for your unborn child, and for Mum.'

But in that moment, the world felt like it was breaking apart in my hands, and I had no strength to stop any of it. I found the strength to stand, even though tears streamed down my face. The thought of losing her was unbearable. She had to pull through. We rushed back to the car and headed home, unable to stay at the wedding any longer. My dad needed me; I couldn't leave him alone. I called each of my mum's sisters while we drove, sharing the news that left them sobbing so hard they could barely speak. In a painful twist, I caught myself consoling them instead.

'She's going to be okay, Thia. You'll see. She's a fighter.'

When we pulled into the driveway, Lil A opened the door and ran straight to his Pappou. He was sitting on a dining chair, one hand on the table, weeping. If I could have died in one moment, I think it would have been then. Seeing one of your parents fall apart is one of the most confronting things a person can witness. It crushes something deep inside you. I wrapped my arms around him and whispered, 'Stop crying. She's going to be okay. We're talking about Mum. She's a fighter, this is who she is.'

Even as exhaustion pressed down on us, our focus never changed. Holding on to the smallest glimmer of hope, we made our way to the hospital at sunrise. By 6 a.m. the ward was overflowing, bursting at the seams. When I say full, I mean completely full. Her sisters gathered around, nieces and nephews arrived to stand by her, and her brother even flew in from Queensland on the first flight he could get. Everyone was determined to be there for her.

I slipped into the ICU just before they wheeled Mum into the operating theatre. I squeezed her hand, whispered a prayer, and kissed her cheek. 'See you on the other side, Mum.' As they guided her away, I sank into the nearest chair, waves of emotion crashing over me. I took a deep breath, gathering my thoughts, bracing myself for whatever lay ahead. There was no room for fear, only hope. Mum was strong; she always pulled through.

Stepping out of the ICU, I wrapped my jacket tighter around me and joined my sprawling family; over 20 of us present, loud and boisterous even in the shadow of crisis. The hospital waiting area wasn't a place for our energy, so I suggested we move to the cafe across the street. We claimed a table and as I settled in, a pungent yet sweet scent of frankincense drifted by. I looked up and saw it: the Greek Orthodox Church in Kogarah, its presence both grand and serene. The moment held me still. I could almost hear the chanting from the service, my skin prickling with goosebumps.

Without thinking, I rose, grabbed my bag, and crossed the road to the church. It felt like God was calling me in. I lit a candle, letting the flickering orange flame become my anchor as I poured out my prayers, pleading for Mum's safe recovery. In that quiet, sacred space, I felt it. Yes, I felt God was with her. The chance choice of our cafe, the path that led me here, felt like divine guidance. Faith had found me in the most unexpected way, and I couldn't deny it.

From that moment, it was out of my hands. It was all in God's. Even in the chaos of life, I realised my strength wasn't optional. It was inherited, sacred, and undeniably mine.

CHAPTER 7

Conquering shadows

The harmonious chants of the church service enveloped me, their ancient cadence like a balm for my restless soul, as we waited for the surgeon's call. The smell of frankincense lingered in the air and the candle flames flickered gently, each one like a whispered prayer. Every note of the hymn pulled at my heartstrings, every pause holding me in a suspended silence. I wasn't prepared for any outcome. Running on autopilot, driven by adrenaline and prayer, I drifted between faith and fear, clinging to the hope that had carried me through Cyprus's warmth and my mother's first collapse.

Surely the call will come soon. Hours had dragged since Mum was wheeled into the operating theatre. Logic told me to be patient: brain surgery is delicate, complex, and demands time. I wanted the surgeons to take as long as they needed, no rush. Yet the gnawing unknown consumed me, a shadow that swallowed everything whole. Her fragile state made the procedure perilous. One wrong move and everything could unravel.

More hours passed. I was back at the cafe when my phone buzzed violently, cutting through the quiet like a jolt of electricity. I fumbled through my oversized bag – *why did I insist on carrying this thing?* – and pulled it out. 'Private number' flashed across the screen. My breath caught, my heart thudding hard against my ribs. It had to be the hospital. I steadied myself and drew a deep breath.

'Hello, Andrea speaking.'

'Hi, Andrea, it's Professor I. Your mum's surgery went well, but the clot was larger than we expected. She sustained a significant head trauma; we'll need to be very cautious. Any further impact could jeopardise her recovery. Let's discuss everything in person when you return. No rush, she's stable and in recovery.'

The line went silent. A tear slid down my cheek as I turned to Dad. Squeezing his trembling hand, I forced a smile. 'She's okay, Papa. I told you.' My father, usually an immovable rock, softened, his relief almost childlike, his eyes glistening with unshed tears.

We sat by Mum's bedside, the steady rhythm of her breathing grounding me. I paced, unable to settle, the sharp smell of antiseptic filling my nose. My aunts gently guided me to a chair. 'Be calm, Andrea. You're pregnant. Your mum would want you strong.'

I stared at her peaceful face, the woman who'd taught me resilience and faith. Matching my breathing to hers, the panic inside me began to ease. Then, her eyes fluttered open.

'Hi,' she whispered, her voice faint but alive.

We leapt to our feet, careful not to overwhelm her. 'Hi, Mum. Good morning. How are you feeling?' I stroked her cheek, my heart swelling.

'I have a headache,' she murmured, a faint smile flickering, a quiet spark of her old strength. Of course she did. She had weathered the storm again, resilient as ever. Recovery would be long; her brain needed time to heal before rehabilitation could begin. Yet here she was, still with us, still fighting, still herself.

♥

Life resumed its insistent pace, as it always does. I juggled part-time work, mornings at the office and afternoons and evenings at St George Hospital. As Mum regained strength, they moved her into a recliner chair. My growing belly left me exhausted, and I felt a guilty flicker of relief when I could rest for a moment. I'd crawl into her bed, and though she was frail, she'd pull the blanket over me, her hands still protective. At five months pregnant, the baby's kicks mixed with sharp pangs of sciatica running down my leg, a constant reminder that life persists even amidst the chaos.

The cycle of preschool runs, work shifts, and hospital vigils blurred into something that felt like a real-life Groundhog Day. At night I collapsed, too exhausted to do anything but let the weight of it all sink in.

One evening after dinner, tidying up, bathing Lil A, and tucking him into bed, I finally stole a moment for myself. A hot shower soothed my aching body and I slipped into bed, curling against my body pillow, my muscles melting into the mattress, grateful for a few minutes of peace. But then a knock shattered the quiet. Dad's voice trembled from the other side of the door: 'Andrea, I need to go to the hospital.'

Groaning, I pushed myself up, heavy as a beached whale. 'Are you kidding? What now?'

'Please...come, come! I'll show you. I'm urinating blood.' His voice trembled as he rushed to the bathroom. I hobbled out of bed, slid into my slippers, and followed him to the door. 'Look,' he said, pointing into the toilet bowl. I didn't know what I was expecting at this hour, but what I saw froze me in place. Blood; bright, red, everywhere. He hadn't exaggerated. He really needed the hospital.

'Oh shit,' I muttered, panic rising. 'Let me get dressed. I'll take you.' We drove to Prince of Wales Emergency Department. The streets were deserted, slick with rain. I didn't want the radio on, just the soft, persistent pitter-patter of rain and the rhythmic swish of the windscreen wipers. No words were exchanged. My mind was in overdrive, spinning internal questions like a horror movie marathon. What nightmare is this? *Nightmare on Elm Street? Child's Play?* The image of bright-red blood kept replaying in my mind, drenching every thought in dread.

Dad hunched forward, clutching his side, his face etched with pain. He rarely complained, so I knew this was serious. I helped him to a seat in the emergency department and approached the triage nurse. It was quiet, a rare mercy. Thankfully, Dad was called nearly immediately. He rose, a flicker of relief in his eyes, as if being seen had lifted an invisible weight from his shoulders. Within minutes, an IV was running, blood was drawn, and scans were ordered. Everything moved swiftly, but I couldn't help tensing, bracing for the results, wondering just how long our luck would last.

We waited in the acute lounge until a bed was available. A porter arrived and whisked Dad away to a ward. I followed in a daze, my footsteps echoing in the quiet halls, barely registering the sterile corridors until Dad was settled. Sleep tugged at me, my body heavy in the hard-backed armchair, but before I could drift off, the doctor appeared, flicking on a dim light. His words hit me like stones: Dad's prostate was severely enlarged and was pressing on his bladder. Antibiotics for the infection, and a specialist referral first thing in the morning.

It was 3 a.m. when Dad insisted I go home. 'Lil A can't wake and not find you there,' he said softly, trying to sound strong. I kissed his forehead, grabbed my bag, and slipped out. The corridor was silent, the low hum of machines echoing in the stillness. Every step felt borrowed, as though I were trespassing on time that didn't belong to me.

I soon realised I was lost. We'd come up earlier by lift, so I pressed the down arrow, hoping instinct would guide me right. The doors opened with a faint ding, and I jabbed 'G' for ground, praying that would take me where I needed to go.

When the lift doors parted, I hesitated. Where was I? Endless grey corridors stretched out on both sides: sterile, identical, soulless. I turned left, the sound of my footsteps bouncing off the walls, each echoing louder than the last. The air felt heavier here, almost thick. The lights flickered, dimmer with every few steps.

Then, a creak. Faint, distant, but enough to freeze me in place. My heart slammed against my ribs. Panic clawed at my throat. I was deep in the hospital's underbelly, alone. I fumbled for my phone, hands shaking, and called Master M. It rang twice before his voice calm, grounding came through.

'Hey, babe, you, okay? Is your dad alright?'

'I'm lost,' I managed to say, my breath shallow. 'I don't know how to get out of here. I'm scared.'

'Okay, breathe. Stay calm,' he said gently. 'What can you see around you?'

'Just...a corridor. Long, empty. I've been walking forever.' My voice cracked. It felt like hours, though it had only been minutes. My sense of time was unravelling, fear distorting everything.

Then I heard a sharp whistle echo down the hallway. My whole body tensed at once, every muscle locking tight. 'Someone's coming to kill me!' I cried into the phone, my heart hammering so hard it hurt.

'What? No one's going to kill you,' he said, steady and firm. 'You're safe. Just breathe.'

But his voice drifted away, fading under the sound that swallowed everything else. The whistle grew louder, sharper, sliding through the walls like it was hunting me. My thoughts spun out of control faster than I could catch them. 'They're whistling!' I screamed, my voice shaking so badly it cracked. 'I see him! It's Freddy Krueger!'

Terror overtook me completely. Logic slipped away, replaced by the wild, choking panic that comes when exhaustion and fear collide.

'It's not Freddy Krueger. Calm down!' he insisted, his voice steady, but the shadow loomed closer.

I froze, a wave of nausea curling in my throat. My legs wobbled like jelly. The whistling, the endless, piercing whistling, cut through my head, each note sharper than the last.

'Please...don't kill me!' I screamed, my hand trembling as the phone slipped from my grip.

The figure stopped abruptly, startled. 'Ma'am...I'm not going to kill you. Are you alright?'

I pressed my back against the cold, sterile wall, tears streaming down my face. 'I'm trapped. I'm pregnant, tired, hungry, and I think I'm losing my mind. Please help me.'

His expression softened, his eyes full of compassion. He pointed at a green button just a few metres away. 'Press this. It'll lead you to the entrance.'

In my panic, I had missed everything: the door, the signs, all of it. My eyes had caught nothing but an endless white corridor, stretching without end.

'Babe? Are you okay?' Master M's voice cut through the fog in my mind. His calm tone reached me first, pulling me back into myself and steadying my breath.

I grabbed the phone, a shaky, near-hysterical laugh slipping out. 'I've totally lost it,' I whispered. 'I'm seeing things. I'll be home in ten.'

When I pulled into the driveway, the sight of the open front door was a lifeline. I bolted inside, throwing myself into Master M's arms, sobbing uncontrollably. My body trembled as I buried my face in his chest. I collapsed onto the kitchen bench, burying my head in my arms, tears soaking the tissues he handed me. Raw and exhausted, I whispered, 'Give me a cigarette.'

'No way,' he said firmly, the words carrying the weight of love and concern.

'Give me one now,' I demanded, my voice hoarse, cracking under the pressure. When he refused again, I snatched the packet and stormed outside.

At 4 a.m., rain mingling with my tears, I lit the cigarette. Two puffs brought a wave of calm. I knew it was wrong, but in that moment no deep breathing could've soothed me. Those puffs were my fragile anchor, a shameful comfort in the chaos.

Do I sleep or not? The sun brushed the horizon. Nearly 5 a.m. If I closed my eyes, I knew I'd be up again soon. Should I collapse on the couch or in bed? Either way, the day was already looming. Dad at Prince of Wales, Mum at St George, the relentless back and forth.

First, I had to call work. My stomach twisted. Was I about to be fired? I wouldn't have to lie to him; the truth was wild enough. Could I admit I couldn't cope? I stalled, my thoughts racing, until 7.30 a.m. when I finally called my boss's direct line.

'Hi, J, it's Andrea,' I said, my voice thin, barely above a whisper.

'Hi, Andrea. How are you?' he asked, immediately noticing the strain in my voice.

'Not great. Mum's stable, thank God. But last night...' I hesitated, then rushed the words out, 'I had to take Dad to the hospital for prostate issues.'

'Oh my,' he murmured, his voice heavy with sorrow. 'Is there more you'll have to face?'

I swallowed the lump in my throat. 'It's...tough,' I admitted. 'But I'll manage. I can't commit to work until Dad's discharged. It's just too much right now.'

Honest. Raw. I'd always prided myself on invincibility, but now even I had cracks. His understanding was a lifeline, easing the weight on my chest. I could juggle hospital runs and childcare, somehow. It wouldn't be easy, but I had to. The leniency I was granted at work eased my stress considerably. I had to be flexible, coordinating visits with my parents around childcare, but I was confident I could manage. I could do this. I had this.

Lil A woke up, and his usual routine was to rush into my dad's room and jump onto him. 'Good morning, Pappou! I'm awake!' It was always the cutest sight. But today he ran into the room only to find it empty. 'Pappou? Pappou, where are you?' he shouted, looking around the house.

I called out to him gently. 'Come here, *agapi mou* (my love). Pappou wasn't feeling well last night, so I took him to the hospital. He'll be back soon.'

'But Yiayia is in the hospital,' he replied, his face scrunched in confusion.

'I know, sweetheart, but Pappou was sick last night too, and the doctor is making him better,' I assured him, trying to calm his worry.

'Are they in the same room, like a sleepover?' His innocent question made me smile. I love how pure children's thoughts could be.

'No, *agapi mou*, Pappou is in another hospital. We'll go see him after school today, okay? Would you like that?'

'Yes!' he exclaimed with a grin, his excitement contagious.

Not only did I pack Lil A's school bag, but I also tucked a snack bag away for myself. The constant back and forth was feeding my hunger, and, honestly, I wasn't one to pass up a good snack.

Master M took Lil A to school since it was out of my way, and he gave the childcare a quick rundown of our family drama so they'd be aware if we ran late. My first stop was Dad's hospital, which was closest to home. I spent a few hours there, discussing his condition and expected outcomes with the doctors. Thankfully, surgery wasn't required, but he needed to stay under observation for a few days. Dad was quick to send me packing, not because he didn't want me there, but because he knew Mum was alone and wanted me to be with her.

I headed to St George Hospital. As I drove, I debated whether to tell Mum about Dad's situation. I was torn – should I share the news or wait? I didn't know what to say or how she'd react. I decided to play it by ear, gauging her condition and going from there.

I walked in, bags weighing me down, a mess of exhaustion and worry. 'Hi, Mum, I'm here!'

'Oh. Hi, love,' she said, her voice steady, though her eyes followed me with quiet concern.

I sank into the chair, the weariness finally catching up with me. 'I'm so tired, Mum.'

Her gaze softened. 'Didn't you sleep?'

I hesitated, then blurted it out, the words tumbling out before I could stop them. 'No. Papa was urinating blood. I took him to the hospital. Stayed all night.'

Her expression changed to alarm, her lips moving instinctively in prayer. '*Kyrie eleison*, is he okay?' Her Greek prayer wrapped around us both, carrying fear and faith in equal measure.

'Yeah, Mum, he's okay. They gave him antibiotics through an IV. He'll be home in a few days.'

'Good, good,' she said softly, closing her eyes in relief. Her lips moved silently again, this time reciting the Lord's Prayer, her faith a quiet anchor in the storm.

I sat by her bedside, the weight of everything pressing down on me. I reached for my phone and called my obstetrician's office nearby. My appointment wasn't due, but the chaos of the night before left me feeling uneasy, unsettled. It was hard to explain, but the nurse on the other end urged me to come in immediately. With a heavy heart, I gathered my things and left, my mind still racing.

In the obstetrician's office, my leg bounced nervously as I flipped through magazines and checked my phone. A faded ultrasound poster curled on the wall, the machine's hum a faint, comforting sound in the background. Dr D called me in.

'Hey, Doc,' I said, forcing a smile.

'I'm fabulous. You?' he replied, gesturing to the scan room.

The words tumbled out. 'I freaked out last night. Dad was rushed to the hospital. I had a panic attack; hallucinated Freddy Krueger, but it was just the porter. I smoked a cigarette. Doc, I feel like I'm going to have this baby early.'

'Take a few deep breaths,' he said calmly. 'You're okay. The baby's okay. Last night was intense. Unorthodox, but that cigarette might've steadied you, kept the baby safe. Not a pack a day, but better than a miscarriage.'

I blinked, trying to process this. 'I'm just so stressed, scared. It's too much.'

He smiled gently. 'I never trust a woman's instinct.'

I let out a laugh, but it was heavy, filled with uncertainty. 'You watch; I'm having this baby early.'

'We'll see,' he replied, his tone reassuring but not dismissive.

I grabbed a decaf coffee, the warmth grounding me, and returned to Mum's room. I fed her dinner, made sure she was comfortable, and then left to pick up Lil A.

He was the last one waiting at preschool, sand still in his curls, his socks mismatched, shoes untied. His face lit up when he saw me. 'We going to see Pappou now?'

'Yes, *agapi mou*. But you must stay quiet, no jumping. Pappou is in pain,' I reminded him softly.

'I jump Pappou?' His eyes were wide with excitement. 'No!' I pulled him back gently. 'Be careful.'

Dad stayed in the hospital for days. Master M and I alternated between caring for him, managing meals, and juggling the responsibilities that never seemed to end. When Dad was finally discharged, relief washed over me. One layer of stress lifted, but there was still so much to handle.

Mum's discharge came soon after a long-awaited milestone – six months in the hospital. My belly was now round with pregnancy and I felt a mix of joy and relief. I'd faced both of my parents' hospitalisations, my own emotional unravelling, and the constant fear that the pregnancy might not make it. Yet, amidst the chaos, there was a quiet strength that held me together.

Back home, I helped Mum settle in. Her frail hand squeezed mine, a silent thank you that spoke volumes in my heart. As we sat together, the memory of the church chants I had heard in that moment of prayer returned. Their cadence was a reminder of the faith that had held us all through the storm. I wondered what strength I would pass on to my unborn child as we faced the days ahead.

CHAPTER 8

Nesting adventures

After six months, Mum finally found comfort in her own bed, bringing an end to the long spell of hospital visits, nurses' observations, and the constant beeping of monitors. The quietness of home and the familiar aromas of home-cooked meals felt like a soothing balm.

With both my parents back in relatively good health, they now had a fresh concern: their house wasn't ready for the arrival of their newest grandchild, thanks to me and my bright ideas. Naturally, when one door closes, another opens. Life is never dull under our roof. Surely there's always time for a quick renovation, a splash of paint and a spring clean before a baby arrives, right? Absolutely.

I thrive on challenges, though sometimes it feels like I'm banging my head against a wall. With just under three months left of my pregnancy, I decided it was the perfect window of opportunity to demolish walls, install larger windows, and repaint the entire house while still living in it. Genius, I know. And since we were at it, why not reconfigure the layout to make room for a crib in our bedroom?

God bless my cousin T and Master M for putting up with me and my constant hounding to ensure the project was finished on time. That's the beauty – and the curse – of working with family. You get the added bonus of my persistent nagging, which I'm rather fabulous at.

A pregnant woman nesting is a woman on a mission. I had my checklist, and the deadline for the baby's birth loomed closer each day. At first, demolishing the walls of my TV room felt like a brilliant idea. The thought of sunlight pouring through newly installed windows and fresh air breezing through the house was irresistible. An open, light, airy home is always the most inviting.

But the dust. Oh, the dust. We sealed the room as best we could, yet the fine particles still found their way everywhere. No matter how much we cleaned, they spread like glitter, though with none of the golden sparkle. I cursed myself more than once, regretting the decision, but deep down I knew the end result would be worth it.

The weeks raced by and I became increasingly anxious that the renovations wouldn't be finished on time. My urgency only grew stronger, fuelled by my intuition that the baby would arrive early. So I piled on the pressure, urging the dynamic duo to keep moving. Then one evening when I walked through the door after work, I felt instant relief. The tarps were down and the new windows were in. What a sight. Though it was already dark, I imagined the sunlight streaming in, filling the space with warmth. I pictured myself opening those windows, the cool breeze brushing my face, the scent of fresh air filling my lungs. Re-energised, I set about the tough job of cleaning and preparing the rooms for painting. But that dust! It had crept into every crevice imaginable. Into cupboards, corners, even places I didn't know existed. What on earth had I got myself into?

Day after day, I scrubbed, vacuumed, and mopped, with no end in sight. The number of cleaning products we went through was ridiculous. Yet eventually, the effort paid off. With a metaphorical wave of my magic wand, I transformed each room, one by one, until they sparkled and stood ready for painting. We tackled the painting room by room, as we were still living in the house. One room completed, then onto the next. Slowly but surely, we worked our way from the front of the house to the back. Bedroom by bedroom, night after night, Master M came home from work and joined me in the mission to make our home ready for the baby.

At one point, Master M grew frustrated with my dad. He never offered to help, only stood back and watched him paint. As much as Master M wanted to snap, *Come on, help me finish this goddamn house!* he never did. He respected my dad far too much, plus he knew very well I'd kill him if he ever spoke to my father disrespectfully. Still, I could sense his annoyance in the occasional spiteful comment that slipped out.

Late one evening, as Master M rolled paint across one of the rooms, Dad walked in and stood admiring his work. He stepped back, smiling from ear to ear. Looking over at Master M, he said warmly, 'I'm so sorry I can't help you paint. It's the one thing I never learned to do. You're doing a brilliant job. Bravo!'

I turned and grinned at Master M, tilting my head and narrowing my eyes as if to say, *Ha! I told you so. Now apologise for thinking he was lazy.* I didn't utter a word, but my look was enough to make my point.

I loved the smell of fresh paint, the scent of new beginnings. The renovations were close to complete, and somehow, I still had a little time left in my pregnancy to rest.

One Sunday in February, a brutal heatwave struck, with temperatures soaring into the high thirties and early forties. Being heavily pregnant, I felt it more intensely than anyone. No air conditioning could bring relief. At one point, I stripped down to my bra and shorts and lay flat on the cool tiles, desperate for respite.

Dad walked in, saw me sprawling on the floor, and nearly had a heart attack, thinking something terrible had happened. That afternoon, we gave up on the house entirely. We drove from one McDonald's to another, downing frozen Cokes and blasting the air conditioning. The heat was unbearable.

The morning after brought some relief, though the humidity still hung heavy. Poor Lil A didn't want to go to kindy. 'Too hot,' he protested. But I was in no state to negotiate, so school attendance was non-negotiable.

Throughout the day I felt strange, unwell in a way I couldn't name. Nauseous. Dizzy. No appetite. My energy was gone and heavy lethargy pulled at me. It was a sensation I had never experienced before. By the time I picked Lil A up from school, I was pale as snow. Normally I would linger for a chat with the other parents, but not that day. I dashed in and out, desperate to sit down. My heart raced as though I'd run a marathon.

Monday evenings were family dinner at my in-laws, which meant no cooking for me. Amen to that. I was grateful for the break. But even at their table, I couldn't shake the unsteadiness. I debated whether to call my obstetrician or wait it out. My body felt like a ship swaying on the sea. *Maybe I'm just hungry*, I told myself. But the thought of food made me queasy. I forced down a few bites of schnitzel. No good. Chewing and swallowing only worsened the nausea. I need to call my obstetrician. It was close to 5.30 p.m., so I should still be able to reach him, I thought.

I dialled his office. To my relief, the receptionist answered quickly. I tried to explain what was wrong, but it was hard to put into words. I didn't know what was happening. She placed me on hold, then returned after consulting Dr D. He wanted me to go to the hospital for observation. Precautionary only, she assured me. I wasn't convinced it was anything serious, but I agreed. Better safe than sorry.

I kissed Lil A repeatedly. 'Make sure you eat your dinner, *agapi mou*. I'll be back soon,' I promised. He grew uneasy, not wanting me to leave, and I couldn't blame him. Every time my parents were hospitalised, especially Mum, I disappeared for days. I didn't want him to feel abandoned.

'We're just going to check that the baby's okay in Mummy's tummy. By the time you've gobbled up all your dinner, I'll be back, okay?' I smothered him with more kisses.

'Okay, Mummy,' he said, waving goodbye with his little hand. Tears welled as I turned away, unsettled by a sense of foreboding.

We pulled into the car park at Hurstville Private. The night sky was clear, stars beginning to pierce the dark. I climbed out of the car and waddled to reception. They were expecting me, and within minutes I was escorted straight into one of the delivery suites.

'Hop onto the bed and get comfortable. I'll let Dr D know you've arrived,' the midwife said. I eased myself onto the bed. Moments later she returned with the belly band heart monitors.

'Okay, let's see what's happening. We'll hook you up to a few machines to monitor you and the baby for a while. How are you feeling now?' she asked gently, fitting the straps around me.

'I honestly don't know,' I admitted. 'It's a weird sensation. No pain, just...uneasy. It's been like this all day.'

She gave me a reassuring smile. 'Dr D will be here in five minutes. Just try to relax. You did the right thing by coming in.'

Five minutes to the second, Dr D walked through the green double doors. 'What's happening, Andrea? How are you feeling?' he asked cheerfully.

'I can't explain it, Doc,' I replied. He crossed the room, studied the monitors, exchanged a glance with the midwife, then fixed his eyes back on me.

'Are you in any pain?'

'Nope. Nothing,' I answered casually.

'Right...interesting,' he murmured. 'Looking at the monitors, you're actively in labour.'

'Excuse me? I'm what?' The words caught in my throat, leaving me stunned.

'Yes. According to the readings, you're contracting every few minutes. You could quite possibly deliver this baby tonight. I need to give you steroids for the baby's lungs, as they're not yet fully developed. We need to be prepared.'

'But I'm only thirty-two weeks!' Panic surged through me, hot and sharp.

'You're in a safe space,' he reassured me firmly. 'You and the baby will be fine. But if you do deliver, you'll both need to be transferred immediately. This hospital doesn't have the facilities for premature babies. What we'll do now is try to stop the contractions. Our goal is to keep the baby inside for at least another two weeks.'

The fear lodged deep inside me. I couldn't make sense of it. How could I be in labour yet feel nothing?

Dr D pulled up a stool, rolled it beside me and took my hand. His eyes softened. 'Andrea, to be honest, I expected this. You've endured an immense amount of stress. There's only so much the body can take. Either way, everything will be all right. Trust me.' He squeezed my hand with a steadiness I clung to.

I looked at Master M in disbelief. I wasn't ready. The baby's clothes weren't washed, the cot wasn't built, nothing was finished. My mind spun.

Through the panic, one thought broke through. I needed Lil A with me. I begged Master M to bring him. I didn't want him to worry. He needed to see with his own eyes that I was okay. And he didn't care that I was in hospital, bless his little heart. He was just thrilled at the thought of becoming a big brother.

The contractions kept rolling through the night. Still no pain, just tightening and some strange sensations, which were bearable. One night turned into two, then three. They weren't slowing. If anything, they'd grown irregular, puzzling the nurses. By the third evening, I insisted Master M go home, eat a proper meal, rest, and spend time with our son. Lil A was thriving with my parents, particularly with his Pappou, who spoiled him with ice cream and chips after school. Why would he miss us? Knowing he was happy and safe brought me a sense of peace. Had he been distressed, I would have unravelled completely, and no doubt I would have sent myself straight into delivery.

That night, my cousin S came to sit with me. Having her there gave Master M the confidence to leave, and it gave me comfort too. She was like the big sister I never had: fierce, loyal, and unshakably protective. She refused to leave until I fell asleep. Rugged up in a blanket against the hospital's chill, she perched on the lounge chair, keeping me company. We laughed, swapped stories, talked rubbish, and turned the sterile room into something almost homely.

When handover time came, we hushed to listen in. I always did that, eavesdropping on the nurses and doctors. I wanted to know everything. The new midwife entered, short blonde hair tucked behind her ears, scrubs under an oversized jacket, clipboard in hand. She grinned.

'Right, I hear you're a bit of a problem patient,' she teased. 'I've had a long day, I'm exhausted. Let's keep tonight cruisy, no surprises.'

'Deal,' I laughed. 'I'd love a cruisy night too.'

She left, and S and I returned to our chatter and Candy Crush. But within 15 minutes, the midwife burst back in, eyes wide.

'I told you no surprises!' she exclaimed, hurrying to the monitor.

'What? I haven't moved!' I said, startled.

'You're contracting every minute. I need to call Dr D.' She dashed out, then reappeared almost instantly, phone pressed to her ear.

'Yep, yep, no problem. I'll call them now and see where we can get her transferred to.'

She hung up, breathless. My stomach dropped.

'What's going on? I don't understand.'

She softened her voice. 'Sweetheart, we can't deliver your baby here. We don't have the neonatal facilities for premature babies. We can only deliver safely from thirty-four weeks onwards, and you're only thirty-two. We need to transfer you so the baby can get the care it needs. You're in safe hands, I promise. Worst-case scenario, I can deliver your baby safely if it happens here, but the transfer is essential, and as soon as possible.'

Her words were calm, but the urgency behind them rang clear. In that whirlwind moment, the absurdity of it all hit me like a wave.

One second I was laughing with S and the next, everything was careening towards something I couldn't yet fully grasp. My heart pounded as I realised how quickly life could flip, its possibilities echoing in my mind even before the real chaos began. I stared at my cousin, stunned. I had to call Master M. He'd only just gotten home. What were the chances he hadn't even showered yet? My cousin rang him. He picked up on the first ring.

'Is everything okay?' His voice was tight with panic.

'M, you need to hurry back. Andrea's contracting every minute. They're organising her transfer.'

Before she could say goodbye, he hung up. His foot was already on the pedal, running every red light from Rosebery to Hurstville. A 10-minute trip, no police, no cameras, no delays.

He burst into the room, breathless. 'I literally just got out of the shower! What's going on?'

'Your guess is as good as mine,' I said with a helpless shrug.

The midwife returned, phone still in hand. 'They can't find a bed anywhere. All the special care units are at capacity.'

'So...what now?' I asked, my pulse hammering.

'I've called in a helicopter. You're being transferred to Canberra.'

'I'm what?' The word cracked from my throat.

My cousin leapt from her seat. She and Master M exchanged a look of sheer terror. A helicopter? Was that even safe?

Moments later, the midwife reappeared, still on the phone. 'No, not a good idea,' she argued sharply. 'She'll probably deliver mid-air. Too dangerous. I'm cancelling. I'll send her to St George. They'll have to accept her.'

She hung up and dialled again, frustration etched across her face.

'Hi, I need patient transport ASAP.' A pause. 'No, now. We can't wait.'

She slammed the receiver down, turned to us, and said, 'There's a delay with transport. You'll need to get to St George immediately. The safest option is for Master M to drive you. I'll contact them; they'll be obligated to take you, private patient or not.'

Slow and steady, I eased myself into the wheelchair. Just minutes ago I'd been laughing with my cousin and now I was hearing words like 'helicopter' and 'Canberra'. Unreal. Who would even believe such a story?

We drove carefully this time – no racing. Mumma on board, contractions ticking along, but we obeyed the speed limits. We pulled up at St George's emergency bay, where staff were already waiting with a chair.

'Hi, Andrea,' a nurse greeted me warmly. 'We'll take good care of you and your baby. Let's get you inside.'

Down corridors, left then right, wheels squeaking on linoleum. We stopped briefly for paperwork, and from a nearby room came the sound of a woman's crying.

'Wtf,' I muttered.

The nurse chuckled. 'Another mum in labour. She's almost ready to deliver.'

They wheeled me into a room. I unfolded myself from the chair, climbed onto the bed, and surrendered to yet another round of monitors.

'You're contracting every minute,' the nurse observed.

'So they say, but I'm not feeling a thing,' I replied.

Moments later, she returned, brow furrowed. 'Your contractions are slowing down.'

'Are you kidding me?' I snapped.

'You're not going anywhere. Dr D will see you in the morning. Let's just watch through the night.'

Unimaginable. One minute I was being threatened with a helicopter transfer, and the next, my contractions decided to ease off. This baby was toying with me. Make up your mind kid: in or out?

That night dragged on. I watched the clock as time crawled by, listening to the guttural moans of the other mother nearby, followed by the sweetest sound of all: a newborn's first cry. Tears pricked my eyes. Aww, bubba. *When would it be my turn?* Clearly not tonight.

By morning, my cousin stirred from a short nap.

'S, I need a favour,' I begged. 'My hair is putrid. I need to wash it and straighten it. I cannot have this baby while looking like a slob. And I am dying for coffee.'

She laughed, rolled her eyes, and set off for my 'emergency supplies.'

Of course it was an emergency. Not long after, my obstetrician walked in, shaking his head. 'Well, well, well. What have we got here?'

'I told you this baby was going to come early!' I shot back.

'You haven't had the baby yet,' he replied dryly.

I was to remain under observation. They needed me to reach 34 weeks. I was nearly 33 weeks, just one more. Initially, they wanted me admitted until then. Over my dead body!

I needed to get home to Lil A. I needed to get back to him. I still had all the baby clothes to wash and prepare. After much back and forth, my obstetrician finally signed my discharge paperwork. Wooooo hoooo! Under strict orders to do nothing, I chirped, 'I promise, I promise,' as I bounced out of bed, ready to leave.

'You do know this is serious,' Master M warned, speaking to me as if I were the misbehaving toddler in the room.

'It's not like I planned it,' I shot back. 'OMG, yes – can you relax? It's not like I'm going to knock down a wall and install a window,' I added, dripping with sarcasm.

'It's already been done,' he said.

Ah, I'm home. Home sweet home. The scent of fresh paint was so good. The breezy air drifted through the TV room, the newly installed windows wide open. I was so impressed with the renovation's outcome. All that rush had been worth it. And the warmth of the sun – oh, how beautiful it felt against my skin. Nothing compares to the satisfaction of being in one's own home, surrounded by the comfort of one's own bed.

'Mummy, you're home!' Lil A bulldozed into me with excitement.

'I'm home, baby. I'm home. I'm not going anywhere.' I smothered him with kisses.

Being ordered to do nothing did not sit well with me. Doing nothing on a good day wasn't even in my brain's capacity. I honestly don't know what the actual meaning of 'doing nothing' truly is. I hear the word 'doing' and I *do,* completely ignoring the *nothing* part.

❤

I loaded the washing machine with the baby's clothes. While that ran, I decided it was a brilliant idea to grab the short stepladder, climb up and clean the bar. Shelf by shelf, I wiped down every bottle and redecorated the back section of the house. There was so much to do; every time I looked around, I added another task to my list. I wasn't being silly. Well, let me rephrase, I was *absolutely* being an idiot. Heavily pregnant, in labour, still contracting, and climbing a ladder. I was a dead-set moron.

My Dad yelled at me. My Mum snapped. And Master M lost his shit. It felt just like my teenage years. I ignored them all and kept going. If I didn't do it, who would? I needed a few days to get the house sorted. A nesting mother is the most productive creature on two legs. Master M called me an 'alien' a few times – a very fitting compliment.

My driving was limited. I didn't feel comfortable being behind the wheel, especially with Lil A in the car. His school being up the road gave me an excuse to get some light exercise in. However, there was one slight problem: I was still contracting every few minutes. Even though there was no pain, the pressure and tightness were constant. What normally took us 10 to 15 minutes to walk would take 30, sometimes 45, because I'd have to stop every few minutes and breathe through each contraction. It was absolutely wild.

I was in high spirits. I continued seeing my obstetrician twice a week. The house was ready. Lil A was settled in Kindy. Things were finally smoothing out. At comfortably over 34 weeks, the pressure eased a little, knowing the baby could arrive safely at any time. Still, the longer I kept the baby in, the better.

The following week I attended my scheduled ultrasound appointment. It was a crucial routine check to make sure the baby's growth remained on track, especially after all the complications. Because I was still uneasy driving alone, my best friend L came with me. As the prospective godmother, her presence meant even more – she got to unofficially meet her unborn godchild during the scan.

We sat in the room waiting for the sonographer, and to be totally honest, I felt slightly anxious. She squeezed the warm, gooey blue gel onto my rounded belly and pressed her probe against my skin. All eyes were glued to the screen. My heartbeat quickened.

'And there's your baby. Here is its little hand – one, two, three, four, five fingers. And over here is the other hand – one, two, three, four, five. The left foot...and there's the right foot. The heart is beating well. Here, listen.'

She turned up the volume and the baby's heartbeat pulsed through the room. I was soothed, as if it were a gentle lullaby. She grew quiet while taking measurements, then retaking them. She tilted her head to the side, then measured again. Her silence spoke volumes. I sensed her concern.

She rolled her stool back and said, 'I'll be back shortly.'

I looked at L as she gently took my hand and squeezed it tight. A moment later, a doctor followed the sonographer back into the room.

'Hi, Andrea. Don't be alarmed. We're just going to remeasure your baby. It appears the measurements are very small considering how far along you are,' he explained, taking the probe in his hand. He pressed it against my belly, any harder and I would have peed on myself. He clicked a few buttons on the computer screen and sat back.

'Okay, so the measurements are small. We just wanted to double-check. We'll send these to Dr D immediately, and he'll reach out to you. Don't panic. Your baby looks healthy and well – it's just on the small side,' he said with warmth as he wiped away the gel.

The entire day moved in a haze. I kept anticipating my obstetrician's call – any minute, any second. Minute after minute, hour after hour...nothing. Maybe everything was fine and I was working myself up for no reason. I glanced at the clock and saw it was 5 p.m. If he hasn't called by now, I'm safe, I told myself. He's probably on his way home. I'm in the clear. The thought settled me, and for a brief moment, I let myself breathe. Just as I found that small pocket of peace, my phone rang. Of course it did. And of course, it was Dr D.

'Hi, Andrea. It's Dr D. I've received your scans from today. As you're aware, your baby is measuring relatively small. You're 35 weeks now, and we've gotten you as far as we can. I don't think we can hold off anymore. It's time to get your baby out. Why don't you come in tomorrow morning so we can discuss everything in person?' As quickly as it began, the call ended.

I now had to mentally prepare for another induction. I started counting the days in my head; it was Thursday, and he usually did inductions on Mondays, so I had a few days to get ready. I told myself I was fine with that.

The next morning I set out to visit my obstetrician, eager to hear his thoughts. When would he schedule my induction? Unfortunately, on this of all days, I had no choice but to drive myself. Dad had a doctor's appointment with Mum, and Master M had errands to run. Still, I felt remarkably optimistic. On arriving at the office, I waited patiently to be called in. I was struck by my own patience. Clearly, things were improving. Soon, I was summoned into his office. I took a seat as he leaned back comfortably, sipping his coffee.

'How are you feeling, Andrea?' he asked, sitting up.

'I'm good. Really good. I haven't felt this good in a long time,' I replied confidently.

'Great. Let's do a quick check. Come over,' he said, rising from his chair.

He performed a quick scan, followed by a dreaded internal. Ouch.

'So, what are your plans for the weekend?' he asked casually, as if he were inviting us over for a barbecue.

'Well, we have a soccer launch dinner tonight, soccer tomorrow with our little one, but otherwise it's pretty chilled,' I replied.

'Great! Cancel your plans. Meet me back at the hospital at one p.m. we're going to deliver your baby,' he blurted out.

'Excuse me, what? Today?' I said, a slight panic creeping into my voice.

'Yes, and be careful walking to the car, your waters may break from the internal,' he added.

I slowly grabbed my bag, swung it over my shoulder, and shuffled my way out, taking tiny steps and keeping my legs closed just in case anything popped. I made my way to the pedestrian lights. Pulling my phone from my back pocket, I quickly dialled Master M's number. He didn't answer. Steam seemed to shoot out of my eyes, nose, and ears. *Answer the fucken phone, will you!* I rang again.

Finally, he picked up. 'Fuck, fuck, fuck,' I rambled into the phone, pressing the pedestrian button like I had Tourette's.

'What's wrong? Why all the fucks?' he asked.

'Um...we're having the baby today. Oh, and...chances are my waters are going to break because he gave me an internal. That's why! I need to get to the car, fast.' I sped through my words as if saying them quicker would help. I just needed to get home safely. It's okay. What's the worst that can happen?

My waters could break while I'm driving...fuck!

I drove home with utmost caution, eyes on every corner, every speed bump. I was almost there. Boy, was I glad to pull into my driveway. I hobbled into the house and jumped straight into the shower.

'What are you doing?!' Master M screamed as I slammed the door.

'I need to wash and straighten my hair! I have to paint my nails and shave my legs! Look at me, do I look ready to have a baby? ... NO!' I yelled, water streaming over my head.

'You're a psycho, woman,' he muttered, walking into the bathroom. Then, softer, he asked, 'Do you need help? What can I do?'.

'Just organise my dad to pick up A from school. Oh, and don't tell *anyone* we're going to the hospital; just your parents, that's it!' I yelled, thinking he couldn't hear me with my head under the running water.

We arrived at the hospital right on 1 p.m., buzzing with excitement. As much as I knew the delivery would hurt, I was ready to meet our baby. Waddling down the corridor towards the nurse's station, I noticed the midwives were just as excited to see me.

'Let's have this baby,' one said, leading me to my delivery suite. Deja vu, again. A scene I knew all too well. I changed into the bedazzling gown and settled onto the bed. The midwife entered, hooked me up to my familiar monitors, and gave me another internal.

Oh, for fuck's sake. No dignity whatsoever. No gel, just a quick piercing of my waters, and pop, just like that, I was sitting in warm liquid. So gross. I was told the labour pains would hit instantly, but I was relatively comfortable. I felt the contractions, but it wasn't the excruciating agony I remembered from Lil A's birth.

Several hours passed and I was still coping, somewhat gracefully. My parents had picked up Lil A from school and were on their way to the hospital. My in-laws were also due to arrive. The news of the baby's delivery had not been shared with anyone else. My phone kept ringing, but I didn't answer, fearing I might accidentally reveal the news. My girlfriends had been incredibly supportive, calling every day to check on me, which was so comforting. This time, however, I wasn't taking anyone's calls.

By 6 p.m. the pains hit hard. I tried to stand, clutching the table for support, leaning forward, rising onto my tiptoes, but I could barely breathe through the intensity. 'Give me the epidural, please, I can't do this anymore,' I begged the midwife.

'Let me check how far you've dilated,' she replied, helping me back into bed. I was too far gone. In just an hour or two, I had gone from a few centimetres to eight. I had no choice but to endure just a little longer. Sweat dripped from my forehead. My eyes rolled back. The pains rocked my world. Remind me again why I wanted another baby? Why do we put ourselves through this, time and time again?

The midwife popped out of the room for a split second to update my obstetrician. 'She is ready,' she informed him.

Then she returned. As she reached my left side, I grabbed her arm. 'Please don't leave me,' I begged, and in the next breath, I screamed, 'I need to push!'

'Okay, let my hand go so we can deliver your baby. Are you ready?' she asked gently, trying to free herself.

'Please hold my hand,' I insisted, squeezing even tighter. It must have seemed like I wasn't letting her leave my side. She was my support person, while Master M delivered our baby with another midwife, my obstetrician nowhere in sight.

I felt a contraction coming. It was time to push. One small push, and the baby's head was out. Oh my God, that burning sensation. How vividly I remembered it from five years earlier. A few deep breaths later, another contraction was well underway.

'Okay, with this next contraction, just a little push. Your baby is small; you don't need to push so hard,' the midwife said, brushing my hair away from my face. I took a deep breath and pushed – just a little one, as instructed. I felt the body slide out, slippery little sucker.

They quickly cut the umbilical cord and took the baby to the table. There were no cries, no ruffles – just silence in the room. I held my breath. Then, after clearing the baby's mouth, that silence broke with the exhilarating first wails of a newborn. In that one tiny outburst, my strength, energy, and calmness returned.

'Is it a boy or a girl?' I asked, catching my breath. Master M stepped forward and placed our newborn in my arms. 'Check!' he said, his voice full of love. Tears slipped onto the blanket as I slowly unwrapped our baby – and discovered we had another son.

Baby R was born on 4 March 2011.

Lil A ran in and jumped on the bed to greet his baby brother. Dr D walked in.

'So, what did we have?'

'You mean I had, I had a boy! We have another son!' I beamed with joy. 'I told you I was going to have this baby early,' I couldn't resist reminding him I was right.

'Yeah, yeah. I never trust a woman's instinct, but you...you are something else,' he said with lightness, love, and laughter.

Never in my life would I have imagined my pregnancy coming with such external hurdles. Yet throughout all 35 weeks, the tiny heartbeat of my growing baby gave me the strength to stand taller, to love deeper, and to cherish everything around me that truly matters.

Welcome to this big world, R. The world is waiting for you. I didn't know what lay ahead, but for now, we were whole.

CHAPTER 9

The quest unfolds

Our sweetest little bundle of joy, just under two kilograms – lighter than a bag of sugar – made his grand entrance into the world, born too soon at just 35 weeks. I barely had time to savour that first warm cuddle before he was whisked away to the Special Care Unit. My heart burned with anguish as they wheeled him out of sight, tearing my world apart in an instant.

My greatest fear was that something might happen to him, or worse, that he could somehow be mistaken for another baby. Stories of such tragedies haunted me, so I insisted that Master M shadow Baby R like a hawk, watching every step of his journey into the Special Care Unit. The drama of his birth had been terrifying enough; I couldn't bear another ordeal. This wasn't overreacting, it was instinct. It was what any protective mother would do.

When the time came for me to push open those heavy doors to the Special Care Unit, they felt as weighty as my own heart. Yet as I crossed the threshold, something in me lifted, as though I were floating. I approached his tiny crib and saw him lying there, so fragile, his little body connected to monitors and nasal feeding tubes. The sight both shattered me and pulled me closer.

I stood vigil beside him, whispering prayers into the quiet hum of the machines. I prayed for his health, for strength and resilience, and for the nurses entrusted with his care. I prayed they would handle him with compassion, skill, and love. And they did. Their dedication was unwavering, their gentleness unmatched. With every touch and every watchful glance, they wrapped him in the safety and tenderness I had hoped for. In that moment, all my fears dissolved. My little bag of sugar was exactly where he was meant to be, safe, cared for, and loved.

The hardest part of my hospital stay was trying to fall asleep at night in an empty room without the comforting presence of my newborn. The silence felt heavy, suffocating, broken only when the nurses gently woke me to feed him. I walked down to the nursery each time, where his tiny hands, his delicate feet, and that soft, lamb-like cry captivated me completely.

Because of his size, he struggled to regulate his body temperature. The nurses asked me to buy onesies, singlets, socks, and beanies to help keep him warm. When I say tiny, I'm not exaggerating. Even the smallest garments, size 00000, hung loosely on his delicate frame. It would take weeks before he could fill them out.

By day three, the dreaded 'third-day blues' struck like a tidal wave. My body betrayed me with tears I couldn't stop, my breath catching in ragged bursts. How could hormones shift so dramatically, flooding me with such despair?

That very day, I was discharged. I left the hospital with empty arms while our precious baby remained behind, needing more time to grow strong. The tears that streamed down my cheeks could have filled an empty lake. My chest ached with every breath.

How was I supposed to walk away? How could they expect me to leave him when he needed me most, my touch, my scent, my love? I needed him just as much. I couldn't breathe without him. Nothing made sense.

The emptiness was unbearable that first night at home. His bassinet stood beside me, hollow and accusing. My body lay in bed, but my spirit hovered over him in the nursery, watching like a guardian angel. Eyes wide open, I finally threw back the covers and pulled the bassinet closer. Rocking it gently, I moved my arm back and forth as if he were lying safely inside. A Greek lullaby slipped from my lips; the same soft melody I once used to lull Lil A to sleep. Its familiar notes wrapped around me, warm and soothing, each line carrying the weight of memory. For a moment, the hospital's cold hum faded, replaced by the quiet comfort of home that still lived in my heart. As I rocked the empty cradle, my breath synced with the rhythm of the song and the room slowly blurred at the edges. My eyelids grew heavy, not from exhaustion alone, but from the ache of holding on to something I could not touch. Still gently rocking, I drifted into sleep.

When morning came, I woke up renewed. The lullaby had cradled me in God's quiet peace, reminding me that even in absence, love bridges every distance, and faith carries us through the night. Upon waking up, my eyes instinctively turned to the bassinet. To my surprise, I felt calm; not fragile, but strong. Unshaken. I was unbreakable.

During our baby's hospital stay, I devoted every waking hour to being by his side. I arrived by 5 a.m. each morning, determined to greet him before his first feed. I took on everything, changing his nappies, learning how to guide the nasal tube feeds, and watching every tiny flutter of his eyelids. My days stretched long, from the first light of dawn until 10.30 at night, when I stayed to help with his final feed. Exhaustion never won; love carried me through. The moments I could cradle him, inhale the sweet scent of his skin, hold him close, were precious but fleeting, mostly limited to nappy changes. The rest of the time, he lay in his crib, surrounded by a tangle of wires and monitors.

Yet the hardest task came in the quiet hours of the night: waking to express milk without him by my side. Each session felt like a wound reopening, the ache of separation mirrored in every pull of the pump. I would sit there, my body heavy with fatigue, wondering, is he sleeping? Is he crying? Does he need me? Despite the heartache, I carried on, driven by the fierce love of a mother and the unshakable belief that my little miracle deserved every ounce of strength I had to give.

As the days passed, the fear that had once gripped me began to soften. He grew stronger. His skin, once translucent and fragile, took on a healthier glow. His temperature stabilised. His cries became bold and insistent, powered by his maturing lungs.

Then came the breakthrough I had long prayed for: his nasal feeding tube was removed. At last I could nurse him in my arms. My worries about his ability to latch, born from my older son's early struggles, melted away as he instinctively found his way. In that moment something altered and an unbreakable bond was forged between mother and child, heart to heart.

Just days before Baby R's long-awaited discharge, the nurses asked me to spend a night in the hospital with him, a chance to practise caring for him independently before bringing him home. At first, I brushed it off. I wasn't a first-time mother; surely I didn't need a trial run? But the staff gently insisted and eventually I agreed. *Easy-peasy,* I thought. *I've got this in the bag, maybe it will even be a little holiday.*

But as the sun slipped below the horizon, my confidence began to unravel. Baby R grew restless, his cries sharp, insistent, and unyielding. I tried everything: changing him, feeding him, and rocking him close. Nothing soothed him. The gentle, lamb-like cries I had once cherished now pierced the night like tiny daggers of worry. The nurses checked in regularly, offering to take him to the nursery so I could rest, but I refused. Stubbornly, I clung to him, determined to weather whatever the night demanded.

And endure I did. The hours stretched endlessly, darkness pressing in on both of us. Sleep never came for either of us. When morning arrived, I was hollowed out by exhaustion. The staff kindly offered me another night to recover, but I shook my head. I was done. I needed my own bed, my own rhythm, and my own space. More than anything, I missed my little boy A with an ache that wouldn't leave me. I was ready. Ready to bring our miracle home. Ready to reunite with the family who had been waiting for us.

At last the sun began to rise, its rays beaming gently through the curtains. For the first time in hours, our room felt peaceful. Baby R slept soundly in his crib, his chest rising and falling in perfect rhythm. I watched him for a moment, then quietly began to pack for our discharge, careful not to disturb him.

I expected Master M to arrive with a coffee any minute. Just as I zipped up my bag and sat back on the bed, he strolled in, though he looked far less relieved than I'd imagined he would.

'You're not going to believe what just happened,' he said. I hushed him and nodded towards the crib.

'Shh, he's finally asleep. We had a nightmare of a night.'

He went on anyway. 'I just got pulled over by the cops.'

'What? For what?'

'I was speeding. I didn't want to be late to pick you up. I told them I was rushing to get you and the baby, and they gave me a warning. They said to drive safely, especially with a baby in the car.'

I exhaled slowly. That was lucky.

Saying goodbye to the midwives and nurses was unexpectedly emotional. The time we'd spent together had forged a kind of family; the highs and lows we'd weathered bound us in ways words couldn't quite capture. As we prepared to leave, they smothered Baby R with hugs and kisses, their affection a sweet reminder of how deeply they'd cared for him.

And then, at last, we began the journey home. I surprised Lil A by picking him up from Kindy. His face lit up when he saw me instead of the expected Pappou. As the bell rang, he burst out of the door, scanning the crowd until his eyes landed on me. He froze for a heartbeat, unsure if it was really me, then broke into a huge smile and sprinted straight into my arms.

'Oh my God, I missed you so much!' I said, scooping him up and holding him tight. 'Quick, let's go home,' I added, showering his face with kisses. 'Your baby brother is waiting for you.'

Back at the house, the faint scent of fresh paint from our recent renovations still lingered in the air, a quiet reminder of the nesting chaos that now felt like a lifetime ago. We gathered in the living room, Lil A peering curiously at his tiny brother nestled in my arms, the family circling us like a warm embrace after weeks apart. Home at last, piecing together our expanded world, one coo and cuddle at a time.

Lil A took to his baby brother with a tenderness that melted me. He doted on him, slipping so naturally into the role of protector. He loved helping with feeds and was always quick to stretch out his little arms, ready for me to place the baby in his care. What he wasn't so keen on, however, was nappy duty. The moment a dirty one appeared, he'd vanish faster than I could call his name.

For the first time in what felt like forever, our little family was whole again. The kids were healthy and happy, my parents were doing relatively well, and Master M's support remained a steady comfort. Amen to that.

❤

Not long after, though, Lil A began to act out. At home, it was manageable – little bursts of defiance, moments of attitude. But at school his behaviour took a worrying turn, so unlike his usual calm self. I hadn't heard from his teachers, so I assumed it couldn't be that bad.

That assumption shattered the day Master M went to pick him up. While waiting, one of the teachers approached him with a polite smile.

'Hi, how are you? How's everything going?' she asked.

'Really good, thanks,' he said. 'We're finding our feet, but all is well.'

'That's great,' she replied. 'And how are Andrea and the baby?'

'Both are doing well. R's finally home and settling in,' Master M answered.

The teacher's smile faded. 'Fabulous. I just wanted to check something A mentioned today. He told me he's being fed dog food at home. I just wanted to make sure everything is okay.'

Master M was stunned. 'We don't even have a dog,' he spluttered.

The teacher gave a kind, knowing smile. 'Exactly, which is why I thought it was odd. He's probably just craving attention with a new baby at home. Don't worry, he'll adjust.'

They came through the front door with a slam so loud I thought the stained glass might shatter.

'Go and tell your Mum what you said at school today,' Master M nudged Lil A as I sat feeding the baby.

'I told my teachers you fed me dog food,' he said, laughing.

'Excuse me, you said what?' I said, trying to stay calm so I wouldn't startle R in my arms. 'That's very silly, A. Why would you say something like that? We don't even have a dog.'

'My friends all laughed,' he replied, shrugging innocently.

'That's not funny,' I said, my tone turning firm. 'Do you know teachers could misunderstand that and think we're not taking care of you? They could get the wrong idea and take you away from us. We could get into very big trouble.'

His face fell, eyes wide. 'But I want to stay with you, Mummy.'

'You better go to school tomorrow and apologise to your teacher. Don't say things like that again. Do I make myself clear?' I snapped.

He nodded, and in that instant, I felt the weight of it all, the fragility of family, and the way a single careless word could ripple into something much larger. I placed the baby down between us, took a deep breath, and reminded myself that we were all still learning how to be a family of four.

Finding the balance between nurturing Lil A and setting boundaries felt like a delicate dance. As their mum, I wanted both boys to feel equally loved and seen – no favourites, no gaps. I had so much love to give these two little rugrats; neither one was loved more than the other.

Looking back, I realised Lil A's misbehaviour stemmed from my long absence during Baby R's early weeks. He'd wake up and I'd be gone. He saw me only when Master M brought him to the hospital for visits. Determined to make it right, I carved out deliberate, sacred moments just for Lil A whenever he was home. When I wasn't nursing, Baby R was blissfully unaware, allowing me to give my full attention to his big brother.

The transition wasn't seamless; tantrums still happened, but slowly, Lil A began to trust again. He learned I wasn't going anywhere. And most importantly, he learned that he was just as loved as his baby brother.

Let's be real: parenting is like trying to solve a puzzle blindfolded while being attacked by a swarm of bees. There's no single 'right' way to do it, and if there were a magic parenting book, I doubt I'd have the time to read it (hello, sleep deprivation!). What I did know was that I loved my kids with every fibre of my being, and I did my best with the sleep-deprived, hormone-addled brain I had at the time. Honestly, that's all any parent can do. We wing it, we make mistakes, and we just hope our kids turn out okay-ish.

❤

When Baby R was nearly six months old, Dad travelled to Cyprus to visit family. He'd been torn about whether to go or stay, but I encouraged him to take the break. Caring for Mum had been intense and he desperately needed some respite. We arranged for Mum to move into a nursing home temporarily, where she'd receive round-the-clock care. I simply couldn't manage her needs on my own, especially with a newborn in my arms.

With Dad's safe arrival in Cyprus, my mum was comfortably settled into respite care, receiving exceptional care and genuine compassion from the staff. I visited her daily with Baby R, whose baby babbles brought her immense joy.

As the flu season took hold, Baby R began showing signs of illness. I made the careful decision to keep him away from my mum, determined to protect her from any potential infection. God forbid anything should happen and it was my fault; I would never have forgiven myself. Following medical advice, I postponed his immunisations.

The following week, when he was still recovering, I took him for his vaccinations. The doctor administered the shots, cautioning me that he might feel a little lethargic over the next 24 hours. He seemed in good spirits throughout the day, so I planned an evening outing to Bondi Junction shops to finalise arrangements for his christening. As sunset approached, Baby R grew increasingly agitated. I decided to ask Master M to join us, turning the outing into a family affair. I had carefully packed the baby's bag, prepared his bottle, and taken every precaution to ensure he would be comfortable and safe.

We arrived at Bondi, and Baby R slept soundly in his pram. Then, without warning, he let out a piercing, ear-splitting screech, the kind of sound that makes your hair stand on end. We stopped at the food court to feed him, thinking he must be hungry after barely eating that day, but he showed no interest in the bottle he usually gulped down. He kept wriggling and wincing, shaking his head from side to side as if to say no.

I put the bottle away and held him close, trying everything to comfort him, but nothing worked. He didn't stop. Panic began to rise, and we decided to leave; getting him home was more important than shopping. After a warm bath, he finally calmed and drifted into sleep.

A few hours later he woke again with sharp, shrill yelps. The sweet, lamb-like noises I loved had turned into cries of pain. Assuming he was hungry, I warmed his bottle, but again he refused, shaking his head and wailing until my chest ached. I paced the corridor, whispering softly, rocking him, desperate to soothe him, but the screaming felt endless.

'I think we should take him to the hospital,' I said to Master M.

'Maybe he's reacting to the injection,' he replied.

I hastily packed his bag, grabbed my keys, and Master M buckled him into his car seat.

'Call me as soon as you hear anything,' he said, closing the door behind me.

Driving to the hospital, Baby R screamed the entire way, gasping for air. I kept glancing over at him, terrified.

'It's okay, baby, it's okay; we're nearly there,' I whispered again and again, as if my words could somehow reach him, could somehow ease his pain. By some miracle, I found a parking space right outside the children's emergency hospital. I leapt from the car, grabbed his bag and scooped him into my arms. His cries grew louder, slicing through the night and sending shivers down my spine.

As I reached the sliding doors, nurses spotted me running. They rushed over, took him from my arms and disappeared inside. Before I could even give his name, an oxygen mask was already pressed to his tiny face.

'What's happening?' I gasped, my voice trembling, fear gripping every inch of me.

'Your son's lungs are collapsing. He needs oxygen,' a nurse said firmly.

'How do you know that?' I asked, my voice barely a whisper.

'I could tell from the way he was crying and struggling to breathe as you came in. Please don't panic. He's going to be okay; you did the right thing bringing him straight here,' she reassured me, her tone calm but firm.

Still in shock, I phoned Master M. Through sobs, the words barely made it past my lips.

'Please come. R is being transferred to ICU. His lungs are collapsing. They said it's bronchiolitis.'

'I'll call Mum to pick up A. I'm coming now,' he said, hanging up immediately.

I hesitated before calling Dad. I didn't want to frighten him, but I needed to hear his voice. My hands trembled as I dialled his number, silently rehearsing how I might say the words.

'Hi, why are you calling at this hour? Has the baby kept you up?' he asked lightly, unaware of the storm on my end of the line.

Tears blurred my vision. 'Papa...R is in the hospital. His lungs are collapsing. He's on an oxygen machine.'

Silence. The line was still connected, but he had dropped the phone. Moments later, it rang again – my father's number. This time, it was my uncle's voice.

'Your dad is in shock. He dropped the phone,' he explained.

I quickly told him what was happening. I could hear my dad crying in the background. 'I'm changing my flights. I'm coming home.'

'No, Papa, stay. Please. He will be okay. I just needed to tell you,' I pleaded, trying to steady myself.

Those days in ICU were my worst nightmare. The antiseptic sting in the air felt sharp against my raw nerves and the relentless glow of monitors cast eerie shadows over his tiny form. A kind nurse squeezed my hand during one endless shift and whispered, 'He's a fighter, just like his mum.'

Watching Baby R struggle was agony unlike anything I had ever known. I longed to take his pain into my own body, to spare him. I would have carried the world's suffering if it meant he could be free of it. Why did he have to endure this? He looked so tiny, so fragile, with wires and tubes running across his little body and a feeding tube once again taped to his nose. My heart broke every time I saw him in that crib, fighting for every breath.

Meanwhile, life demanded balance. With Dad overseas, Master M and I had to divide ourselves between both children. By day, I stayed at the hospital with Baby R. At night we switched and I went home to Lil A. It was a harsh routine, but somehow, we managed.

After days of fear and exhaustion, Baby R was finally stable enough to leave ICU. He was moved to a ward for a short time before we could take him home.

The whole ordeal had unfolded so quickly. One moment he was crying in my arms, the next he was being swept away by nurses. The fear in those moments was indescribable, a terror I would never wish on anyone. And yet, through it all, my little boy revealed himself as a force of nature. Despite his tiny frame, his resilience was breathtaking. Watching him recover reminded me that even in the darkest hours, strength can emerge in the most unexpected ways. Though fear and doubt had clouded me, I knew in my heart that I had done everything possible to protect my baby. And in that truth, I found a flicker of peace.

For a while, I couldn't shake the feeling that it was all my fault. Had I done something wrong that made my baby sick? I replayed the past few weeks over and over in my head. Had I not dressed him warmly enough? Had I somehow compromised his health?

My children are my everything, and the thought of putting them in harm's way was unbearable. I'm a Greek Mumma, after all. I bundle them up in layers: socks, singlets, long sleeves, beanies, and snuggly blankets. You know, just in case. Yet even though I knew deep down it wasn't my fault, I couldn't silence the self-blame. Those old insecurities crept back in, whispering that I was undeserving, unworthy, and that perhaps motherhood was beyond my reach.

♥

Dad's trip flew by in a whirlwind, and when he finally returned home, an overwhelming sense of relief washed over me. Having him close again was such a blessing. My parents became my pillars of strength during that difficult time, offering the support I so desperately needed. Despite our frequent bickering, Dad remains my rock, and my mother my guiding light. Together, they give me strength and inspiration to keep moving forward.

Amid the guilt and emotional turmoil, their unwavering support shone like a beacon of hope. Whenever the weight of Baby R's illness felt crushing, their presence reminded me that I was still capable, still worthy, still a mother. I will forever be grateful to have been raised by two selfless and inspiring individuals whose love and resilience continue to anchor me.

It's ironic how, in my younger years, I couldn't wait to spread my wings and leave home, yet in my darkest moments, all I craved was the comfort and reassurance of their love. Their presence wrapped me in a deep sense of peace and security, a reminder that no matter how far I wandered, I would always have a safe place to return to.

Our daily routine slowly began to return. Dad helped with school drop-offs and pick-ups while Baby R adjusted to life after his hospital stay. Lil A's behaviour was relatively calm, though the occasional outburst reminded me that parenthood is always a rollercoaster. But isn't that normal?

One afternoon while I was feeding Baby R and Mum napped, Dad went to collect Lil A from school. The house was peaceful, until I heard a muffled commotion outside. Then, SLAM! The front door banged shut with such force that it jolted me from the quiet. Dad's face told me everything before he even spoke. Normally patient with his grandchildren, he was fuming.

'You won't believe what your son did at school today,' he said, his voice tight with anger.

'What happened?' I asked, my tone sharper than I intended, startling Baby R in my arms.

'The teacher told me he graffitied on the school wall,' Dad snapped.

I turned to Lil A, who looked up at me with a cheeky grin.

'What did you do?' I asked.

'I drew on the wall,' he replied, his voice bouncing with mischief.

Without hesitation, I stood. 'Right, that's it. I'm taking you to the police station. You vandalised the wall, and that's unacceptable. Every action has a consequence.' I placed the baby gently in the bouncer and reached for my phone.

'No, you're not!' he said with a smirk.

'Oh yes I am. Watch me,' I shot back, keeping a straight face as I dialled Mascot Police Station. The officer listened patiently as I explained the situation. He agreed with my approach but, due to workload, suggested I contact Maroubra Police Station instead. By this point, Lil A's grin only fuelled my determination.

'Ha-ha, you're not going to take me,' he taunted.

I dialled the second station. This time, the officer's reply was firm: 'Great, we'll be waiting for you.' I grabbed my keys, scooped Lil A into the car, and drove off. His smugness quickly gave way to fear.

'Where are you taking me?' he asked, his voice trembling.

'To the police station, like I told you,' I said, glaring at him through the rear-view mirror.

His eyes welled with tears. 'But I thought police were supposed to help people?'

'They are helping you,' I snapped. 'Helping you understand that destroying property and stealing from the classroom has consequences. You need to learn this lesson now.'

At the station, an officer greeted us. 'You must be A,' he said, eyeing my son sternly.

'Yes,' Lil A whispered, his bravado gone.

We were shown into a small room, the cold metal chairs scraping against the floor, his quiet sobs echoing off the bare walls like a stark wake-up call. The moment we sat down, Lil A clung tightly to my jacket. Before the officers could even begin, he broke down completely.

'I'm so sorry! I'll never do it again! Please, I don't want to go to jail!'

The officers exchanged a glance before one leaned forward, his voice firm but measured. 'Your mum told us what happened. That behaviour is unacceptable. If you were older, you'd be facing charges.'

The second officer spoke, his tone stern yet softened by compassion. 'We'll be speaking with your principal, and we'll be checking in. We expect your best behaviour from now on. This is your first and last warning.'

Lil A wept, promising over and over to behave and to listen. As we left, one officer gave a small, knowing smile.

'We hope so,' he said. And for the first time that day, I saw the lesson take root.

'Mummy, I don't want to go to jail,' Lil A whimpered, tugging at my jacket as we walked out of the police station.

'You were warned. You heard what the officer said, he's going to check on you,' I replied, clipping him into his car seat.

The drive home was painfully silent. It hurt to follow through, but I knew I'd done what needed to be done. I was raised to respect others and to understand that every action has a consequence, and I wasn't about to let him drift down a path of misbehaviour. I'm all for kids' banter and a bit of cheeky fun, but I would never stand by and watch him spiral. Where I could intervene, I would be there, front and centre, doing my best to guide him.

Driving home, I realised that being a mother isn't about having all the answers; it's about showing up even when you feel broken. In that moment, I felt shattered, as if I'd failed him. Doubts crept in: Am I falling short as a mother? Am I doing enough? But I refused to sweep it under the rug or make excuses. I wanted to hold my children accountable and raise them to be compassionate, respectful, and humble. I promised myself then to be the kind of mum who embodies both tough love and gentle love, everything in between; the kind of love that guides them through life's ups and downs.

Parenting is a rollercoaster of hard moments and small triumphs, but love and unity have always been our anchors. Through every challenge, we've discovered a deep well of strength and resilience. And in doing so, we're quietly building a kinder, more supportive world for our children. With that foundation, I believe we can face whatever hurdles life throws our way.

CHAPTER 10

The heartfelt shift

Time flies, doesn't it? When we're young, the days seem endless, yet once children arrive, life becomes a whirlwind: joyful, demanding, and full of purpose. Every moment suddenly feels precious.

Watching Baby R reach his milestones nourished my soul. This tiny bundle of sweetness was blossoming into a unique and lovable little personality. His chubby cheeks and radiant smile melted hearts wherever we went, his giggles echoing through the house like a melody over the hum of daily chaos. Despite the challenges of those early months, he was by nature an easygoing baby. Truth be told, both of my children blessed me with textbook routines. Feeding schedules ticked along like clockwork and their sleep patterns were miraculously predictable. It was as though some fairy godmother had sprinkled angel dust over our household.

Lil A had been sleeping through the night from six weeks, and Baby R from 12. Perhaps that fairy godmother had taken pity on me; surely it couldn't be a relentless struggle 24/7? Honestly, I doubt I would have coped otherwise.

♥

As Baby R's first birthday approached and my return to work loomed, I wrestled with the idea of placing him in childcare. He was small for his age, healthy, yes, but still small, and my heart could not bear the thought of leaving him.

With about a month left before my maternity leave ended, I kept in touch with my team, who were eager for my return. I felt pulled in every direction: part of me wanted to stay home because he still seemed too young for day care; another part knew that if I went back to work and left Baby R with Dad, it would place an undue burden on him. Dad was already caring for Mum after her fall. Her condition had deteriorated and she now needed round-the-clock care. I couldn't expect him to shoulder both our son and Mum on top of everything else.

Financially and practically, returning to work, even part-time, felt necessary. I wanted to contribute and support the family, but the decision tore me apart. A quiet storm of guilt and duty swirled in my mind as I weighed my love for my son against the family's needs.

One morning, in the middle of the usual chaos of motherhood, my phone rang. My boss's number lit up the screen, and my stomach dropped. I was certain this was the call, the one to lock in my dreaded return date. Hesitantly, I answered, bracing myself for his chirpy excitement. Instead, I was blindsided. The dealership had gone into liquidation. I hadn't just lost the choice of returning part-time; I had no job to return to at all.

A rush of emotions swirled through me: shock, fear, and even a strange relief I didn't dare name. If I had chosen not to go back, at least it would have been on my terms. But being forced felt entirely different. The ground had been taken from beneath me. For the first time in years, I had no plans. I've always thrived on routine, structure, and control, and now I was drifting, moving from one day to the next with two children depending on me. I told myself firmly that I needed to get my life together. I needed a plan, and I needed to make one quickly.

After countless sleepless nights of debate and prayerful reflection, staring at the ceiling while the house slept, Master M and I decided I would take a step back from my career. It wasn't an easy choice; my work had always given me purpose and fulfillment. But when I looked at the bigger picture, I began to see it differently. Perhaps this was a blessing in disguise. This unexpected pause allowed me to devote myself to what mattered most: my family.

I hadn't grown up with stability or consistent parental presence, but I was determined that my children would. I vowed to break that cycle to rewrite my own story by creating the kind of home I had longed for as a child. Love. Stability. Presence. This became my new career, my higher calling.

And then, one ordinary day, the extraordinary found me. I had set out on a routine grocery run to Eastgardens, but for reasons I couldn't explain, I felt compelled to instead drive to East Village. On my way home, I turned down the street where Master M worked and, out of nowhere, a huge pink sign caught my eye: a female silhouette, bold against the background, with the words 'Fernwood Women's Fitness.'

How had I never noticed it before? I had driven down this street countless times. Without hesitation, I flicked on my blinker and turned into the car park. Something greater than me seemed to be at work. Was it instinct? Divine guidance? Whatever it was, I knew I was being led. In that moment, it felt as though my soul had stepped outside my body and whispered, *Here is something for you. A spark of self-discovery. A door to new possibilities.*

Exercise had never been my forte. In fact, I'd always had a deep-seated dislike for it. If you'd known me back in high school, you'd probably laugh at the idea of me ever setting foot in a gym. So, what on earth was I doing walking into one now?

The gym felt like another world, as if I'd wandered into a parallel universe. The air hummed with upbeat music, the clink of weights, and the chatter of women laughing mid-workout, their energy pulling me in like a warm tide. I was greeted with smiles and given a tour, which left me both fascinated and bewildered. As I walked through, I noticed the women inside. They weren't intimidating athletes or fitness fanatics. They were ordinary women, much like me, going about their routines or enjoying what looked like lively, fun classes. And for the first time in ages, I felt a surge of excitement.

It hit me then that I had been drawn to this place for a reason. I was lonely, restless, and unfulfilled. Somewhere along the way, buried beneath my motherly duties, I had lost sight of myself. I needed something that was just for me, an outlet, an escape, a path back to my own identity. And if joining the gym also made me healthier, then all the better.

They handed me a 14-day complimentary pass, but I didn't need a trial. I was ready. This was my chance to step into something new, something life-giving. Bursting with excitement, I couldn't wait to tell Master M. I rang him at work. He answered, his voice tinged with concern, no doubt fearing something was wrong with the children. I quickly reassured him.

'You're not going to believe what I just did,' I said, barely able to contain myself.

'Oh God, what now?' he asked cautiously.

'I just joined the gym, the one across the road from your work!'

'No! You? You joined the gym?' He laughed down the phone. 'I'll believe it when I see it.'

'Don't laugh,' I shot back. 'Watch me. I'm going. You'll see.'

'We'll see,' he teased before hanging up.

What a shithead. He had no faith in me. I couldn't really blame him; this was completely out of left field, but I was determined to prove him wrong. Master M's playful doubt only fuelled my resolve, his teasing grin flashing in my mind as I pictured myself striding into that gym, ready to reclaim a piece of me.

Baby R's mornings were wonderfully predictable. He would usually wake around 7 or 7.30 each morning, so I slotted in my gym visits before then. With the baby, school runs, and caring for Mum, I knew the middle of the day was impossible.

Very quickly, this new adventure began to change me. I wasn't doing it to lose weight; it was for my mental health. My energy levels rose, carrying me through the chaos of daily life. I was beginning to feel alive again. I was sleeping better. I felt physically stronger, especially when carrying Baby R, and most of all, I felt good within myself. For the first time in years, I felt like me again. Reborn. And I loved it.

To everyone's surprise, perhaps most of all my own, I kept at it. What started as two sessions a week became three, then four, then five. As Baby R grew, I grew in confidence, leaving him happily in the creche while I joined group classes, did personal training sessions, or worked out on my own. Exercise stopped being a novelty and became a deliberate, positive habit. This wasn't an obsession; it was a transformation.

And then came the moment of realisation. That day when the bright pink sign caught my eye, it was as if my guardian angels had been steering me towards something greater. I had my ultimate epiphany: I didn't just want to change my life; I wanted to help change other women's lives. I wanted to inspire women like me to become the healthiest, strongest versions of themselves. That clarity lit a fire in me. I decided I would study for my fitness certificate.

What a game changer.

Through Fernwood Fitness, I applied for online studies and, as a member, was offered a front-desk role. That job gave me the perfect foundation: basic skills, industry knowledge, and the confidence to work my way up from the ground to be an instructor and personal trainer.

Once I earned my Certificate III in Fitness, new opportunities opened. I was entrusted with running my own classes on the timetable. At first, I was terrified. What if I forgot the exercises? What if people didn't enjoy the class? But as I stood on stage leading my first high-intensity interval training session, something clicked. The music, the laughter, the banter – it was electric. My nerves melted as I connected with the women in front of me. Soon my classes were packed at any time of day. I couldn't quite believe it. The same woman who once hated exercise was now thriving, on stage, leading high-energy workouts, alive with joy. Who even was I?

In my final year of Certificate IV studies, I didn't just instruct, I managed personal training clients. It was incredibly rewarding to witness the positive impact on each woman's life. Supporting every client on her own health journey felt like a privilege. What an honour.

Throughout my professional journey, I discovered an uncommon satisfaction: work that never felt like a chore because it came from passion. That sense of purpose felt like a personal triumph and echoed something Mum used to say: 'When you do something you love, it doesn't feel like work.'

Suddenly, I understood why she was drawn to dressmaking: it was her passion. Likewise, I had found my own. It may have taken me 30 years, 12 years after leaving school, but I finally found my path. I can only imagine my teachers' faces if they'd known that I would end up in health and fitness. They'd probably be stunned.

❤

As I moved through this pivotal time, I forged a deeper connection with myself and uncovered my core values and passions. That clarity gave me direction and helped me balance my role as a mother. It also brought a surprising peace. I learned my strengths, recognised my weaknesses, and identified my emotional triggers. By acknowledging and releasing emotions I'd long suppressed to preserve harmony and avoid conflict, I felt a new lightness, joy, and fulfillment as I prioritised my own needs for the first time.

Joy and pain are inextricably linked. The fantasy that life is a constant stream of sunshine and butterflies is unrealistic. In our house, we know this painfully well. When challenges come, they often arrive all at once, leaving you gasping for air, as though the weight of the world is crushing you.

I tried to strike a balance between coursework and household duties while I was studying from home. Mum's health declined and her falls became more frequent. Each tumble sent a jolt of fear through us as we recalled the surgeon's warning. It wasn't just that she needed constant care; we could no longer leave her unattended. The vigilance was exhausting and the house felt heavy with worry.

Dad shouldered the physically demanding tasks. His grunts of effort and the visible strain in his muscles were constant reminders that he, too, was aging. The responsibility took a heavy toll on him, both physically and emotionally.

Once, Dad popped out for a haircut, for no longer than 30 minutes. In that short time, Mum fell, and I couldn't get her up on my own. I couldn't leave her on the floor until he returned, so I ran next door and knocked persistently until someone answered. Luckily, the neighbour was home. I explained what had happened and he came straight over to help me lift her. Thankfully, Mum was uninjured.

Another time, Mum was slowly making her way down the hallway through the house. She moved with a limp, her feet shuffling softly against the floor, creating a gentle, rhythmic sound that reassured me she was alright. She never used a walking stick, worried it might trip her, and instead steadied herself by sliding her hand along the wall. As she reached the entrance to the living room, I looked up from where I sat, preparing to feed Baby R, who was bouncing happily in his bouncer. Mum's eyes met mine, and she gave me one of her warm smiles, her eyes crinkling at the corners, a flicker of her old, vibrant self shining through. She continued on her way as I reached for Baby R's food on the table beside me and lifted him from the bouncer.

The next moment, a shadow loomed. I glanced up to see Mum collapsing. A jolt of shock surged through me, and I screamed, 'Mum!' throwing my arms forward in a desperate attempt to catch her. But it happened too quickly. She fell with such force that she almost landed on Baby R, missing his head by only a few centimetres. The heavy thud of her body filled the room. By God's grace, the armchair broke her fall and kept her from striking the baby. At the sound of my scream, Dad came running, his footsteps pounding against the tiles. He found me kneeling beside Mum, trying to lift her. She had suffered a seizure and lost control.

That incident shook us deeply. It made us realise our home was no longer safe for her. The thought of placing Mum in a nursing home troubled us, but we knew we had to prioritise her safety and wellbeing. The decision wasn't made lightly. One evening, as Master M and I sat at the kitchen table surrounded by the faint scent of fresh paint and the soft hum of the fridge, we faced the painful truth.

Family members called, their voices sharp with judgment: 'How could you even think of putting her in a home? She raised you, and now you're abandoning her?' Their words cut like a knife, echoing the doubts already gnawing at me. I wanted to scream back to explain the sleepless nights, the fear of another fall, the impossibility of watching Mum every second while raising two young boys. But I stayed silent, the weight of their accusation sinking deep.

When we finally made that agonising decision, our extended family responded with harsh criticism. They condemned us as careless, accusing us of neglect and selfishness. Their words stung and their hostility left us raw. Not once did they stop to consider what would truly be best for Mum, or the overwhelming strain of providing 24-hour care. They judged without walking a mile in our shoes.

At the end of the day, the choice wasn't about them. It was about Mum. I made sure the nursing home we chose was close by so we could visit her at any time. Even so, moving her felt like tearing a piece of myself away. As I held her hand during the transition, I felt the warmth of her skin, the faint tremble of her fingers, and I whispered, 'Be safe. I'll see you later.' Tears blurred my vision, the antiseptic smell of the nursing home lingering in my nose, the distant clatter of trays, and the murmurs of other residents amplifying the ache. It wasn't a final goodbye, but it carried the weight of one. Despite the hurtful words of others, I knew in my heart we were doing the right thing. Her care had to come first.

Dad visited her faithfully twice a day, every day. He sat with her at lunch and dinner, helping her with her meals and keeping her company. She seemed content and comfortable, which gave him peace of mind. I, too, visited her regularly, making sure I was there at least three or four times a week.

♥

Many people believe that placing a loved one in a nursing home makes life easier. The truth is it doesn't. It doesn't ease the strain; it simply changes its shape. At home you carry the weight of direct responsibility. In a nursing home you shoulder the burden of trust: wondering whether they are truly being cared for with dignity and compassion. And while you no longer bear the daily physical demands, life doesn't pause; there's still work, children, and household responsibilities, all while you carve out time to be present for your partner. For me, this arrangement was never easier. If anything, I longed to have Mum back at home where I could care for her myself with my own hands and heart.

Mum was, in many ways, the easiest person to care for. She was never a difficult resident. Unlike some individuals with dementia who became disoriented, agitated, or even aggressive, she remained gentle and soft-hearted. She was never rude, never bitter. Gratitude seemed to flow naturally from her. Yet the reality was heartbreaking. She could do virtually nothing for herself. Still, each time someone assisted her, she would smile and say, 'God bless you.' She repeated those words countless times a day, offering them to nurses, carers, and visitors alike. Watching her give thanks so freely despite her dependency reminded me how much we take our health, our independence, and the simple act of being able to move freely through life for granted.

Even in such trying circumstances, Mum's spirit never faltered. Her faith remained unshakable. She stayed resilient, steadfast, and strong-willed, teaching me silently that the soul can still shine even when the body fails.

Life's unexpected twists often bring us back to the drawing board and force us to reassess our path. It's natural to grumble about hardships, the curveballs, disappointments, the days that test our strength. As human beings, we are wired to respond emotionally, and it's only natural. To struggle is part of being human. But what's remarkable is the uniqueness of our responses. Each of us walks through adversity differently, and that difference shapes who we are.

For my mum, life changed abruptly in her thirties. By her fifties, she had gone from being a confident, independent woman to someone who had lost her identity, her dignity, and her freedom, relying on strangers for her most basic care. To witness that decline was devastating. Yet from the heartbreak, a new passion was born in me.

If I could rewrite her story, I would. If I could turn back time, I would have done everything in my power to change the course of her health. But since I cannot, I have devoted myself to empowering women to age strong with their vitality and dignity intact. My focus is on mobility, dementia prevention, and reducing the risks of osteoporosis so they can remain independent, capable, and full of life for as long as possible.

As my reflections quieten, I am left with a profound truth: health is not simply about physical appearance. It is about nurturing the whole self; body, mind, and spirit. A healthy lifestyle is not a superficial pursuit; it's a foundation for living vibrantly. Energy, joy, and strength are the fruits of self-care, and they ripple outward, touching everyone around us.

This realisation has become my purpose. My calling is to inspire and guide others to unlock their potential, to embrace vitality, and to live fully. It is not just a mission; it is my passion, my purpose, and my gift to the world born from the heart of a family reshaped by love and loss, where every shift, tough or tender, builds a stronger tomorrow.

CHAPTER 11

Colostomy miracles

Do you ever imagine yourself sailing across serene, crystal-blue waters like you're on a grand yacht, only to realise you're actually in a small red dinghy with white sails, drifting across a quiet lake? The dinghy may lack the luxury of the yacht, but it has its own charm. It pulls you closer to nature. As you glide through the water, the icy spray cools your cheeks, the air fills your lungs with freshness, and you're surrounded by life's vivid colours: the deep orange-brown of old tree trunks, the rich green of leaves, and the soft carpet of grass beneath them. Each leaf drifts slowly to the ground, almost like a sacred moment. For a brief while, everything is calm. How peaceful. How I long to stay in that stillness, knowing that soon my alarm will go off and the shit show will start.

At 5.30 a.m. the alarm shattered the silence, its vibration jolting me awake, rattling through every muscle in my body. *Come on! Wake up!* My morning mantra was simple: *I'm up, I'm up!* A small ritual to launch the day.

♥

Tuesdays were intense, packed from start to finish. I started early at the gym, rushed home to get Lil A ready for school and Baby R set for day care, then headed back for more hours of work. After school pickup, I'd return once again for my favourite classes: Tabata, Spin, and Swiss Ball. My day was a whirlwind, but I thrived on the energy. Each class became a lifeline, steadying me through the storms of family life.

I still laugh thinking back to the day exhaustion caught me mid-Swiss Ball class. As an instructor, you're meant to radiate strength and composure. Instead, mid-demonstration, I wobbled, lost my balance, and tumbled right off the ball. The class gasped, and I couldn't help but burst out laughing. Once I'd composed myself, I grinned and said, 'And that is exactly what not to do.'

That fall reminded both me and my clients that I wasn't superhuman. I was real. Some joked that I was the devil in disguise, but I carried that slip with me as one of my favourite teaching memories, a moment of levity that fuelled my resilience when Mum's hospital stays loomed.

Then there was the Monday morning fiasco. Two early classes, a 4.30 a.m. start, getting dressed in the dark so as not to wake Master M, and rushing out the door. Spin class was fine. It always lit me up. But during the next class, as we wound down with stretches, I caught sight of my tights. They were inside out. A wardrobe malfunction of epic proportions. My expression must have given me away because the girls began to giggle. Before they could say anything, I confessed with a laugh, 'You're all very polite; not one of you mentioned my tights were on inside out!' Then I teased, 'Just wait till next session!' Lesson learned: no more dressing in the dark.

Those light-hearted moments at the gym became my anchor, a reminder to keep smiling even as Mum's health wavered. Despite the chaos, working at the gym gave me a sense of balance. It let me blend family and career without losing sight of either. It was a win-win: I could chase my passion for fitness while still being there for my family, the sweat and laughter of each class recharging me to face the worries waiting at home.

We eventually found our rhythm. I worked four days a week. Lil A was settled at school. Baby R spent two days in day care and the other two with me at work, happily tucked into the creche. Life felt smooth, just like that calm lake.

Until one day, a wave rose out of nowhere, rocking our little boat and jolting us off our seats. During this season, Mum's condition was fairly stable, but winter proved to be her greatest enemy. She caught an illness that lingered and worsened despite every effort. It turned into pneumonia. Her hospital stay was long, and her recovery was slowed by her limited mobility. It was a painful, uphill climb, but her medical team worked tirelessly to restore her health.

When Mum was hospitalised, my priority was being by her side. My boss was incredibly understanding and together we found a way forward. I kept teaching my group fitness classes but stepped back from personal training so I could spend more time with Mum. It was a balance that gave me peace. I could still do what I loved while being fully present for her. The gym became my refuge, each upbeat session helping me process the worry of seeing her frail frame in that sterile hospital bed.

I was relieved that this arrangement worked well. I could visit Mum regularly, stay informed about her treatment, and still find release through my work. Many see work as a source of stress, but for me, it was the opposite. Work became my outlet. Teaching and staying active gave me balance, strength, and the energy to keep going through such a difficult season. It served as a lifeline, carrying me from her bedside to the demands of home.

Just as it seemed we were sailing calmly once more, the lake shifted beneath us. The boat rocked violently from side to side. This time, the wave came out of left field: Master M began experiencing excruciating abdominal pain. It lingered for days before he finally went to the hospital, where he was diagnosed with diverticulitis, something I had never heard of in my 32 years. I quickly learned it was an inflammation caused by irregular, bulging pouches in the wall of the large intestine. After a short stay to manage the pain and a course of antibiotics, he was discharged. The doctors explained that the root cause lay in his longstanding dietary habits. His love of steak and potatoes and dislike for vegetables meant he had a consistently low fibre intake. His habits had led to health problems more common in men twice his age. Significant changes to his diet were now essential to prevent further complications.

At first, it seemed like he was recovering. The stabbing pains came in waves, less severe but still noticeable. But just as he began to relax, another storm struck. The agony returned, sharper and more crippling than before.

I was at the gym when he rang. Thankfully, I happened to be at the desk preparing for my class, so I could answer right away. His voice was ragged and broken, spilling through the phone. I could hear him breathing heavily, practically in tears, and it takes a lot for him to admit he's in pain.

'I need to go to the hospital. Something's not right.'

Panic shot through me. 'I'm just about to walk into class. I can't leave now. I don't know what to do.'

'Stay at work,' he insisted, trying to calm me despite his agony. 'Do what you have to do. You can't keep leaving work for everyone. I'll ask someone to take me. Just meet me at the hospital after class.'

'Are you sure? I feel awful.'

'Yes. Go to your class. I'll keep you updated.'

And with that, he hung up, leaving me helpless.

Every part of me wanted to run to him, but I couldn't abandon my class at such short notice. I was torn, always trying to do right by everyone, and this time I felt like I was failing my husband. What kind of wife stays behind while her husband is rushed to the hospital?

Thankfully, a close friend drove him there and stayed with him until I arrived. She remained by his side, offering reassurance as we waited for updates. What had first seemed manageable quickly became far more serious. The doctors connected him to an IV, giving him stronger antibiotics before transferring him to a ward.

At first, I underestimated how serious it was. But during consultation, the medical team explained that, if left untreated, the infection could have caused a bowel perforation, the worst possible outcome.

Meanwhile, Master M's suffering was relentless. The painkillers delivered through the IV barely touched the agony. He lay in bed drenched in sweat, the stale smell of broth lingering from his food tray, his body trembling as the ward's incessant buzzer echoed through the thin curtains. There was no relief in sight. In his despair, he began to give up.

'Just let me die,' he whispered again and again, his voice barely audible over the hum of machines. Each time those words left his mouth, something inside me snapped. I lashed out – fierce, unrelenting. I've never compared myself to an animal, but the anger he provoked made me feel like a dog baring its teeth. How dare he even speak of giving up? We had two children at home. He was their father. He was my husband. Dying was not an option. He had to fight. He had no choice.

Morning came, though whether it was day or night hardly mattered. The pain clung to him like a foul odour that refused to lift. As he lay in bed, a single broken sigh escaped his lips. His eyes brimmed with tears. Then, in an instant, the agony that had already been unbearable surged from a 10 out of 10 to something beyond the scale, like a rocket firing inside his body.

With trembling hands, he reached for the nurse's buzzer, pressing it again and again, its shrill beep cutting through the ward's hum. The staff rushed in, recognising at once that something had changed. This was not normal pain. The doctor was called, and within minutes he ordered an urgent scan. Almost immediately, a porter arrived to wheel him away. I stayed behind, my heart pounding with dread. The waiting gnawed at me, so I made my way down two floors to see Mum, who was still in her ward. I was running back and forth like a boomerang between the two of them, but I needed her. Just seeing her face soothed me, even though I knew she couldn't fix what was happening.

I held her hand and quietly told her what was unfolding upstairs. I didn't want to burden her, but I had always confided in her, every worry, every pain. As always, her words were simple yet powerful: 'God is always listening.'

I stayed only briefly. As much as I wanted to remain by her side, I had to go back. It was time to face the music. When I returned, Master M was being wheeled back into the ward, hunched over, his face contorted in pain. Moments later, the doctor entered, his expression sombre. He pulled up a chair beside the bed, and his words struck like the sharp chime of a clock, unforgettable.

'The scan shows your bowel has ruptured,' he said, his voice heavy with compassion. 'That explains the pain you're experiencing. We need to operate as soon as possible. But the inflammation is a concern. It needs to settle before surgery so the procedure is less complicated.'

I leaned forward. 'What exactly will you be doing in surgery?'

'We'll remove the ruptured part of the bowel and, if possible, reconnect the two ends,' he explained. 'But with this level of inflammation, I can't be certain we'll manage to reconnect.'

A knot tightened in my stomach. 'What does that mean?' I asked.

His expression grew more serious. 'It means you must be prepared for the possibility of waking up with a temporary colostomy bag.'

Master M's composure finally cracked. His voice broke as he blurted out, 'So I'll have to carry my shit around with me?'

The doctor offered a gentle smile, trying to reassure him. 'If it comes to that, it will only be temporary, no more than six months. It would give your bowel time to heal. We'll do everything we can to avoid it, but you need to be prepared. A specialist will come today to explain, take measurements, and show you what to expect, just in case.'

As he stood to leave, the doctor patted Master M's leg softly. 'Rest. You have a big day ahead tomorrow.'

The air grew heavy with silence, thick with the weight of the unknown. I fought to hold myself together. I couldn't imagine how he felt; fear, anger, and grief all tangled together. I didn't want him to see me unravel; I knew my tears would only break him further. Drawing on every ounce of strength, I reached for his hand, squeezed it firmly, and whispered, 'Everything will be okay. You heard the doctor; he'll do all he can to avoid the bag. What matters is getting you well again. No matter what it takes, we'll get through this. The children need you. I need you.'

He sat there, stunned, silent. The weight of all that information had paralysed him. I could almost see his mind straining to make sense of it, his thoughts like tangled threads. Then the colostomy specialist entered. She carried with her a calm, gentle presence that softened the edges of the room. Sitting beside Master M, she pulled a colostomy bag from her sample kit. His reaction was immediate, raw, and unfiltered.

'What the fuck? I'm going to have to carry that shit around?'

Her voice was soft but steady. 'Please don't panic. This is just a precaution. You might not need it at all. I'm simply here to take measurements and answer questions. Your surgeon is excellent, one of the best. I'm confident he'll do everything possible to avoid this. But we need to be prepared for every outcome.'

Something in her tone seemed to calm him. He still shook his head, but the fear in his eyes eased a little. She stayed only long enough to explain, answer our questions, and offer reassurance before quietly slipping out.

Master M exhaled sharply, shaking his head again. 'What did she just say?'. I leaned closer, steadying my voice.

'It's only a precaution. He's the best there is. I have faith this will go well.' I wanted to sound strong for both of us, even though part of me trembled inside.

That night dragged endlessly. I doubt he slept much, though he never admitted it. If it had been me, I'd have begged the nurses for something to knock me out, just to silence the constant churn of worry. Though I knew he was terrified, Master M held himself with remarkable composure. His calmness under pressure humbled me.

By dawn, I was at the hospital. My chest tightened as I walked down the corridor towards his room. Before opening the door, I paused, took a long breath, and reminded myself that he needed strength, not my fear.

The porters arrived shortly after six. He was first on the list. The room was heavy with anticipation. I sat beside him, my lips moving silently as I prayed the Lord's Prayer.

It was 14 September, a date forever carved into our memories, the Feast of the Holy Cross. On that sacred day, our church remembers Christ's crucifixion. I whispered, 'Lord, have mercy on Thy servant, M.'

I couldn't help but think of Mum, how her surgery, too, had fallen on a feast day. Somehow, that connection gave me strength, as though God's hand was already guiding us. My only choice was to wait, pray, and trust.

The waiting room was torment. Every minute felt like an hour. I checked my phone over and over, willing it to light up, desperate for news. Six hours crawled past like six days. Finally, my phone rang. My hands shook as I snatched it up. 'Hello?'

'Hi, Andrea, it's Dr M,' came the surgeon's voice, calm and steady. 'I'm calling with an update. M is in recovery, and the surgery went well. It was more complex than expected; we had to remove fifty centimetres of his bowel.'

Before he could go on, I blurted out the only question that mattered. 'Did he need the colostomy bag?'

His answer washed over me like sunlight breaking through storm clouds. 'No. M will be thrilled to know we reconnected the bowel perfectly. No bag was needed.'

The relief was overwhelming. Tears streamed freely as I stammered, 'Thank you…thank you…thank you.'

Dr M's reply was gentle. 'No thanks needed. I'm just grateful it was a success.'

The weight of gratitude was crushing. I sat in the chair, tears spilling down my face, thanking God over and over for what I could only see as a miracle. Master M's surgery had been a success, and I knew it wasn't just medicine that saved him, but grace. I believed with all my heart that Jesus had been beside him the entire time, guiding the surgeon's hands and watching over him. For what felt like an hour, I whispered my thanks, my voice trembling with emotion. It was a sacred moment, one of those rare times when heaven feels so close you could almost reach out and touch it. My heart overflowed with joy. Master M's kind heart and gentle nature made this blessing even more precious. 'Thank you, sweet Jesus,' I whispered again, letting the words wash through me like a hymn.

Still trembling with relief, I glanced at the clock. If I hurried, I might just have enough time to share the good news with Mum before Master M returned to his room. At the lift, I pressed the button again and again, as though my urgency would make it arrive faster. When the sweet ding finally rang out, I just about leaped inside, pressing Mum's floor number and jabbing the 'close' button with all my might. The doors opened, and I all but ran down the corridor. Mum was in the dining room, her head resting on the table, drifting into sleep.

'Mum!' I cried softly, shaking her shoulders. She startled awake, blinking at me.

'Yes, love?' she murmured drowsily.

'I'm so sorry to wake you,' I rushed out, 'but I had to tell you straight away, M's surgery went well! He didn't need the colostomy bag. He's going to be okay.' The words tumbled from me in one breath, barely leaving space for air.

Mum straightened slightly, her tired eyes softening with relief. 'That's wonderful news. *Perastika tou*, may he have a healthy recovery. God bless him.'

She leaned her head back onto the table, too weary to stay upright. I rubbed her back, kissed her cheek, and whispered, 'I'll go back up now, Mum. I'll see you tomorrow morning.'

'Alright, love. Take care,' she murmured, already drifting off again.

Our relationship has never followed the conventional mould, but it's real, and it's precious to me. I share everything with her. She knows me like no one else, even though the haze of her memory lapses. However much her mind drifts, I make sure she feels loved, included, and valued.

That day, I couldn't wait to share the news with her. She understood what it meant to witness a miracle, and in her quiet way, she celebrated with me. Our bond might be unorthodox, but it's ours, and I wouldn't trade it for anything.

Back upstairs, I walked into Master M's room with a smile stretched across my face. Deep in thought, I almost didn't notice that he had already been wheeled back in and was fast asleep. I wondered if he knew, somewhere deep inside, that the surgery had gone well. I settled into the chair beside his bed, watching the muted television flicker in the background. A slight twitch of his feet caught my eye, and I jumped up instinctively. 'Hey! Welcome back!' I whispered, leaning closer. 'How are you feeling?'

'So sore,' he grunted, his voice rough and faint, 'but I'm here.'

'Of course you are. You've just had major surgery, but all went well. Just rest.' I bent down and kissed his forehead gently.

His lips curved into a weak smile. 'No bag!'

'No bag,' I said firmly, smiling back. 'The doctor was very pleased. It's going to be a long recovery, but slowly, slowly, you'll bounce back.'

He turned his head into the pillow, that faint smile still lingering as sleep pulled him under once more.

Recovery was a gruelling process. Master M endured unending pain and discomfort, first confined to bed, then slowly transitioning to a wheelchair. The aftermath of having 50 centimetres of bowel removed came with its own challenges.

He was placed on a clear fluid diet, which he despised. The absurdity of being handed a knife and fork for meals that consisted of little more than watery broth wasn't lost on him. One evening, lying in the hospital bed as I set a bowl of bland broth before him, he groaned, 'This tastes like shit,' pushing it away while Lil A giggled, sneaking him a carrot stick from his own snack bag.

By the final days of that diet, the sight of jelly and broth had become unbearable. He longed for real food, something hearty and satisfying...Mmm, steak!

As the days passed, his behaviour began to change. He grew short-tempered, snapping at me each time I entered his room. At first, I was taken aback; it wasn't like him. Eventually, I had to set boundaries, telling him plainly that I wouldn't keep visiting if he continued speaking to me that way. Deep down, I knew something else was going on. It didn't take long to discover the truth. His outbursts, I soon learned, were withdrawal symptoms. Going from 10 cigarettes a day to none overnight was a shock his body simply couldn't handle.

The nurses suggested nicotine patches, but they only made him itchy and more irritable. Frustrated, he tore them off and demanded that I bring him cigarettes. At first, I refused, determined to stay firm. But when his words turned sharp, 'If you don't bring my smokes, don't bother coming,' I felt cornered. It broke me. Despite my disappointment, I eventually gave in and brought him a packet the next day.

I would wheel him out of the ward, and together we'd find a quiet spot outside where he could light his cigarette. The moment he pulled in that first drag, I watched his whole body loosen. His mood lifted so fast it felt unreal, and for the first time in days, I caught a small, familiar glimpse of the man I knew. I was tired, bone-deep tired, but I chose peace over another argument. And lucky for him, because a part of me was ready to knock him out if he pushed any further. For that brief moment, he was himself again.

After a month in the hospital, Master M was finally discharged. He had lost nearly 10 kilos, his frame leaner, his spirit changed. Given a second chance and spared from the colostomy bag, he seemed determined to live differently. He started revamping his diet, adding fruits and vegetables to his meals for the first time.

One night, as we sat around the dinner table, the kids munching on broccoli without complaint, he looked at me and said, 'I never thought I'd crave a salad, but here we are.' That shift didn't just help his recovery; it made my life easier too. Our children watched us eat more than just meat and carbs, and slowly, healthy habits became part of our family rhythm.

He also began exercising in the garage with the old equipment I'd stored away. It felt like a fresh beginning, a new page turned. I was proud of him for choosing to fight, for embracing change, and for valuing the gift of health.

As Master M continued to heal, the days grew lighter and the nights less heavy. Our family found comfort in one another's company, cherishing the laughter that returned to our home and the love that bound us closer. What we had endured tested us to the core, yet it revealed the resilience we carried as a family and the strength that faith had given us.

Each morning as we woke, gratitude became our first prayer. With every day that passed we grew stronger, not only in body but also in spirit. And once again, it felt as though we were sailing on calm waters. Together, we knew we could weather any storm.

CHAPTER 12

Tropical twist

I'd long neglected the need for a proper break, but after years of turmoil, my family and I were desperate for a restorative getaway. When I started looking into domestic travel options in Australia, I was stunned by how expensive everything had become. For all the country's beauty, it was disappointing to realise that exploring our own backyard now felt out of reach. A seven-day trip would have cost us thousands, a hefty price for a holiday that wouldn't even take us beyond Australian shores.

After chatting with friends about family-friendly destinations, one place kept coming up: Fiji. With its warm hospitality, appealing holiday packages, and short distance from Australia, it quickly became a strong contender. We started digging into the options, weighing up what would best suit our little family.

Thankfully, I had the freedom to plan our trip exactly how I wanted. Master M was easygoing and flexible, happy to go along with whatever I organised. To keep our budget in check, I always created detailed itineraries, a must when travelling with two young kids.

Our travel agent soon found a deal that was simply too good to ignore: The Outrigger, on the Coral Coast. It felt like a dream come true. We booked an ocean view room with breakfast and dinner included, transfers sorted, and even 50 per cent off two massage treatments. To top it off, the flights were on special.

Lil A already had his passport, having travelled abroad before. Lucky boy! That just left Baby R. Filling out the forms was easy enough, but the passport photo was another story. Getting him to sit still was like pulling teeth. One minute he was crying, the next giggling, then closing his eyes at the crucial second. After 30 tiring minutes of coaxing and bribing, we finally got a decent shot of Baby R; calm, facing forward, and acceptable by the strict requirements. What a mission.

While I'd love to say both kids were bursting with excitement, the truth was Baby R hadn't a clue what was going on. Being a baby meant no responsibilities, no worries, just pure simplicity. Lil A, on the other hand, was full of anticipation.

As for me, my OCD instincts went into overdrive during packing. I over-prepared for Baby R; tins of food, custards, fruit gels, all packed carefully into the hand luggage, just in case. He'd only just started solids, and I wasn't sure how he'd cope with new foods abroad. I wasn't about to risk hunger meltdowns at 35,000 feet. And because I like to be over-prepared, I packed more than a hundred nappies. Slightly delusional, yes. I knew I could buy more in Fiji but being over-prepared gave me peace of mind.

Our long-awaited trip was finally within reach. Lil A was counting down the sleeps until his next aeroplane adventure, his excitement bubbling over at every mention of it. I was dreaming of sun-soaked afternoons by the pool, a book in one hand and the sound of laughter in the background. Master M was simply looking forward to switching off from the world for a little while, savouring uninterrupted time with his children. His quiet smile hinted at a rare chance to just be.

♥

Trip day has never been my favourite. Whether we're heading interstate or crossing oceans, the lead-up is always a nightmare for me. Until I'm buckled in and the plane is in the air, I'm wound tight, pacing, restless, and irritable. It isn't a fear of flying that grips me, but the overwhelming desire for everything to run smoothly. I know I'm the architect of my own stress, yet I can't silence the part of me that obsesses over every detail.

I'm always ready hours before I need to be. I triple-check our luggage, weigh the bags again and again, and secure every lock as though those extra clicks could guarantee peace of mind. Even though we live close to the airport, I still insist on arriving far earlier than necessary, padding our time to cover every possible obstacle like traffic, queues, you name it. Some might call it over the top; I call it being a mum. It's not about being a control freak, but a precautionary one. And honestly, I've made peace with that part of me. It's who I am.

Once we arrived at the airport, the atmosphere shifted. Excitement started to settle in, softening the edges of my anxiety. While I wasn't completely relaxed, anticipation slowly began to replace tension. With the luggage checked and customs cleared, all that was left was to wait. Lil A's voice grew louder with every word, as though the volume button inside him had been turned up a notch. He was practically shouting, but in the most endearing way. His joy was contagious; a breath of fresh air that reminded me to embrace the moment instead of trying to control it.

We sat together at the gate, waiting for our boarding call. The clock ticked steadily, the minutes stretching with expectancy. Then came the announcement: a slight delay due to storms and strong winds. The reassurance followed that everything was under control and boarding would begin soon.

I took a deep breath, willing myself to surrender to the waiting, whispering patience to quiet my racing heart, reminding myself that sometimes the delays we dread are simply another lesson in stillness. Two hours slipped by nearly unnoticed. The children kept us entertained, their energy lightening the mood. Between Lil A's animated chatter and Baby R's restless stroller adventures, the time drifted past, distracting me from what would normally have been mounting anxiety. Where I might usually have been frantic, I found myself surprisingly calm. Unexpectedly calm.

As the three-hour delay drew near its end, an announcement finally came: boarding for our flight bound for Nadi, Fiji would begin shortly. Lil A leaped out of his chair, his husky little voice booming with delight. 'Yess, it's time, Mummy!' He bolted towards the queue for the gate, unable to contain his excitement. While we waited, Baby R grew wriggly and irritable, his cheerful babble quickly turning into cries. My heart sank. Please don't let him be that crying child on the plane.

Once we boarded, Lil A, still buzzing with excitement, looked up at me and asked eagerly, 'Can I sit by the window? I want to see outside.'

It was already dark, but I wasn't going to take away something that lit him up so much. I helped him buckle in, watching his small hands fumble with the seatbelt before he finally clicked it shut. Then I settled Baby R onto my lap.

He grew uneasy the moment the plane began to move. As we raced down the runway, his little body stiffened, and by the time we lifted into the air, he was crying in full panic – loud, breathless, shaking in my arms. I held him close, rubbing his back, whispering to him over the roar of the engines, feeling every tremble in his tiny frame. But once we levelled off, something in him softened. His cries faded to small hiccups. He nestled into my chest, his cheek warm against me and his fingers curling into my shirt. Within minutes, his breathing slowed and he drifted into a deep, peaceful sleep.

I sat, frozen, barely daring to move in case I woke him. My legs ached and I longed for a bathroom break, but the last thing I needed was a mid-flight tantrum disturbing tired passengers.

As we began our descent into Nadi, the captain's voice filled the cabin. He warned of a rough landing due to severe storms and strong winds. My stomach tightened as he continued, explaining that heavy rainfall had caused flash flooding, submerging the main bridge connecting Nadi to the Coral Coast, the very route we needed to reach our resort. I glanced at Master M in horror. This was supposed to be a blissful holiday, yet it was already starting to feel like a disaster.

The plane jolted violently, rattling against the wind. I clutched Baby R tightly, shielding him with every motherly instinct. He slept soundly, oblivious to the bumps. Lil A, however, perched at the edge of his seat, grinning as though he were on the world's wildest rollercoaster.

'Whoa, this is fun!' he exclaimed, his excitement cutting through my nerves. For a moment his innocent joy became our in-flight entertainment, dissolving the tension that had gripped me so tightly.

At last, we landed safely in Nadi, but the scene that greeted us was chaotic. The winds were fierce and the signs of flooding were undeniable. The terminal was packed with confused passengers, all scrambling to arrange onward travel. We joined the crowd, searching for our hotel transfer amid the noise and commotion.

Our driver appeared at the designated meeting point with a wide, reassuring smile, his warm *'Bula!'* cutting through the chaos like a beacon. His calm presence was a comfort. Once everyone had gathered, he raised his voice above the chatter.

'Bula, Bula! Welcome to Fiji. I am your driver. Due to the severe weather conditions and flooding, the bridge is still underwater. We cannot cross tonight. We'll take you to a nearby motel where you can rest. In the morning, if the waters recede, we'll continue your journey.'

Though my chest tightened with unease, his words made sense. We had no choice but to wait. Tomorrow would bring new options and new decisions. For now, we had to trust the process. As the bus rolled into the darkness, the devastation around us was undeniable. Though it was only 8 p.m., it felt long past midnight. The wind howled, trees swayed violently, and floodwaters shimmered under the weak glow of the headlights. Broken branches littered the road, reminders of nature's strength. This wasn't the paradise I had imagined, but we were safe and at this time, safety was enough.

❤

We arrived at a small motel in Nadi, a modest place with only a few rooms. It was far from the resort we'd pictured, but gratitude outweighed disappointment. The courtyard was dimly lit, shadows stretching across the space, making it hard to tell what shape the building was in. We were shown to our rooms and called it a night.

Lil A, in his innocent excitement, saw nothing but adventure. To him, the little room was a palace straight out of a fairytale. He bounced on the beds, laughing and shouting before we'd even turned on the lights. When I flicked the switch, the glow was dull, leaving half the room in shadow. What might have been intended as romantic lighting only added to my unease. The room was small, and though it didn't look dirty, I couldn't shake the feeling that something was crawling on me. One step into the bathroom confirmed my discomfort. I stepped right back out, refusing to shower. I'm no princess, but as a mother, I expect a basic level of cleanliness, not just for me but for my children. After giving the kids a quick clean with wet wipes and dressing them in their pyjamas, I settled them for the night. Lil A slept wrapped in rolled-up beach towels, my makeshift way of protecting him from imaginary bed bugs, while Baby R rested peacefully in his stroller.

I spent the night sitting on the floor, leaning against the bed. The hum of the ceiling fan did little to calm my nerves. Once the children drifted off, my panic crept in like a slow poison. *Where had I brought my family? How had I led us here, stranded in a shabby motel, far from home?* All I wanted at that moment was to go back. I dug my phone out of my bag and sent an email to our travel agent, explaining everything in detail. Though it was late in Sydney, I didn't expect a reply. To my surprise, her message came through minutes later: 'Try to get some rest. We'll discuss this in the morning.'

Her words were kind, but sleep refused to come. The night stretched endlessly, every minute dragging as if the darkness itself had extra hours. When morning finally broke, Lil A was the first to rise. He shot out of bed, full of energy, his excitement lighting up the tiny room. I, on the other hand, felt as though I'd spent the night locked in a dungeon. Still, his joy was infectious, a little spark cutting through my exhaustion.

As Baby R stirred, Lil A made sure his brother woke quickly, clapping and chatting loudly. Once both boys were ready, I gathered our things and stepped outside.

The morning light revealed what the night had hidden. The motel was built in a U-shape, with a small pool in the centre. Lush greenery framed the property, giving it a jungle-like look. Picturesque maybe, but it wasn't what I'd signed up for.

Lil A spotted the pool and almost burst with excitement. 'This is the best place, Mum! Can we stay here?' he begged, eyes wide with wonder. I muttered under my breath, 'Over my dead body,' and let his question hang in the air.

Soon after, I struck up a conversation with another guest, a woman travelling with her son. Our boys clicked instantly, chatting as if they'd known each other for years. She told me she was also from Australia and, as fate would have it, had booked the same resort as us – the Outrigger.

As we waited for management to arrive with news about the bridge, we compared our options: transferring to another hotel on the Nadi side or returning home early. One thing was certain: I wasn't staying in that motel.

When management finally arrived, they invited us into the office. I went in with my new friend, B. The update was disappointing: the bridge was still submerged and there was no way across. We exchanged blank stares. B offered to help find accommodation on this side of the island, but the last-minute options were ridiculously expensive. By then, I was done; tired, hungry, and irritable beyond measure. We walked out of the office with long faces. Master M, who'd been watching the three kids, came over to hear the latest.

Just as we were beginning to settle into the uncertainty, the manager returned with a spring in her step. Suddenly, the mood lightened, a flicker of hope returning. She sat down and said, 'I've been thinking of ways to get you to your resort. The only viable option is by air. What do you think about taking a helicopter?'

We looked at one another as though she'd just suggested flying to the moon, but she pressed on. 'Please note, this is the only way to reach the resort. Your travel insurance should cover the helicopter costs, but you should check with your provider first.'

Back in our room, I rifled through our travel documents and rang the insurer. The customer service agent was kind, apologising for the ordeal and confirming the manager was right. The helicopter transfer would indeed be covered, since it was the only available option. Relief washed over me. Finally, there was a way forward.

B and I stepped out of our rooms almost in sync, eyes wide with excitement. We strode into the manager's office and gave the go-ahead. She negotiated a reasonable deal and we agreed to split the cost evenly between our families. Our transport to the helipad would arrive within the hour.

I felt like a giddy child, having never flown in a helicopter before. The kids, blissfully unaware of what lay ahead, sulked as we packed up. They were devastated to leave the motel, convinced we were ruining their holiday.

'Can't we just stay by the pool?' they pleaded.

'No, not today. We've got a surprise,' we teased, a promise that bought us a temporary truce. Children have an extraordinary way of finding joy in the simplest things. Their innocence reminded me again that the present moment is where life truly happens.

As we drew closer to the helipad, both boys spotted the helicopter sitting in an open field, its blades gleaming under the humid Fijian sun. At first, they didn't pay it much attention, distracted by the wide-open space around them. But when the car stopped, their heads snapped up like meerkats.

'Where are we?' they asked, puzzled.

'We're taking a trip,' we replied, opening the door.

'On a helicopter?' one of them gasped.

'Yes, how lucky are you boys?'

'WOW! Just like the movies!' Their eyes shone with wonder.

We hauled our luggage across the field while they hopped and skipped beside us. But as the rotors began to spin, whipping the air into a frenzy, Baby R's face crumpled. Within seconds, he was screaming uncontrollably. Master M scooped him up, holding him tight as the pilot strapped him in first and gently placed earmuffs over his tiny ears. It made no difference; he was petrified. All we could do was keep him safe until it was over. The older two clambered into their seats, buckled up, slipped on their earmuffs and sat grinning from ear to ear, ready for lift-off. Their joy could have lit up the sky.

The chaos of the past few days faded. What had begun as a mishap had turned into a once-in-a-lifetime experience. Watching the boys' excitement and hearing their laughter, I realised how lucky we truly were. What a moment.

As we lifted off, our eyes stayed glued to the windows, drinking in every detail of the world below. The higher we climbed, the more the devastation unfolded. Homes lay shattered, streets were submerged, and fields once heavy with crops now drowned beneath muddy water. The destruction was overwhelming.

The thirty-minute helicopter ride passed mostly in silence, broken only by the rhythmic hum of the propellers. That image of vast brown water swallowing entire communities will forever be seared into my memory.

As we approached the resort's helipad, the scene below shifted dramatically. A landscape of serene beauty stretched out below: lush green grass, tall swaying palms, and elegant buildings painted in vivid hues against an endless blue sky. The contrast, from devastation to paradise, left me unsettled. My heart ached for the families we had flown over, grappling with loss while we were arriving for a holiday.

After a long and winding journey, relief washed over me. We had finally made it, together, safe and sound. At check-in, the front office manager greeted us warmly, her cheerful *'Bula!'* echoing the driver's earlier welcome and grounding us once more in Fiji's signature warmth, even after all the chaos. With genuine gratitude, she thanked us for persevering through the road and bridge closures. As a gesture, she upgraded us to a beachfront bure, an unexpected gift after the stress of travel.

While we waited for the golf buggy, we simply breathed. Around us, vibrant flowers burst with colour, lush greenery shimmered under the sun, and a cloudless sky stretched endlessly above. For the first time in days, everything felt still, almost unreal.

When we finally arrived at our accommodation, delight replaced exhaustion. We discovered two bures connected by a central room, perfectly designed to give each family their own space while the boys shared a retreat of their own. What had begun as two separate families travelling together suddenly felt like one happy family of six.

The boys were ecstatic, racing towards the pool before we'd even unpacked. Their joy was infectious. Their giggles and splashy 'bombs' echoed across the resort like music. Baby R floated happily in his little float seat while the older boys competed to make the biggest splash. We either joined them in the water or sat nearby, sipping drinks by the bar.

Luxury enveloped us. Our bure came with exceptional amenities: a butler, a nanny service, and full access to the kids' club. I couldn't have planned it better myself.

One of the most rewarding parts of the holiday was the people we met. Many were Australian families, and one in particular became fast friends. They had two girls and a boy, and our children bonded instantly, playing endless games in the pool by day and snooker by night. The parents connected just as quickly; it felt as though we'd known each other for years.

The highlight of the trip came on Australia Day. The resort hosted an all-day celebration bursting with games, music, and laughter. The atmosphere was electric. Children squealed with delight, adults joined in the fun, and joy rippled through the place like sunlight on water. It felt like one big family gathering, only without the usual dramas such events so often bring. Sitting back and watching it all unfold was bliss. It was pure community, pure joy.

As the evening rolled on, conversations turned to where we were all from. It amazed us how small the world suddenly felt.

'Where are you from?' 'Australia.'

'Us too. Whereabouts?' 'Sydney.'

'Same! Which suburb?'

'Oh, you wouldn't know it. It's a little place near the airport called Eastlakes.'

'You're kidding! We're from Rosebery, right next door.'

'No way, we own the cafe on Maloney Street!'

The connections felt fated. What had begun as a challenging journey had led to unexpected joy, new friendships, and unforgettable moments of connection.

What were the chances of bumping into this family on Australia Day, in Fiji of all places, after crossing an ocean without ever having met them before? If I hadn't already believed the world was small, this moment certainly taught me so. Incredible stuff.

From that day on, our families remained in contact. We stayed in touch for a while and even visited their cafe when we returned home. Sadly, contact faded after they sold the business and moved interstate.

A few days into our trip, everything felt like heaven. The hospitality was outstanding, the food exquisite, and life was simply brilliant.

One afternoon, as we sat by the poolside watching the boys splash about, the wind suddenly picked up. We rushed to get the children out and wrapped them in towels, still laughing a little at how quickly the weather had changed. But then the resort's sirens blared through the speakers, sharp and ear-splitting, announcing a cyclone alert. What the...? Moments before, the atmosphere had been calm. Now, guests were hurrying towards their rooms, staff moved with urgency, and I struggled to grasp what was happening. The supervisor confirmed a cyclone warning. He explained that there was one final flight leaving the island in two hours for those who wished to evacuate; otherwise, we would need to stay put. We had only minutes to decide.

I looked at Master M in shock. His usually calm eyes betrayed a flicker of doubt as he glanced at the darkening sky. Then I turned to B, who froze mid-motion as she dried her son's hair.

'What should we do?' I asked.

'I don't know,' she admitted quietly.

Master M stepped closer, calm but firm. 'Look, the resort is equipped for emergencies. They'll escort us to a safe area if needed.' He pointed towards the designated shelter.

'How do you know that?' I demanded.

'The supervisor just told me. Apparently, this is fairly common; they're prepared, and we'll be safe.'

I exhaled and turned to B. 'Let's stay. We've come this far. Surely we can't be that unlucky.'

Together, we made the conscious decision to remain at the resort. Back in our rooms, we gathered everyone's passports and placed them all in one secure spot for both families. We were determined to stick together. With the cyclone expected to hit that evening, the resort instructed guests to stay indoors and avoid roaming the property. After dinner, we kept the children safe in their rooms while we, the foolish adults, tested nature's patience by sitting out on the verandah, chatting away as though the winds weren't building around us. A strong gust rattled the chairs, and B laughed nervously. 'Maybe we're tempting fate a bit too much,' she said, her words swallowed by the growing howl of the storm.

By morning, the storm had passed. The winds had eased and the sun rose brilliantly, painting the sky in breathtaking colours. Although branches had been torn from trees and scattered across the grounds, the damage was minimal. The air carried the faint scent of wet earth and broken leaves. The cyclone had veered off course and spared us its full force. Relief washed over me.

The next morning over a breakfast of tropical fruit and warm pastries, we debriefed as a family. The boys chattered excitedly about the 'big wind,' while Master M and I exchanged quiet smiles, grateful for the calm after the storm. That moment, surrounded by the clink of plates, the hum of conversation, and the children's laughter, cemented a truth I'll never forget we had faced the unknown together and come out stronger.

In hindsight, I was deeply grateful we hadn't panicked and fled. Sometimes fear urges us to run when patience teaches us the storm isn't always as fierce as it seems. What was meant to be just a family holiday became something more – a lesson in surrender, resilience, and perspective.

Life doesn't come with guarantees; you never know what's waiting around the corner. But I've learned that embracing the present moment is the key to growth. Every experience, even the frightening ones, carries the potential to teach us something new. While financial wealth has never been my reality, I count myself rich in life's experiences, and that, I've come to realise, is a treasure in itself.

CHAPTER 13

Euphoria

A short break can be a powerful reset for the mind, body, and soul. Our little getaway rewired my system, immersing me in nature's beauty and serenity. It was the pause I didn't know I needed, a moment to refocus, to recharge, to simply breathe. With life constantly throwing curveballs, a hard reset was exactly what we needed, and a chance to draw closer together as a family.

I often wake up wondering, *What's next?* It's as though I expect chaos to waltz in across the dance floor of some enchanted masquerade ball. Maybe I jinx myself every day, if that's even a thing. I long for calmness, for a life that feels like a smooth, scenic drive down an open highway. But then again, wouldn't that be boring? Where's the entertainment in that? Who needs a bingeworthy series when my life serves up its own drama?

All I have to do is close my eyes and watch my memories flash past like a reel. Sometimes I look back at the hills, trenches, and hurdles and just laugh, muttering, *What the fuck?* Other times I joke that I'd be better off strapped in a white straitjacket, though, honestly, crisp white wouldn't suit my complexion, plus it wouldn't stay clean anyway. I am, without doubt, one of the clumsiest people around.

Yet I did enjoy the normality of life after our trip. There's nothing quite like your own bed, even if waking by the ocean is magic. Nothing tugs at the heartstrings quite like being home.

❤

Mum's health was as good as could be expected. Her days varied, much like anyone else's. The kids, God love them, were simply being kids. Lil A threw himself into both soccer and football, sometimes merging the two on match days. Meanwhile, poor Baby R was dragged around in the pram. I still remember those freezing winter nights at training: Baby R bundled up like a little Eskimo, covered from head to toe, while Lil A sprinted across the pitch, soaked in sweat, the crowd's Aussie-accented cheers echoing through the chilly air.

One Sunday morning stands out vividly in my mind. Lil A had a football game at Yarra Bay. He was younger and smaller than many of his teammates, but he had remarkable speed and strength. As we arrived, I noticed him pause by the car like a statue, gripping the door handle. I was busy unbuckling Baby R and didn't immediately catch on until he whispered, 'I don't want to play today.'

Puzzled, I scanned the field. Then I saw what he had seen: the size of the opposing team.

'Why, agapi mou?' I asked gently, crouching in front of him.

'Look at them, they're huge!' he exclaimed.

I took his hand, kissed his forehead, and reassured him. It was obvious he was intimidated. 'They may be bigger than you, but that doesn't mean anything. You're not alone out there; your teammates are with you. It's a team effort.' With that, I walked him over to the coach. Part of me wanted to check birth certificates to make sure those giants really belonged in the Under 7s.

When the whistle blew, my nerves spiked. My palms began to sweat as I watched the boys dash back and forth, our team scoring early and riding a confidence high. Parents cheered from the sidelines, urging them on, their voices a rowdy chorus of 'Go Jets, go!' and 'Kick it!' For a while, it worked. But as the game wore on, the opposition clawed back goal after goal. Our boys began to deflate.

Then came the moment. Lil A sprinted down the field, the try line in sight. Suddenly, four boys piled on top of him, tackling him hard. My heart jumped into my throat. I leapt to my feet, holding my breath, fighting the urge to run onto the pitch.

When the pile cleared, Lil A dragged himself up and walked straight to me. With glassy eyes, he whispered, 'Mummy, I don't want to play football anymore.' My poor boy was mortified. As much as I wanted to scoop him up and promise he'd never have to play again, I knew that wasn't the right response.

After the game, I pulled him close and said softly, 'I know you were scared in that tackle. Anyone would be. But you were so brave. I'm proud of you. Your teammates need you. You made a commitment, and sticking with it makes you stronger and braver. That's what good sportsmanship is about.'

He looked at me, his head tilted, and muttered, 'But I got smashed to the ground.'

'Yes,' I replied, smiling. 'But you got back up, didn't you?'

The sparkle slowly returned to his eyes. On the drive home, he stayed quiet, processing everything. We didn't push him; we knew he needed time. Later, he came to me on his own and said, 'Okay, Mummy, I'll keep playing with my team.'

I hadn't needed to dramatise or lecture. In that moment, all I could do was guide him and hope he absorbed the lesson. To my surprise, he did. At seven years old, he understood the message: courage isn't about never being afraid, it's about standing back up.

❤

Meanwhile, my dad kept himself busy with his usual routine; tending to his garden, catching up with friends, playing lawn bowls, and visiting my mum in the nursing home every day. He was easygoing, respectful of our space, and the kids adored him. They also knew that if I said no to something, they could usually run to Pappou and get a different answer.

When I raised my voice, something I often did with Lil A, who still carried that rebellious streak (and I still wonder where he got that from), Dad would step in and tell me to stop yelling. And every time, it lit a spark. I'd whirl around, already on edge, and snap, 'Did your mother ever intervene when we were growing up? No? Then butt out.' He only wanted me to be gentler with the children, but in those moments, Lil A would often stand by his side, wearing a cheeky grin that seemed to say, *Ha! Pappou's got my back.* That little rascal.

Over time, though, I noticed changes in my dad. His behaviour became erratic in ways I couldn't quite put my finger on. Certain conversations seemed to spark heightened reactions, his mood swinging quickly from sombre to unnervingly elevated. More and more often, he spoke about the Greek alphabet and its connection to God. The pattern unsettled me, but I pushed it aside. Until his sister phoned me one day. To my horror, she voiced the very same concerns. She told me that in church, he acted as though the priest was speaking directly to him, completely absorbed in a way that went beyond devotion. Hearing it from her confirmed what I had tried to dismiss: something was deeply troubling my dad.

He began channelling his energy into writing poetry, even though he wasn't a writer. His words often carried fragments of wisdom, but they were always heavy with faith and religion. At first, it felt thoughtful. But whenever I questioned or challenged him, he grew agitated, his eyes flashing an intense crystal blue. He started calling me 'the devil.' It was jarring. My calm, grounded father had become someone I barely recognised, a man whose emotions seemed heightened, almost electric. And around the children, it frightened me.

Then one day, while tidying up, I noticed a small box tucked into the corner of the bar – one I was sure hadn't been there before. Curiosity slowed my steps. I reached for it and eased the lid open, the faint dusty scent rising from the cardboard and drifting towards me. It carried a memory, soft but sharp enough to stop my breath for a moment. Dad's old cigarette packs he used to store in that same spot years ago.

Inside, I discovered a packet of medication labelled Champix. I didn't recognise the name, so I unfolded the leaflet. It was a treatment to help people stop smoking. My Dad, a lifelong smoker now in his sixties, had decided to quit – something I hadn't known he'd even discussed with a doctor. Looking at the pack, I realised he was in his third week of the program. My mind rewound, pulling at threads. Suddenly it clicked: everything had started three weeks earlier. Shaken, I called his sister and shared what I'd found. She wasn't surprised. Calmly, she advised me to keep an eye on him and reassured me that I could reach out anytime. Her steady voice grounded me, reminding me that I wasn't imagining it, that I wasn't losing the plot. Someone else could see it too.

Later, when I confronted him, he proudly confirmed that he was on the medication and doing well with quitting. For a brief moment, I felt relieved. But when I mentioned the possible side effects, everything shifted. It was as if he'd slipped on a cape and *boom!* transformed into something out of a horror film. He erupted, accusing me of not knowing what I was talking about, insisting I was the one with psychological issues, and again calling me 'the devil.' Each time those words left his mouth, they cut deeper. Rationally, I knew that it was the medication speaking, not my dad. But still, it pierced my heart.

One morning after dropping the kids at school and preschool, I headed to the gym for a shift. The familiar smell of sweat and iron grounded me. Dad was still asleep when I left, so I figured there was little chance of trouble. I returned home by midday, unease gnawing at me. As I fumbled with the key, my mind raced with worst-case scenarios. Normally, I'd be greeted by the loud blare of the Greek channel from the TV. Instead, silence. Unsettling, suffocating silence.

I stepped inside, bracing myself, scanning for chaos. But there he was, sitting at the kitchen bench, quiet, still, his face unreadable. The silence between us was heavier than any shouting could have been. I walked over to him cautiously. 'Hi, Papa, what are you doing?' I asked, keeping my tone calm.

He was frantically typing on his phone. He glanced up with those crystal-blue eyes. In his usual calm state, they were grey. That blue was never a good sign. Panic tightened inside me. He thrust the phone towards me.

'See, he's talking to me,' he said. I was terrified of what would be on the screen, but I forced myself to look.

'See? God is responding to me. I write something, and God already knows what I'm going to say and writes it for me,' he went on.

'Papa, that isn't God, it's predictive text. All phones do it. My phone does that too,' I said, keeping my voice calm, trying not to trigger him further.

He screamed, 'You are the devil! Get away from me!' and shot to his feet.

I grabbed my phone and called Master M. He picked up straightaway because he knew what our situation could look like. I was shaking as I blurted out, 'Can you come home? Dad isn't well. I don't know what to do.'

'Okay. I'm on my way. Call your aunt and tell her what's happening,' he said, calm as always.

'Good idea,' I said, and hung up.

I ran to my room and called my aunt. I told her Dad was having another manic episode and I didn't know how to handle it. She said she would send my uncle, and she would come from work too as soon as she could. She also suggested I ask the doctor whether he could do a home visit. As soon as I dropped the phone, the front door slammed. My heart jumped. Oh God...did he leave? I rushed into the hall, breath tight in my chest. Thank God, Master M had just arrived.

Dad was pacing back and forth, talking to himself under his breath, lost in his own storm. Everything spun too fast to follow. One second he was reaching for his keys, ready to walk out of the house, and the next... Something fierce sparked inside me.

'No. You're not leaving,' I breathed, more to myself than to him. I threw myself forward with all the strength fear had given me. I wrapped my arms around him like a lioness guarding what she loved, dragging him down, planting him on his knees before he could slip away from us. Tears poured out before I even felt them, hot and sharp, running down my face in a rush I couldn't stop.

'Papa, please, you need help. I need to take you to the doctor. The medication is affecting you,' I pleaded.

He pushed me away and yelled, slurring, 'Y-O-U'R-E T-H-E D-E-V-I-L.'

I wiped my face with my sleeve then looked to Master M, who stood guarding the door, his hand briefly squeezing mine to steady me. I had to get the doctor. I needed help. I ran around the corner as if racing for a gold medal and burst into the surgery. The waiting room was full. I told the receptionist it was urgent and begged her to send someone. She told me the doctor couldn't do a home visit. Fury and helplessness collided inside me. Tears streamed down my face as I kept repeating, 'He needs help.'

The receptionist asked if there had been any violence. I told her Dad had pushed me. Her response was muted. I left the surgery feeling defeated and utterly unsure how to help him.

I rushed back to the house to find Master M still guarding Dad's bedroom door, as if he were an enraged animal locked in a cage. I had no idea how I was going to calm him or how I was going to help. All I knew was that he needed help.

A few moments later, there was a knock at the front door. Dad shouted from his room, 'Who did you tell, you devil?' His voice rose sharply and my uncle heard him. He opened the door slowly, walked in, and sat on the bed. Dad was bouncing off the walls. Thank God my uncle had come.

Dad continued to insist that I was the one who needed help, that I was the devil, and that God had given him a message. He rattled on about biblical literature, waving around 'signs' that he claimed God had sent him.

The doorbell rang again. Who on earth was that now? Two shadowy figures stood outside. I hesitated to open the door; Dad's state was already volatile. But I did. Two police officers stood on the doorstep, arms relaxed, voices calm. They introduced themselves and asked if I was alright. I was bewildered. Where had this come from?

They explained they'd received a call from the surgery reporting possible violence and had come to conduct a welfare check. I was speechless.

Dad heard unfamiliar voices and shuffled to his bedroom doorway. He greeted the officers with a broad smile. 'Come, come in, let us make you a coffee,' he said. The officers glanced at me, their concern evident. As Dad led them through the house, speaking passionately about God, I gave them a quick debrief. They sat with him and chatted. For a moment, I thought they were just humouring him. But really, they were assessing the situation.

'Welcome into my home,' Dad announced proudly. 'I was sent to shed the light of love.' He went on, enthusiastically explaining some connection between the alphabet and God. One of the officers stepped out to make a call, then returned quickly. Both looked at me, one stepped forward and said, 'Your Dad seems to be experiencing a psychotic episode and needs medical attention. What medication is he on?'

I fetched the box from the bar and showed it to them. They nodded, then told me an ambulance was on its way to take him to the hospital, for his safety and mine.

'I'm worried he might refuse,' I said quietly.

The doorbell rang again. This time, it was the ambulance. Dad's eyes lit up, thrilled by the gathering. The paramedics entered and began to assess him. He remained euphoric, delighted that everyone had come to hear his words. I looked at the paramedics with a pleading expression; they could see the torment written across my face. One of them approached Dad gently.

'We're going to take you to the hospital to see a doctor,' they said softly. 'The medication you're on is causing some side effects.'

I braced myself for a confrontation, but Dad surprised me.

'Yes, yes, I'll go wherever you want me to go,' he said eagerly. 'I can tell the doctors what God told me. The more people I tell, the more people will know that God exists.' His eyes shone with conviction. 'This is good, very good,' he added in his broken English.

As I helped Dad into the ambulance, the minute-by-minute developments felt impossible to process. I turned to Master M. 'Please look after the kids,' I said. My eyes filled with tears as the paramedic closed the doors and we drove away. What now? I whispered to myself, the question looping like a mantra.

My Dad was unusually quiet during the ambulance ride. He looked over at me once or twice, but he didn't say a word. We lived only a few suburbs away from the hospital, so we reached the emergency department within minutes. As the paramedic processed his admission, we waited in the narrow waiting space, counting down the seconds until it was our turn to see the doctor. I sat there motionless beside him, shivering from the weight of stress pressing through my body. I could hear everything around me, yet none of it felt clear or real. I was locked in a numb state when my dad suddenly glanced at me and pointed to an electrical outlet on the wall. 'See, there are three. They symbolise the Holy Trinity,' he murmured.

I held his hand gently and whispered, 'Yes, Dad. Yes, I know,' hoping my voice would calm him even a little.

Thirty minutes passed, though it seemed endless. People walked back and forth, voices echoing from every corner. My thoughts felt scattered and for a moment I wondered if I was losing my grip. Another patient arrived and sat beside my father. My dad nodded politely at him. Inside, I whispered to myself, *Please, Dad, just stay calm. Don't draw attention. Not now.* But soon they began to talk. The conversation between them flowed easily. Dad pointed at the paintings on the wall, offering commentary, and the man nodded along. 'Yes, yes, I see,' he said. Then Dad gestured towards a three-legged stool where a nurse had been sitting and declared it a divine symbol, another sign of the Holy Trinity. They laughed together, seemingly on the same wavelength. I sat there feeling like an outsider, panic rising in my chest. I'm the one who's losing it, I thought. Maybe it's me, not him.

'Mr A,' the doctor called. Dad sprang up. 'Yes, that's me,' he replied. I rose slowly, dragging my feet.

The doctor led us into a private room and asked for a brief rundown. I explained the changes in Dad's behaviour and mentioned he had been taking Champix. He listened carefully, then told us that the staff in the waiting area had been observing Dad and believed he was experiencing a psychotic episode. Their intention, he said, was to admit him to the mental health unit as an involuntary patient. I didn't fully understand what that meant. The doctor went on to explain that sometimes, when a person's condition made them a risk to themselves or others, admission without consent was necessary. He assured me the unit was a secure facility designed to provide intensive care and support for patients in acute mental distress.

Dad seemed calmer now, even though little bursts of excitement still slipped through; moments the doctor had seen for himself.

I knew I wasn't imagining anything. The medication was affecting him, twisting his mind in ways I couldn't understand. This was my dad, the most steady, reasonable man I had ever known. 'How could this be happening to him?' I whispered.

Accompanied by two security guards and the doctor, Dad was escorted to the Kiloh Centre, an acute mental health unit. I texted Master M to update him as we walked through the hospital corridors, my hands trembling. He had already arranged for a friend to pick me up, knowing I had no car. He needed to stay home with the kids. It was bad enough that I was gone; we didn't want both of us away, leaving the children to worry.

The doctor buzzed us through the first door and a shiver ran down my spine. Door after door, lock after lock, it felt as though we were walking into a jail. By evening, most patients had returned to their rooms and doors were closed. Guards patrolled quietly, their footsteps echoing against the linoleum floors. The air carried an icy stillness, pierced only by the faint hum of fluorescent lights overhead. The doctor led Dad to his room and I helped him settle in. I kissed him goodnight, my heart splintering at the sight of him sitting alone on the bed.

As I was escorted out, my hysteria rose with every step. My friend was waiting outside the front entrance, her eyes already filled with tears. I walked towards her, mine spilling freely. It felt as if I were moving through a fog, seeing right through her, just walking one slow step at a time towards the curb. We didn't speak. I sat down on the roadside, feet on the tarmac, and my quiet tears turned into sobs.

'My dad...my dad,' I cried. My friend wrapped her arms around me as I swayed and wailed. I couldn't seem to catch my breath. My rock, my strength, had been taken away. Tears accompanied me all the way home. I couldn't make sense of what had happened. How could this have happened to my dad?

When I stepped into the house, Lil A came barrelling down the hallway.

'Mummy!' he squealed, leaping into my arms. I held him close, kissing his warm forehead.

'I'm home, baby,' I whispered, trying to still my trembling voice. With his tiny hand tucked in mine, we walked slowly through the house.

My aunt and uncle were there. The moment I saw them, I collapsed into my aunt's arms and sobbed.

'He's going to be okay,' she said softly, her voice full of warmth. 'He'll get all the help he needs.'

We sat together and talked about treatment, about what would come next and how to handle telling Dad's brothers; three men who hadn't spoken in over seven years. My aunt promised she wouldn't reach out without discussing it with me first. After a long conversation, I decided it was best to notify his brothers. Dad needed the family's support now more than ever.

The next morning I went back to the hospital straight after dropping the children at school. I had packed a small bag of essentials for Dad. He was seated in the same position as the night before. Had he sat there all night? When he saw me, he smiled. Although he seemed calm, I knew he could snap at any moment. My visit had to be brief; I still needed to get to Mum's nursing home to help with lunch. Before I left, I promised to return that afternoon. He asked me to bring playing cards.

'Of course, Papa,' I said, kissing him goodbye.

Racing from the mental hospital to the nursing home felt like being trapped in a scene from *Nightmare on Elm Street*, and I was running on autopilot. I buzzed into the home with my access card and climbed the stairs. How had I managed to get from point A to point B without falling apart? I felt like a pilot announcing to passengers, *This is your captain speaking. We're experiencing extreme turbulence. Please fasten your seatbelts.*

When I entered the dining room, my face felt frozen in a blank expression. Mum was in her chair, wearing her brown jacket, her head resting gently on the table. I laid a hand on her back and whispered, 'Hi, Mum, I'm here.'

Her big brown eyes lifted towards me. 'Hi, love,' she said.

'How are you?' I asked.

'I'm good,' she replied.

I didn't tell her about Dad. Instead, I said, 'Papa isn't feeling well today. He didn't want to risk getting you sick, but he'll come tomorrow.' I felt guilty for the lie, but I didn't want to break her heart.

'Oh no, that's not good. I hope he's okay,' she said softly.

When the lunch trays arrived, I tried to sound cheerful. 'Ooh, Mum, what have you got today?'

She sniffed and smiled. 'Mmm, it smells nice.'

I cut her food into smaller pieces and handed her the fork. She tried to feed herself, as I helped guide the fork. 'God bless you,' she kept saying as I fed her.

The clock made me panic; there never seemed to be enough hours in the day. I had to rush home, make dinner, pick up the children, return to see Dad, and then go back to Mum. This became our new normal. Lil A understood that Pappou was unwell and in the hospital. He kept himself quietly occupied. Baby R was too young to comprehend.

♥

Visiting Dad every day was frightening. The ward felt unpredictable, the air thick with tension and the faint crayon-like scent of patients' artwork pinned to the walls. One visit stands out vividly in my mind. I was playing cards with him in the lounge when a patient, sitting a short distance away, suddenly leapt to his feet, screamed, grabbed a chair, and hurled it across the room.

I froze. Every hair on my arms stood on end. My heart hammered and my breath caught midair. A security guard intervened and quickly escorted the man away. In the next moment, the guard led Dad back to his room and guided me out of the area. The violence had erupted so suddenly. Just moments earlier, the patient had been laughing with us, and then, in a blink, it felt as if we might all be killed. I left the ward shaken and afraid.

A later visit left me speechless. Dad seemed to be having another episode; his tone was overly enthusiastic, practically theatrical. I asked about his morning and he said the doctor had visited, that they'd walked in the yard.

'That's nice, Papa. What did you talk about?' I asked.

He looked at me and said, 'She's skuoopid! She asked me what I saw,' he said, pointing towards the mural on the wall.

'Oh yes, it's beautiful. What did you tell her?' I probed gently.

He sprang up, animated, and pointed to different parts of the painting. 'Can't you see? It's Alexander the Great and all the soldiers,' he declared.

I stared, perplexed. The mural depicted a peaceful beach with palm trees, a bright sun, golden sand, and crystal-blue water. Sailing boats with colourful sails. How on earth could he see Alexander the Great in that? My mind raced for an explanation, but I had none.

He took my hand and pointed to a framed picture. 'Come, she showed me this,' he said.

'Oh yeah? And?' I prompted.

'Can't you see it? It's a woman's womb, and there's a baby inside,' he said with absolute certainty.

I stepped back and looked again. It was nothing more than an arrangement of neutral-coloured shells.

I couldn't make sense of the mental pathways that led to his words. He was clearly disoriented. I felt a swell of emotion rising, but I swallowed it back. I couldn't let him see me fall apart.

Once Dad was settled, I phoned my aunt and gave her permission for his brothers to visit on the condition that their brother-in-law come as well. Dad was comfortable with his brother-in-law. It had been years since he'd seen his brothers and I had no idea how he would react. The meeting could go one of two ways: he might explode and come unhinged, or he might simply buckle under the weight of despair.

As my father's brothers walked in, a wave of anxiety washed over me. I hadn't seen them in years, and I didn't know how to prepare myself for that moment. When I buzzed them through and finally looked into their eyes, the emptiness I saw there broke me. I burst into tears. They immediately wrapped me in a hug; gentle, warm, and unexpectedly tender. I had never felt that kind of softness from them before, and it confused me. It felt unfamiliar, yet comforting. 'He will be okay,' they whispered.

Before Dad arrived, I had warned them that he might be triggered and asked them not to take anything personally. They listened with patience and compassion. They waited quietly in the waiting area while I went to bring my father through. I tried to lighten the moment and said, 'I have a surprise for you, Papa.'

'*Ti?*' he asked, what?

'Come, come and see.'

I walked ahead of him, instinctively protecting him. When he saw his brothers and his brother-in-law, I held my breath. My heart was pounding. What was he going to do? Had I done the right thing? For a second, panic grabbed me.

But yes, I'd done the right thing. He froze, then suddenly crumbled with emotion. He fell into his brothers' arms, sobbing in a way I had never witnessed before. His cries were raw, childlike, pouring out years of quiet pain. The room was thick with emotion. These grown men – strong, rough, the kind you'd expect to hold everything in – were fighting their own tears, only to finally let them fall. The change in the air was powerful. Three grown butchers became vulnerable children again, meeting in a place of pure honesty.

They talked, but their tears said far more than their words ever could. This visit carried a weight nothing else could match. For the first time, I felt a deep peace settle inside me. My father wasn't alone. His whole family was standing with him, not just a few siblings. What happened in that room softened years of tension and unspoken conflict. It took a heartbreaking situation to bring them back together, but it also reminded them of what truly mattered.

As they prepared to leave, my father smiled a soft, hopeful smile, and said, 'I'll see you again.'

He was nearing his 30-day milestone in the hospital. Time moved so quickly that I barely understood what was happening. I didn't even know the real purpose of the tribunal he had to attend until the very day of the hearing. It was meant to make sure patients received the right care, stayed in the hospital only when necessary, and were discharged safely. Even so, I felt anxious. This was my first tribunal meeting and I had no idea what to expect.

When we entered, the magistrate called the doctor forward. He explained that my father had been experiencing psychotic episodes caused by the side effects of Champix. The magistrate's reaction stunned me. 'Another one?' he snapped. 'This is the third case this month.'

My mind stopped. The third case this month? What on earth was happening? As the discussion continued, I learned that Champix, a medication meant to help people quit smoking, carried serious side effects: psychosis, hallucinations, and even suicidal thoughts.

Jesus Christ. My dad had two out of the three. Why was this still allowed on the market? Honestly, that shit needed to be pulled off the shelves immediately.

It took time for the chemicals to clear from his body. During that period, his energy swung from one extreme to the other. Some days he was so tired he could barely stay awake; other days he was bursting with ideas, creating things with a level of focus that felt both amazing and heartbreaking.

One day, I walked in to find he had built several 'robots' out of tissue boxes and toilet rolls. He looked so proud of them. Then he asked me if I could bring extra art supplies because the hospital materials weren't up to his standard.

Righty-ooo. I went out and bought him Textas, paint and crayons, and gathered every spare art item from home, anything he could use to bring his robot world to life.

There was one entire visit where he didn't breathe a single word to me. He was completely lost in his creativity, sitting at his little table, cutting, gluing, colouring. He looked peaceful, almost content, in a way that made the silence feel gentle instead of cold. Watching him like that gave me a strange kind of strength, a reminder to keep going even when everything inside me felt drained.

My mum's dementia kept her from fully understanding what was happening with my dad. In a painful and unexpected way, this became a blessing. She couldn't keep track of who had visited, so she never had to face the ache of knowing he hadn't shown up. It would have broken her if she had realised the truth.

One evening during our usual dinner visit, we talked about random things; whatever drifted into her mind, I followed. As I fed her, I casually asked if anyone had come by that day.

'Yes,' she said.

'Oh yeah? Who?' I asked, curious and hopeful.

'Your dad just left.'

I froze. Then, trying to keep myself steady, I tilted my head and said, 'Oh really? I must have just missed him.'

I wished the earth would open wide and swallow me whole. As insensitive, selfish, or even horrible as it might sound, her dementia truly became her shelter. It spared her from a heartbreak she did not deserve.

Far out...what on earth was going through both my parents' minds? I felt myself slipping, going through the motions. I wondered if I was about to completely lose my mind, if I hadn't already.

My father's hospital admission became the longest and most traumatic experience I had ever lived through. It felt unreal – the kind of thing people only watch on TV but never imagine themselves surviving.

During one of my visits, a young woman approached me, visibly distressed, saying she couldn't find her wallet. I offered to help her search for it. As we looked around, she leaned closer and whispered that she had watched aliens come down in a spaceship. She said she saw it land with her own two eyes. According to her, an alien had stepped out, gone through her bag, taken her wallet and left with it. I stood there, torn between concern and confusion. She genuinely believed her wallet was gone, but the poor thing was clearly trapped in a frightening delusional episode. She became frantic, insisting her identity, room cards, and everything important to her were now in the hands of extraterrestrial beings. Her voice trembled as she added that she needed help from the President of the United States so she could communicate with the spaceship. In her mind, every part of that story was as real as the walls around us. Her hallucinations painted vivid pictures that she could not separate from reality. Instead of challenging her or deepening her fear, I chose to speak gently. I assured her that the kind lady, the nurse, would help her get access to a phone.

But beneath that calm tone, I was suffocating. A wave of nausea hit me out of nowhere. I wanted to be kind, but I also desperately wanted to leave. I wanted to breathe again. And most of all, I wanted to get back to my dad.

♥

I've seen things I can't unsee and felt emotions that remain heavy inside me. This experience left a fear that lingers in quiet ways. The truth is, everyone carries their own battles; some hidden, some loud, and many too complicated for others to fully understand. You never really know what someone is carrying, or what storms they're fighting in their mind. And the way trauma, addiction, and medication can disrupt the brain's balance, making a person fragile in ways they never asked for, is a reality that still startles me.

Those 12 weeks felt endless. That was how long it took before my father's brain even began to return to itself. And even then, the harm was already done. Once the brain changes, some parts don't go back to what they once were. That truth carved itself into him, and into me.

For a long time, I felt as though I was walking on eggshells around him, trying to measure every breath and shape every word with care. Each topic felt fragile, something I had to hold gently because the wrong one could send him slipping back into the darkness he fought so hard to leave behind. I stayed on high alert, reading his mood, watching his eyes, listening for the quiet signs that most people would miss. It drained me in ways I couldn't explain, yet the fear of seeing him fall again pressed heavier on me than exhaustion ever could.

Yet, as I look back on this dark and terrifying chapter, something unexpected rises from it; a kind of fragile beauty. What once felt like the breaking point somehow became the bridge that healed longstanding tension between the siblings. One powerful moment forced them to see how small their old conflicts were compared to what truly mattered. Their reunion became a quiet blessing, especially because my yiayia spent years hoping and praying for that peace. In the end, love stood where fear once lived. LOVE conquers ALL!

CHAPTER 14

The turning point

How is it possible that one minute I'm cradling Baby R in my arms, soothing his soft cries to sleep, and the next, we're celebrating his graduation from day care? It feels as though time simply blinked and overnight, he grew up. Where have those days gone, the ones at his change table, cleaning him up while he kicked and cried, shouting, 'I want to go to the gym with you, Mummy!' Those tender, clingy toddler days have vanished, swept away as he steps into a new adventure. I use the word 'adventure' deliberately, rather than 'chapter,' because this child doesn't just move through life; he lives it fully. He draws people in, leaving a mark wherever he goes. If any five-year-old could rule the world, it would be Sir R.

One memory that still makes me laugh is when his preschool teacher asked him about his future ambitions. Without hesitation and with total confidence, he declared, 'I want to be a FIXER.' The specifics of this mysterious profession were unclear, but it was obvious that chaos followed him wherever he went. The irony still gets me, because his name means 'peace'. Ha! Clearly, I got that one wrong. Sir R was, in truth, Armageddon in disguise.

Our little miracle had sped through his early years, leaving a trail of glittering moments behind him. On the final day of day care he strutted out the doors, singing, 'I'm a big kid now!' I knew this day would come, but I never expected it to arrive quite so soon. I didn't care about the passing years or the increasing number of candles on my birthday cake. The truth was that both of my children were now schoolkids. And while I braced myself for the homework battles ahead, a quiet pang of grief nudged at me, the realisation that my children were becoming less dependent on me. Sir R's fearless march into school, so different from my own childhood spent clinging to safety, lit something inside me: a yearning to reclaim parts of myself; to define a life that honoured both family and purpose.

It's strange how we encourage our children to grow up quickly only to feel shocked when they actually do. I caught myself thinking, *I can't wait until you grow up!* only to swallow those words later. Don't wish time away. One day you'll regret it.

These days, I gently remind other parents to savour the ride. Embrace the sleepless nights. Lean into the tantrums. Because, sooner than you think, it will all be over. These tiny humans will grow into miniature versions of themselves, full of opinions, backchat, and a whole new way of stretching our patience. Someone wise once told me, 'When children are little, you face small problems. As they get older, the problems get bigger.' How true is that!

❤

Sir R was ready to take on school life. Without needing his older brother's guidance or my comforting hand, he strode straight through the school gates, the hum of Sydney traffic fading behind him, showing exactly who was in charge. I exchanged a blank, speechless glance with Master M, both of us quietly stunned by how unfazed he was. Around us, some of his classmates clung to their parents, eyes red and wet with tears. But not Sir R. His priorities were crystal clear: learning could wait; play came first. I watched my little one, once a baby in my arms, stand on the top step of his classroom building, grinning, waving enthusiastically, 'Bye, Mummy! Love you! See you later! Don't forget to pick me up!' And just like that, he turned and marched through the classroom doors.

It hit me like a tidal wave. My breath caught as though I'd swallowed a mouthful of salty seawater, except it was my tears, the ones I'd been fighting so hard to hold back. All morning I'd managed to, but the moment he disappeared from sight, the dam broke. I became that blubbering Kindy mum. Anyone watching would've thought I was the one suffering from separation anxiety, not him.

Sir R was thrilled to be starting big school alongside his older brother. I, on the other hand, was still struggling to let him go. When did he grow up? It felt like only yesterday we brought him home from the hospital. Now, he stood there dressed in his crisp blue uniform, an oversized school bag hanging from his shoulders, his whole being radiating the confidence of a child ready to conquer the world. *Who is this kid? God help me.* Lil A had been rebellious, so what on earth was this one going to be like?

Filled with a cocktail of mixed emotions, and after taking time to truly sit with myself, I finally admitted that the shift work at the gym was no longer serving me. The split hours had worked for a short while, but eventually I found myself struggling to keep up, always rushing between responsibilities and racing against time. I felt as though I was constantly juggling, trying to keep everything in the air. If someone had offered me a job in a circus, I'm certain I would have mastered the act by now. But beneath the humour, I knew the truth – I needed a real change.

♥

I had grown deeply attached to my career. It had given me a renewed sense of purpose; it brought me back to life. Mentally, physically, even spiritually, it nourished me. More than that, it felt meaningful. I was making a tangible, positive impact on others, and that meant more to me than I could ever put into words.

Honestly, it was a miracle I hadn't been fired yet, given everything happening in my life. The constant unpredictability meant I was always swapping shifts, asking for time off, or juggling last-minute emergencies. Splitting myself in two – or three – would have been useful. If only I had that superpower. I've always joked that if I could clone myself, life would be infinitely easier.

It was around this time that I began training with a mentor and a friend. He encouraged me to spread my wings, to picture a future where I could run my own fitness hub. I hesitated at first. Did I really have enough experience to do this on my own? Why would anyone choose to train with me when there were so many more qualified professionals out there? Was I setting myself up for failure before I even began?

My biggest challenge was the internal conflict I faced. On one hand, this new path felt exhilarating, overflowing with possibilities I had never dared to dream of. The thought of creating a fitness studio that aligned beautifully with my family life lit a spark in me. But on the other hand, I was terrified. I had no background in running a business, and self-doubt crept in constantly.

Master M proved to be a truly supportive husband, never doubting my abilities and always offering encouragement. One evening, as I sat at the dinner table tangled in my doubts, he leaned forward and said, 'You've got this. You've always found a way to make things work – look at how you juggle the kids and the gym. This is just the next step.' His words gave me the freedom to explore my passions, even when my confidence was shaky. He trusted my instincts and my decision-making, allowing me to choose paths that aligned with what I believed was best for us. Knowing he was in my corner, cheering me on, gave me that extra push I needed to step outside my comfort zone and dream boldly.

It didn't take long to realise that my fate was already sealed. My path was set. I took a leap of faith, pushing aside my fears and focusing instead on the bigger, brighter picture, one I hadn't even known existed. The possibility of greater flexibility and balance in my life slowly began to eclipse my doubts.

With my mentor's guidance, I found the courage to hand in my resignation. My contract included a three-month, five-kilometre radius restriction on starting my own business, but strangely, it worked in my favour. It gave me time. Time to enjoy Christmas with my family, to breathe, and to settle Sir R into Kindy before diving headfirst into the unknown world of solo entrepreneurship.

Never in my wildest dreams did I imagine I'd one day be my own boss. When I first studied for my Certificate IV in Fitness, the business module felt like a load of nonsense. I had no intention of starting my own venture. And yet, when I dusted off those notes later, I realised just how valuable that module had been. I could finally appreciate all the boxes it helped me tick off.

Registered my business name: Check.

Set up insurance: Check.

First Aid and CPR up to date: Check.

The final step was creating my home gym space, and honestly, it felt like the most exciting part of the entire journey. I kept things simple and intentional, focusing only on what would truly serve me. I wasn't trying to recreate a commercial gym; I just wanted a functional, comfortable space where I could move, grow, and stay consistent.

So, I started with the basics. A squat rack, a sturdy bench and a barbell with plates. A few pairs of dumbbells and kettlebells. Some resistance bands. Nothing fancy, just the essential tools that would support real progress. It was minimal, practical, and exactly what I needed.

With the setup complete and everything falling into place, I realised this was the boldest move I had ever made. For the first time in a long time, I truly believed in myself – and it was exhilarating. As someone who was usually the motivator, hyping others up and pushing them towards their goals, it was a delightful surprise to be on the receiving end of that energy.

I couldn't wait for the waiting period to end and the doors to finally open. I was eager to start transforming women's lives. Every ounce of passion and dedication I had was poured into my fitness studio, my new baby. I had invested everything into creating a space that was successful, supportive, and inspiring.

Launching the social media pages and promoting the event had generated such a buzz. I was overwhelmed by the outpouring of love and support from friends, family, and former clients. Word was spreading fast.

With my opening day on the horizon, I was fuelled by excitement and determination. Yet, on the night before, I lay awake, heart pounding, wondering whether the roller door would open to an empty driveway. What if no one showed up?

That Saturday morning my opening day felt nothing short of glorious. A radiant March sun shone down, filling the day with promise, hope, and fresh beginnings. As the new kid on the block, I was buzzing with excitement, like the Energizer Bunny ready to take centre stage. I hit play on Spotify, letting the music drift through the speakers and fill the space, the steady thump of the bass vibrating softly through the backyard. The faint scent of ink clung to the whiteboard as I finished scribbling the day's workout. I triple-checked that everything was in place before opening the door. My heart was racing and a flutter of nerves danced in my stomach. I pressed the button and watched the roller door slowly rise, half expecting an empty driveway, fearing I might have to close before I even started. But then, they came. One by one, people arrived. Familiar faces. Neighbours. Local residents filling the garage, spilling into the backyard. The space buzzed with life.

The sight of it all revitalised me. It anchored me. In that moment, I stepped fully into who I was meant to be. I wasn't just the trainer anymore; I was the face of my business.

As I greeted the class, my smile did its best to hide the nerves. Every cell in my body trembled with anticipation, but I was determined not to let fear overshadow the moment. I wanted them to feel what training with me would be like: real, energetic, and a little bit cheeky.

My dynamic personality came alive, naturally blending humour and warmth. Conversations bubbled during exercises, creating this beautiful, harmonious energy. How incredible was this? Everyone was connecting, laughing, and supporting one another. There were bursts of laughter, playful f-bombs flying, and smiles stretching across every face. At one point, a client's infectious giggle over a clumsy kettlebell swing set the whole group off, and my signature eyeroll only added fuel to the laughter. It was, without a doubt, the most exhilarating 30-minute high-intensity interval training session I had ever led. Hearts were racing, sweat was dripping, and joy filled the room. I was ecstatic.

By the end of the session, every participant had signed up for a complimentary two-week foundation membership.

I was a proud coach. I was so damn proud of myself.

♥

After I closed the roller door, I sat back with a steaming cup of black coffee. That first sip touched my soul, it was pure bliss. As the warmth settled inside me, I began replaying every moment of the morning like a highlight reel. I realised I couldn't have asked for a better outcome. Had I not taken that leap and trusted myself, I'd probably still be stuck in split-shift hell, juggling work and home life, teetering on the edge of burnout. Instead, I chose belief. I chose to back myself, to embrace creativity and innovation.

I truly believe people come into our lives at the exact moment we need them. And my mentor arrived with divine timing. Just when I was unsure, he gave me guidance and encouragement to do something bigger than I ever imagined for myself. APBT became the perfect platform to express my character and style. I envisioned my studio as a sanctuary: warm, welcoming, and empowering for women of all ages and fitness levels. A place where they could feel supported, seen, and safe. My mission was to breathe new life into the fitness industry, to shake things up and offer something fresh, meaningful, and exciting.

I built my timetable with care, weaving it around school drop-offs, errands, visits to Mum, and the everyday rhythms of family life. Being my own boss was both terrifying and deeply satisfying. Every time the roller door opened, I was reminded that I was helping shape someone's personal journey and truly, there is no greater reward.

My love for fitness was never just about exercise; it was about changing lives. Now, my mission is to build a strong, supportive Fitfam community in Rosebery; a place where women can come together, set aside their worries, grow stronger, physically and mentally, and do it all in a space that is non-competitive and free of judgement. Having felt the intimidation of walking into a commercial gym, I understood that apprehension. I've never been one for make-up at the gym; I'm there to sweat, not to impress. Even as a fitness coach, I've had my own moments of self-doubt, wondering if I was strong enough, lean enough, or if I even looked like I belonged there.

But what truly bothered me wasn't about me, it was watching others suffer in silence. I saw women feeling inadequate because their bodies weren't cooperating – sore shoulders, tight hip flexors. I didn't want my tribe to feel that way. My dream was simple yet deeply personal: to create a space where women could just be themselves. This studio is more than a business to me. It's my sanctuary, my home. And from the moment someone walks through that roller door, I want them to feel it too: the warmth, the ease, the quiet promise that you belong here, just as you are.

Time flew by and before I knew it months had passed, bringing me closer to my first anniversary at APBT. My clients saw me for who I truly was, a down-to-earth woman and a mum with a family to care for, just like them.

It became a running joke that I had bipolar, because when my kids would interrupt mid-class, shouting things like, 'Mum, I'm hungry!' or 'Mum, how do you spell…?' the back sliding door would open, and a little head would peek through, and in an instant, I'd switch from trainer mode to mum mode. It always amazed me how seamlessly I could toggle between the two worlds.

Sir R, now past his toddler years and full of determination, often joined us at the end of class. With his natural charm and infectious enthusiasm, he'd win the ladies over, coaxing them into basketball games or skipping competitions. His energy was irresistible, turning a regular workout into something playful and memorable. They got a two-for-one deal: a session with me and bonus playtime with Sir R, which often became an unexpected extra workout, a two-for-one deal. And if someone couldn't stay to play, Sir R would remember and gently hold them accountable, eagerly asking them to follow through next time.

As membership numbers grew, I realised traditional advertising wasn't necessary. The joy, laughter, and connection in our classes spoke louder than any poster or social media post ever could. Word of mouth became our strongest marketing tool. The energy, camaraderie, and genuine care in our sessions naturally drew in new clients.

My clients became my biggest cheerleaders, and their support and referrals were the heartbeat of our Fitfam community. I worked hard to earn their trust and loyalty, and it proved priceless. Many of them attended multiple sessions each week, and somewhere along the way we became more than just a gym. We became a family. In fact, I often spent more time with these incredible women than I did with my own extended family.

Who would have imagined that exercise could actually be fun? How could 'exercise' and 'fun' even belong in the same sentence? Yet there they were. We had transformed a typically dreaded activity into something captivating, and when the girls started seeing results, the reward only multiplied.

With multiple sessions running, I've never repeated the same workout twice. I still chuckle every time I write 'DRIVEWAY RUNS' on the whiteboard. The girls are convinced my driveway magically grows longer with each session! My signature eyeroll always makes an appearance, and I absolutely thrive on the banter. I challenge my girls, train alongside them, and when we're done, we hype ourselves up with our battle cry: 'WE ARE ELITE!'

It's remarkable what we can accomplish in just 30 minutes, and even more inspiring to witness what the human body is capable of when fuelled by determination. Together, we hit our goals, push our limits, and remind each other to reach for new heights.

Sometimes, Sir R would leap onto the push sled while the girls were mid-set, adding extra resistance just for fun. He'd giggle and carry on like a little pork chop, shouting, 'Go faster! Push me faster!' He was clearly having the time of his life, while the girls found it hilariously torturous.

I often remind my girls that my fitness 'bible' is an endless book of creativity. I pour my heart into designing new sessions, blending different elements like ICE (Intense Cardio Exercise using bodyweight), FIRE (Focused Intense Resistance Exercise for small groups), and women's fitness bootcamps, a 30-minute fusion of cardio and strength. Every session is thoughtfully crafted, with modifications for injuries or pre-existing conditions so each woman can work at her own pace and to her capability. Each individual is unique and that uniqueness is exactly what makes our community so special. One of the things I treasure most about our community is the absence of pressure. The only competition is with ourselves.

I've had to adjust my own workouts because of the strain in my shoulder and the tennis elbow I got from overuse. But that doesn't make me any less of a trainer. If anything, it makes me more human and easier to connect with. By listening to my body and giving it what it needs, I show my girls that strength also comes from rest, patience, and honesty with yourself.

I emphasise the importance of sharing any injuries or discomforts with me so I can tailor the sessions to suit their needs. My clients come to feel better and to improve their daily function, not to add more stress to their lives. That's why I work closely with sports physicians, ensuring everyone receives proper care and can return feeling strong, supported, and in tip-top shape.

The transformation in my life has been nothing short of profound. I've traded juggling multiple shifts for running a thriving home gym studio, creating balance not just for myself, but for my family too. By sharing my passion for fitness, I'm inspiring women and showing my kids that exercise can be both enjoyable and sustainable. As a mum, modelling a healthy lifestyle feels deeply important to me. What makes it even more special is that I get to do it in a way that's fun, real, and accessible – right in our own backyard.

Sometimes the leap that intimidates you the most is exactly the turning point you need. So go ahead, manifest your inner greatness.

Behind the smile

As Jnr A tried on his high school uniform in the change-room, I waited outside, listening to the telltale sounds of struggle, grunts, huffs, and puffs, followed by the soft swoosh of the curtain. How did we get here already? He is no longer a little boy, but a young man in the making. When he finally stepped out, dressed in his grey trousers and light blue shirt, the crisp starch of his collar catching the light, he looked every inch the high school student.

Oh my! I wanted to pull him into a hug, but I held back. I didn't want to embarrass him. He was a big kid now. With his tall stance and newfound confidence, Jnr A looked ready to take on high school, and I couldn't help but marvel at how quickly time had slipped by.

Since our children's school only went up to Year 6, Master M and I had to choose a high school. Our local public school was our backup option, and I had no issues with it. But this time, we made it a family decision. We involved Jnr A, wanting him to feel comfortable and proud of the place he'd call his second home for the next six years.

After attending three open days at a local public school, another public school a little further away, and a Catholic boys' high school, we finally had a clearer picture of our options. At first, I was sceptical about the all-boys' school. In a world that demands emotional intelligence and social awareness, I believed that daily interaction with girls was essential. Master M, who had attended an all-boys school himself, shared similar concerns. He opened up about his own experiences, how he struggled with confidence around girls, and how isolating it could feel. Master M admitted he often felt uneasy approaching girls outside of school, except for family friends.

His honesty shifted something in me. Growing up in a co-ed high school, I valued the social skills I had developed; skills that served me well beyond school. For Jnr A, I wanted an environment rich in cultural diversity and alive with different languages, English flowing into Greek and beyond, boys and girls learning side by side. That's the kind of upbringing I had, where friendships with boys were simply part of everyday life. To be clear, I grew up in a strict household where romantic relationships were out of the question; our friendships were innocent, respectful, and completely normal. And that's exactly the kind of normality I wanted for my children.

The open day visits were a valuable opportunity to evaluate each school's environment in depth. One public school, however, fell short in several areas. Its small size, limited range of subjects, and a less-than-stellar reputation combined to place it at the very bottom of my list. Another public school, however, stood out. Despite being boys-only, it offered a larger campus, a wider range of subjects and sports, and what I especially liked, it sat right next to a girls' school. The students could mingle at lunchtime. Some classes were even taught collaboratively, giving them a healthy taste of co-education.

Still, the large enrolment numbers worried me. With so many students, would a boy like Jnr A get lost in the crowd?

Jnr A's interest in the school seemed to be driven more by friendships and extracurricular activities than academics. Even so, I was grateful that we were involving him in the decision, allowing him to take ownership of this new chapter of his life.

The last school we visited was a small-to-medium-sized all-boys Catholic high school, and it immediately felt like a good fit. As we walked through the gates, we were greeted by a warm, welcoming atmosphere that radiated comfort and safety. There was something about it that touched us all deeply, giving that rare, warm-fuzzy feeling of, 'This feels right.'

Jnr A was instantly drawn to the school's curriculum and sports program. After the tour, he turned to us and said, 'I really like this school. I want to go here.' Master M and I were taken aback. We hadn't expected him to choose this school, especially knowing that most of his primary school friends wouldn't be joining him. Yet, there he was calm, certain, and unwavering.

We chose to support him and take his decision seriously. Pride swelled within us as we watched him choose with his heart, not out of convenience or peer pressure. It was a bold step and such an admirable trait to see in our son.

Jnr A had begun as a bit of a ratbag, but over the years he grew into a bright, confident boy with a strong will. Life in our family home had shaped him, fostering resilience and a quiet empathy that made me certain he would flourish wherever life took him.

The beginning of his high school journey felt momentous. His grandparents and my dad were there for the welcoming ceremony. As he stepped onto the school grounds, joy radiated from him. His excitement for this new chapter was unmistakable. If anyone was nervous, it was me. He, on the other hand, exuded calm and quiet confidence. In that moment, I knew he had made the right choice and my pride overflowed.

At first, everything seemed perfect. He eagerly rode the bus to and from school, forging friendships along the way. His happiness was evident, and as a parent, there is no greater relief than knowing your child is content and thriving.

Until he wasn't.

It slowly came to my attention that he was frequently complaining of stomach pains and asking to stay home. At first I brushed it off, assuming it was just the sensitivity I knew ran in our family. But as time went on, his absences became more frequent. A small part of me wondered whether he might be avoiding school because of unfinished assessments.

We began noticing subtle changes in his behaviour. He grew quieter, more withdrawn, often returning home in a sour mood. Soccer, once his greatest passion, no longer ignited any excitement in him. This was the same child who had lived and breathed the sport, yet now he seemed completely disconnected from it. I couldn't make sense of it.

Soon he refused to take the bus. If I didn't drive him to and from school, he simply wouldn't go. This was so unlike him. Something was clearly wrong, and yet I still couldn't see what it was.

Weeks passed, and the situation became increasingly concerning. We were barely past the halfway point of term one in Year 7, with a long road still ahead. Something had to change. We needed answers. But every attempt to talk to him was met with silence. He shut down completely, insisting everything was fine when it was painfully obvious it wasn't.

One afternoon, just as I was about to start work, I heard Master M's car pull into the driveway. The car doors slammed shut louder than usual and immediately my curiosity was piqued. I waited, bracing myself for raised voices or hurried footsteps, but instead, there was only silence. An eerie, unsettling silence, broken only by the faint hum of traffic from the busy road nearby. The front door didn't slam the way it usually did when emotions were high. Odd. The contradiction left me puzzled. What on earth was going on?

As I made my way towards the hallway, Jnr A appeared in front of me. His eyes were red and glassy. I instinctively stepped back, startled.

'What's happened?' I asked softly.

'Mum, you need to come to school tomorrow...the principal wants to see you,' he said, his voice barely holding steady.

'What the hell have you done?' I blurted out, panic instantly taking over as my mind rushed to the worst possible conclusions.

'Thank God I was at soccer training to pick him up,' Master M said.

'Why?' I asked, my heart thudding in my chest.

'There was a group of kids waiting to jump him after training,' he replied.

A cold wave of horror washed over me. 'I need to know exactly what's going on,' I said, turning to Jnr A. 'What happened, and why would they want to hurt you?'

Jnr A sat beside me, visibly distressed. I had never seen him like this before. Slowly, he began to explain. A particular boy had been bullying him for weeks, both at school and online through social media. Suddenly, the recent 'tummy pains' made sense. I asked to see the messages. Reading them in black and white, I was appalled. My son had been subjected to ruthless bullying.

And all this over what, exactly? From what we could piece together, the boy had a girlfriend. She had stumbled across Jnr A's profile online and commented that he was 'cute.' That apparently sparked jealousy in her boyfriend, and from that moment, the bullying began. Jnr A didn't even know this girl; he had no connection to her at all. I sat there, shaking my head in disbelief. Something so childish had escalated to such a frightening degree.

The next day, I arrived at the school meeting with a knot of apprehension in my stomach, wondering what the principal would tell us. We sat in the stuffy office, tense and on edge, the chair creaking under my fidgeting weight as we waited for our turn. When the principal finally entered, we were greeted warmly, a small reassurance in an otherwise nerve-racking moment.

The principal began to brief us on the situation, referencing the teacher–coach's account of the previous day's events. The teacher had noticed several boys lingering unusually around the field. More concerning, however, was Jnr A's pronounced fear response upon seeing them. Alarm bells had rung immediately. As the session ended and the boys approached, Jnr A's panic intensified, confirming the teacher's concerns.

Usually, Master M would have waited in the car for Jnr A, but by coincidence he happened to be outside and witnessed the incident firsthand. What a blessing in disguise. The teacher approached him, explained what had happened, and mentioned that a formal report would be filed, hence why we were sitting in the principal's office that day.

I leaned back, fuming. Okay...so what was actually going to be done about this? I needed a resolution. We couldn't go on like this. I shared with the principal everything I had observed over the past few weeks, highlighting how all the pieces of the puzzle were finally coming together. He proposed bringing the boys in for an open conversation to clarify the situation. I agreed, waiting anxiously to hear the outcome.

From that day on, Jnr A didn't feel safe catching the bus. I had to drop him off at the school gate in the mornings. In the afternoons, it wasn't enough for me to wait in the car; he needed me to walk to the gate, meet him and escort him back. This was not normal.

The meeting with the boys reportedly went well, though it was unclear whose perspective this reflected. In the classroom, it seemed as though they had put their differences aside. But the real torment persisted on social media. As a precaution, I advised Jnr A to block all relevant accounts to prevent further contact.

I distinctly recall one day as if it were yesterday. I was working on my laptop at the dining room table, sunlight streaming through the back sliding door, when my phone dinged with a message from Jnr A. My heart leapt; he was supposed to be in class. Panicked, I opened the message. I could barely comprehend it at first.

'Mum...one of the boys said he has a knife.' Was this a joke? Was he serious?

I jumped out of my skin, a mix of fury and fear flooding through me. I immediately contacted the school, insisting they remove him from class. I told them I would pick him up due to the potential threat. I couldn't confirm whether the claim was true or simply a scare tactic, but the school's response mirrored my concern. They were equally bewildered.

My thoughts raced uncontrollably as I rushed to the school, my hands trembling on the wheel during the tense drive. A torrent of anger and fear built inside me, like a volcano ready to erupt. The idea that my child, or any child, could go through such a traumatic experience was utterly crushing. I felt shattered, ground down into dust. To think he had been silently carrying all of this inside him was unbearable. My stomach churned, yet I knew I had to remain calm, level-headed, and strong for him. As his mother, I needed to be his protector, his safe haven amidst the chaos.

I pulled up at the school, slammed on the brakes, jumped out, and let the car door crash behind me. I stormed through the office doors, no greetings, no pleasantries, just me, Mrs Panteli, A's mum, letting the thunder roar right out of my mouth: 'Where is my son?'

I made it crystal clear that A would not return to school until I was satisfied the matter was being handled properly. I was assured the situation would be investigated thoroughly.

Days went by. Nothing. Did they even do anything about it? Who knows. I called the school multiple times, left messages, sent emails. No response. Absolutely disgusting.

Finally, after a few days, the principal called. My fury bubbled as his voice crackled through the phone, explaining that they had tried to contact the other students' parents but were unsuccessful. Hmm...weird, and not good enough.

Meanwhile, I explored options to transfer Jnr A to a different school. Term 1 was drawing to a close, and it was disheartening to see him struggle so early in his high school journey. Not even a term in and he was already facing a grenade of a start. Talk about a shit beginning, right?

Master M and I made the joint decision to transfer him to my private co-ed high school, removing him from the toxic nightmare he had been living. He was relieved to leave that environment behind.

He had expected us to leave him there to fight his own battles, because we've always emphasised facing life's challenges head-on. But this wasn't a challenge; it was a catastrophe. There was no way we could leave our child in an unsafe environment. We faced the problem with tenderness and an unwavering focus on our child's welfare. As parents, our children are everything. The mere thought of them in pain is unbearable. I couldn't breathe, let alone live.

Watching him slip away from himself was like squeezing a lemon directly onto an open wound, the sting piercing straight to my core. His radiant smile had disappeared. The spirited, mischievous boy I once knew was trapped, muted, and distant, leaving me struggling to recognise my own child.

When he began attending his new school, a fresh beginning unfolded. The bitter memories of the previous term were behind him. He was determined to move forward, unaffected. The school, fully informed of his circumstances, prioritised his safety. He felt protected, and that was all that mattered.

Being the new kid is always a mix of nerves and excitement. He received attention from his female peers (eye roll), forged friendships with the boys, and gradually found his rhythm in school life. One evening at dinner, his proud grin as he recounted scoring a goal in soccer lit up the room, the spark of the old Jnr A returning. Although the transition presented obstacles, he tackled them with determination and grit. Some teachers, who remembered my own schooldays, were struck by his athleticism, a stark contrast to my own disinterest in sports.

Jnr A, once a victim of bullying, has emerged as a strong, resilient young individual, tempered and strengthened by adversity. I recall the countless sleepless nights, the endless worries, and the heartache that came with his struggles. Yet now I watched him radiate happiness and confidence, and it is clear that every difficult decision, every moment of uncertainty, was a stepping stone to this milestone. Our choice to remove him from that toxic environment was undeniably the right one. He was thriving in a supportive, safe, and nurturing educational space.

Seeing his restored happiness and confidence brought us immense relief. The dark days were behind us, and for the first time in weeks, we could breathe. Jnr A had found his footing, and we knew he would continue to grow and succeed. Each morning, as I watched him stride through the school gates, pride and gratitude swelled in me. Challenges would still arise, of course, but I felt certain that together we could face whatever came our way.

❤

That heart-wrenching experience became a turning point for our family, forcing us to confront the importance of open, honest communication. It was painful, yes, but it ultimately brought us closer together. Jnr A learned that he could trust us with anything, knowing we would support him every step of the way. As a parent, there is no greater joy than seeing your child feel safe enough to share their thoughts and feelings with you.

When they stumble, we work together to find a way forward. Honesty is the foundation of our relationship, and I want my children to always know that they can count on me to listen, guide, and support them. Becoming a parent means preparing your children for the world, not shielding them from it. I am a tough love mum, but my boys know that my love and support are unwavering. I owe this unshakable resolve to my dad, who taught me the value of resilience and compassion. Thank you, Papa.

CHAPTER 16

My mother's legacy

For me, life's greatest pleasure lies in indulging my tastebuds in the rich aromas and flavours of mouthwatering food. True solace is found in the kitchen, where the sizzle of onions and garlic fills the air as I prepare meals for my family. The warmth of the stove, the soft clinking of pots and pans, and the vibrant colours of fresh vegetables create a symphony of sensations that transport me to a place of peace and joy. The kitchen is my sanctuary (aside from the gym) where I delight in the simple yet profound act of cooking.

I am forever grateful for the lessons passed down to me, teaching me how to prepare the most amazing dishes from our Greek culture. Yet one dish stands out above all: my mother's famous chicken pastitsio, the best Greek pasta bake anyone has ever tasted. The layered tenderness of pasta, the flavourful chicken bathed in her homemade diced tomato sauce, topped with rich bechamel and baked to golden perfection, evokes memories of family gatherings and celebrations. I can smell it now, the aroma of the oven mingling with melted haloumi and a hint of cinnamon, a scent that lingers like our heritage. She would spend hours in the kitchen, carefully layering each element, the anticipation building as the bubbling golden dish emerged.

I remember being a bit of a slob back then, getting splattered with vibrant tomato sauce while Mum, always pristine in her apron, insisted on precision. At the time, I thought her fussing was a chore, but now I see it as one of the greatest gifts she ever gave me. Today, as I recreate her chicken pastitsio, I feel her presence in the kitchen, guiding my hands, softly reminding me to layer the pasta and sauce just so.

Her handwritten recipe book, *G's Recipes*, fills me with warmth. The page for chicken pastitsio is dog-eared and stained; notes scribbled in the margins. I can hear her voice reminding me: 'Make sure you use penne!' and *'Vale poliko haloumi'*, don't skimp on the haloumi. Every time I reach for a tea towel and see the pink book tucked in the drawer, my heart swells with love and gratitude. It feels as if she is still with me, guiding me silently, lovingly.

❤

Over time, my mum's health declined. She began losing weight excessively and struggling to swallow. Mealtimes became a challenge: her food had to be carefully cut into small, chewable pieces to prevent choking. After thorough consultations with occupational therapists, we were forced to transition to a soft-food plan. This shift was brutal. Not only was she paralysed and immobile, but now the simple joy of tasting food as she once had was gone.

Trays of food would arrive at lunch and dinner, and my stomach would instinctively churn. Any anticipation of satisfying hunger turned to disappointment when confronted with pureed mince and mashed potato. Watching her eat, spoonful by spoonful, struck every chord of my heart. If we were repulsed by it, I could only imagine how she must have felt.

Thickening her fluids brought its own challenges. We would lift the cup and guide the straw to her lips, but honestly, how could that ever quench her thirst?

Meals that should have lasted 20 minutes often stretched to an hour. Even with pureed food, her body instinctively rolled it around her mouth, breaking it down further, making it safer to swallow. It was a quiet reminder of how miraculous our bodies are, always striving to protect us. This demanded patience, something I struggled with at times. Yet patience was the only gift I could truly offer her. None of this was within her control. And still, with every spoonful, she whispered, 'God bless you.' Her gratitude in the midst of so much loss was humbling. How could a woman facing such misfortune remain so strong-willed?

More than once, we rushed her to hospital with aspiration pneumonia, the cruel result of her swallowing difficulties and limited mobility.

As the main family contact with the nursing home, I made it my duty to protect everyone else from the bluntness of medical updates. Calls came to me first, giving me time to soften the truth before sharing it with Dad. Yet every time their number flashed on my screen, my stomach sank, bracing for the worst.

During a visit one afternoon, she seemed especially lethargic. Her eyes drooped and her body seemed drained of energy. I told myself it was her poor food intake and that fatigue was to be expected. Still, seeing her so diminished was painful. And yet, hand in hand, we prayed together. With what little strength she had, she finished the 'Our Father' with a resounding 'Amen.'

Later that day, while I was getting the boys ready for soccer training, the phone rang. My heart beat in rhythm with the ringtone as I read the nursing home's number. The nurse's voice was calm but weighted: my mother's condition had worsened, and the doctor was on his way. Without hesitation, I turned to Dad.

'It's Mum. I'm going to the nursing home. Stay here, I'll keep you posted.' I grabbed the keys and bolted. In my haste, I flung the car door straight into my hip. The shock shot through me like fire. I wanted to scream, but time was too precious. The slam echoed, *swoosh...slam*, a reminder of my own clumsiness in the chaos.

Clutching my hip, I hobbled through the corridor towards her room. Normally the home was calm, but that day it buzzed with urgency. Nurses moved quickly, exchanging clipped updates, their voices overlapping like a rally at Wimbledon. I stood back, trying to catch every word. Then my phone rang again, Dad.

'*Ela, Papa,*' I said softly. 'I'm here. Nothing yet. The doctor's with Mum now. I'll call you back soon.'

I had always tried to shield my parents, to carry the weight of worry for them. Nothing pained me more than seeing them worry more than they needed to. For now, I held that weight alone, my voice calm, my heart breaking. It was better for my dad to stay at home and remain calm until we knew more about what was happening. The GP finished examining Mum and walked over to me, the stethoscope hanging around his neck.

'Andrea, your mum is really unwell. We need to send her to hospital. She's developed severe dysphagia, which is preventing her from swallowing. I recommend considering a PEG tube to help with feeding. With constant aspiration, pneumonia remains a serious risk. Let's focus on what's best for her.' His tone was calm, but his eyes carried genuine concern.

I took a deep breath, *inhale, hold, exhale. Three, two, one.* My throat tightened, my eyes filled. Even swallowing my own saliva felt impossible.

When the ambulance arrived to transfer Mum to hospital, I rang Dad. I softened my voice as much as I could, not wanting to alarm him.

'*Ela*, Papa. Don't panic. They're taking Mum in because of her swallowing problems. The specialist will assess her and decide the best approach. Meet me at the hospital.'

One blessing of ambulance transport is bypassing the long wait. Mum was quickly assessed by the emergency department doctors and sent for scans. Before the results were back, an occupational therapist carried out a bedside swallow test. My heart splintered into pieces. Once she could chew steak, peel her beloved prawns, savour all the foods she loved. Now, she struggled with pureed fruit, custard, and even thickened fluids left her choking. I had never seen her so diminished.

When the ED doctors returned, Dad and I leapt to our feet. Their conclusion was clear: Mum's case would be handed to the gastroenterology team to discuss inserting a PEG tube. For now, she needed close monitoring. Aspiration pneumonia had set in, and she had to recover before any surgery could be attempted.

She lay motionless, fully conscious but not always grasping the gravity of it all. Still, I explained every step to her, including her in every conversation. Even when she only nodded, she was part of the decision-making. More than anything we wanted her to remain pain-free, without distress.

By then the children were older, old enough to understand Yiayia's illness, and old enough to notice how often I was absent. My life became a rhythm of hospital visits, hurried showers at home, and teaching classes in between. Dad and I tag-teamed so Mum was never alone.

After three weeks battling pneumonia, we turned her hospital room into our second home. We came to know the nurses by name. Slowly, Mum began to recover. Her cheeks regained their warmth, her familiar glow returning. In the fourth week the specialist team scheduled the PEG tube surgery. They brought in a Greek interpreter to review the consent form with Dad, ensuring he fully understood the risks, even though Mum herself spoke excellent English. I stood quietly in the corner as the words were translated, my body swaying as though the floor beneath me had shifted. Then the surgeon posed the question I dreaded most.

'What are your wishes in the event of complications during surgery?'

The words hung in the air like a stone dropping into water. I couldn't contain myself. 'What do you mean?' I blurted, denial coursing through me. He looked at me with deep compassion in his eyes.

'In the event of a complication, if your mother's heart were to stop on the table, would you want us to attempt resuscitation?'

It was as though a curtain of deja vu fell over me. Flashbacks stormed my mind: the childhood nightmares, the whispered talk of divorce papers, my mother nearly signing her freedom from a marriage. And now, a vivid memory of us in the kitchen, her hands guiding mine to layer her famous chicken pastitsio, her laughter filling the air as tomato sauce splattered my cheek. But this was different. Now it was about releasing her soul entirely. My throat seized, my eyes blurred. The words I feared most hovered on the edge of the surgeon's lips.

The interpreter translated the surgeon's words with visible reluctance. Hearing them once was painful enough; hearing them a second time in Greek was just about unbearable. As the words lingered in the air, my eyes locked onto Mum. She slowly shook her head, side to side, a firm, unmistakable refusal of resuscitation.

With age comes wisdom, and I have since come to appreciate the strength behind her choice. Her suffering had already been prolonged beyond reason. How much more strain could her fragile body take?

I held my breath, forcing composure. Quietly, I walked out of the room, desperate to hide my tears from her. A nurse followed and placed a calm hand on my shoulder, rubbing my back gently as muffled sobs escaped.

'Stay strong, for your mum's sake,' she whispered.

'I'm trying…I'm trying. I just don't know how much more I can take,' I whispered back, low enough so Mum wouldn't hear. I steadied myself. However heavy the grief, I knew I had to be her strength.

Mum's PEG surgery was set for the next morning. The thought that she might never eat by mouth again, never taste the comfort and joy of food and instead rely on a tube in her stomach, was almost too much to bear.

❤

In Greek culture, food is so much more than sustenance. It is connection, love, memory, laughter, and belonging. It is the clatter of cutlery at family tables, the fragrance of cinnamon and tomato in the oven, the chatter over coffee and sweet pastries. For my mother to lose that was not only to lose pleasure but also part of her identity. Despite this cruel deprivation, my mother, always a figure of elegance and grace, reminding me of Princess Diana in her poise, continued to face her daily battles with astonishing tenacity.

That afternoon, I phoned our local priest, believing a blessing would give her peace before surgery. Father A, one of the most compassionate priests I have ever known, was deeply moved by her situation and came promptly. He offered prayers, a blessing, and finally Holy Communion. As he entered, Mum's face softened into a gentle smile, and the atmosphere in the room lifted. Hope, love, and quiet strength filled the air. To our amazement, when the Holy Communion touched her lips, it slid down her throat with ease, without the usual struggle to swallow. It felt like a miracle, a sign of God's presence with her and a quiet reassurance that she was not walking in to surgery alone.

That night, sleep evaded me entirely. My mind was restless with anticipation, fear, and prayer. Before dawn broke, I was at the hospital, determined to greet her with fresh energy and faith. I wanted and needed to be there before she was wheeled into surgery. I refused to let her go without us reciting the 'Our Father' together.

With a strength that belied her fragile frame, she prayed aloud, her voice carrying passion and certainty. She finished with a resounding 'AMEN,' a smile resting on her lips. I was perched on the edge of her bed, her hand clasped in mine, when the porter arrived to escort her down. I expected to be left behind, but to my surprise he said, 'You can come too.'

Relief washed over me. With a sudden lightness, I jumped up.

'Mum, I'm coming, wait for me.'

She reached her hand out from beneath the blanket, and together we walked the corridor, hand in hand.

'You're going to be all right, Mum,' I told her with certainty.

She nodded firmly, her eyes clear, her lips whispering without sound: '*Yes, I am!*'

I had assumed I would need to leave Mum at the door while she was prepared for surgery, but once again I was pleasantly surprised. They allowed me to accompany her into the prep room. Because Mum was almost non-verbal, the staff encouraged me to stay close to help keep her calm. I remained by her side until the anaesthetic was about to be administered, its sterile scent sharp in the air, my hand faintly trembling as I held hers. The moment they asked me to step away I told myself to put on my 'big girl pants', but in truth, they slipped off at once, leaving me exposed and vulnerable. I kissed Mum on the forehead and squeezed her hand tightly. I couldn't bring myself to say goodbye. Instead, I whispered, 'See you later,' and she nodded in agreement.

The surgical procedure lasted several hours. My dad arrived midway through the operation, though it was still early morning. Knowing how long the day ahead would be, I had insisted he rest after a late night, but his presence reassured me. When I stood to ask for news, the nurse reached me first, smiling as she said the words I longed to hear: the surgery had gone well and Mum was in recovery. I turned to Dad, and in that instant, a tear glistened in his eye, his quiet nod echoing my relief. Memories of childhood rushed back. Hugging him tightly, I silently affirmed, 'She's alright, Papa. She's going to be alright.'

Not long after, I spotted a hospital bed being wheeled down the corridor. Pacing nervously, I recognised Mum's hair and cried out, 'She's here!' She lay still, her face peaceful, though she was groggy from the anaesthetic. Relief flooded me until my eyes caught the tube. I had forgotten the PEG insertion, forgotten the tangle of tubes that would now be part of her reality. The sight sent a rush of blood to my head. A stand beside the bed held equipment waiting to be connected, a stark reminder of how life had changed.

When the bustle quietened, I climbed onto Mum's bed, cradling her head against my chest as I gently stroked her hair. Dad had stepped out for a walk, leaving just the two of us. I whispered softly, unsure if she could hear, tears slipping silently into her hair. Then I felt it: her thumb brushing lightly across the back of my hand. The touch was delicate, almost angelic, and it raised goosebumps along my arms. With it came the faintest voice: 'I'm here.'

Her eyes fluttered open and joy surged through me. This time, I wanted her to see my tears, not of sorrow, but of relief and gratitude.

'Yes, you are here. You're not leaving me,' I told her.

As she squeezed my hand, she whispered, 'Keep cooking, my love,' a faint echo of her kitchen legacy, tying us back to those pasticho days.

Caring for Mum has shown me the extraordinary power of love. Even in suffering, her spirit has been a constant teacher. The kitchen, once filled with laughter and the aromas of our shared meals, remains a symbol of our bond, our resilience, and our faith. Strength, I have learned, is not loud or unyielding; it is revealed in the grace with which we endure adversity.

My mother's legacy lives on in every prayer, every act of kindness, every moment of quiet courage. Her love continues to guide me, and I am endlessly grateful for the time we shared. To honour her memory is to face life's trials with the same unwavering spirit she embodied, carrying forward her light through resilience, compassion, and faith.

CHAPTER 17

Perspective in pandemic times

I'm not someone who settles for half-full. I'm the kind of person who overflows, who strives to live fully rather than accept mediocrity.

It was a warm summer Monday evening in Sydney's Inner South, the hum of distant traffic filtering through the open roller door of my APBT as a soft breeze cooled our post-workout glow. During our cool down, I seized the moment to make a big announcement I'd been itching to share. Though it had nothing to do with training or APBT, my ladies are my people. I can share anything with them: the highs, the lows, and everything in between. They know more about me than my own family sometimes. Without judgement, always with love, acceptance, and encouragement, they've been my fiercest cheerleaders, inspiring me to strive and uncover the best version of myself.

This felt like the perfect moment to share my news. As we chatted away, I eased into my favourite stretch, the pigeon pose, and casually dropped, 'Sooooo, girls, because I have all the time in the world (cue sarcasm and a giggle), Master M and I have decided to buy into a restaurant.'

Their faces were priceless. The room froze for a second before erupting into noise, like a rainbow had suddenly appeared.

'What?!'

'No way!'

'That's incredible!'

They bombarded me with words, their enthusiasm tumbling out in disbelief. None of them had ever imagined I'd step into hospitality, and honestly, neither had I. Most assumed I was about to announce APBT's closure, not the start of a brand-new venture.

One client, herself the co-owner of a restaurant, cafe, and catering business, fixed me with her crystal-blue eyes, laughed, and said, 'Are you crazy? Pregnancy would've been the easier choice!'

Yet deep down I knew this was alignment, a sense of purpose nudging me forward. The time felt right. We'd kept our lips sealed until the contracts and loans were finalised, but after months of hurdles, we finally signed on the dotted line. Suddenly, we weren't just dreaming. We were proud co-owners of an Eastern Mediterranean restaurant.

The idea hadn't come out of nowhere. For over a year, our cousins, who would now be our business partners, had joked about joining forces. We'd tossed around business ideas, brainstormed names, and mused over locations. Then, as though the stars had conspired, the opportunity to buy into an established restaurant we already adored fell into our laps.

February 2020 marked the milestone. Fittingly, it coincided with our 15th wedding anniversary, a celebration within a celebration. Signing the contracts wasn't just a legal step; it was the sealing of a dream. Our families were already tightly knit. G and Master M were second cousins, and she and I had grown up Greek dancing side by side. Her husband, D, was like a brother to Master M, and we always joked that I was his *nouna*, his godmother. Being married into a Cypriot family, he loved the meaning behind faith, family, love, culture, and tradition.

The joke grew over time, then during a family holiday it turned into a full mock christening, complete with laughter, cheering, and a loud leap into the pool. When they were together, our four children behaved like siblings, fighting one moment, clinging to each other the next.

Now we were about to merge our everyday lives with a business partnership, something that could either make us stronger or drive us mental. But as we stood in that little restaurant in Sydney's Inner West, ready to begin this new chapter, all I felt was a rush of excitement. We weren't just building a business; we were shaping a shared future.

The restaurant closed briefly for renovations, giving us the chance to refine its aesthetic and add our own touch to an already beautiful space. With the clock against us, we worked relentlessly, determined to be ready on time. One of the boldest changes we made was to add a takeaway menu, a significant shift in our business strategy. This move transformed what had been purely fine dining into something more relaxed and family-friendly, making it accessible to more people. It also gave us the chance to weave in dishes rooted in our homeland, deepening our cultural connection through food.

Master M and I had no prior experience in hospitality. We stepped into unknown territory and had to learn fast, everything from running the point-of-sale system to making coffee, clearing tables, and understanding restaurant procedures. After weeks of long hours and endless effort, adding our final touches of 'spice,' the time came to swing open the heavy glass door to the public.

That Friday night, the grand reopening was electric. My heart was pounding, and I was frothing with excitement, watching family, friends, and our local community pour in. The joy on their faces was priceless. Guests told us they felt transported back to Cyprus. Our chef's creations were flawless, each dish carrying flavours that stirred my own memories of the village. Pride welled in my heart as I imagined my yiayia's spirit smiling down on me with warmth and approval: '*Bravo, koukla mou.*' (Bravo, my sweet girl.)

Just as we were beginning to settle into our new routines, balancing full-time jobs with the added responsibility of managing payroll, accounts, staff, and facilities, we were blindsided by a news story about a strange dish on the other side of the world. I remember sitting outside the restaurant with G, a cup of tea in hand, chatting casually as the news played.

'Bat soup?' I spluttered. 'Wtf is wrong with people? That's frickin' disgusting!' We laughed it off, not realising how those words would come back to haunt us.

On a Sunday afternoon a few weeks later, as we prepared to close for the day, the news broke: COVID-19 had reached Australian shores. Not long after, the Prime Minister addressed the nation. The words rang in my ears: 'We are entering lockdown.'

That night is etched into my memory as though it happened yesterday. The four of us sat there in shock, our minds racing. We had just reopened our business, only to be forced to shut it down. Panic consumed us as we tried to imagine how we would survive this blow. Meanwhile, our four kids were jumping around the restaurant's dining room, high-fiving each other as though they'd won the lottery. For them, school closures meant holidays; for us, it felt like doomsday. Their dreams were coming true while our nightmares had only just begun.

❤

As the restaurant faced restrictions, my anxiety turned towards APBT. The weight of both businesses pressed heavily on me, but the gym felt even more personal. Unlike the restaurant, which was shared among four partners, APBT was mine alone, my baby. Its survival depended entirely on me, and I felt a profound sense of responsibility to my clients. They had always looked to me for strength, and I knew they needed me more than ever now.

The hardest part was the sudden silence. Overnight, I lost the daily connection with my clan, the faces I saw every single day. I sat at my desk trying to draft a message to our private Fitfam Facebook group, but every attempt ended with me deleting the words. I, who never struggled to find something to say, was suddenly speechless. How could I tell them the roller doors would close indefinitely? Would there even be a business to come back to when this storm passed?

The thought was suffocating. Everything I had worked so hard for felt like it was crumbling before my eyes, and I was powerless to stop it. The absence of my team was already palpable, and if I was struggling, I could only imagine what they were going through, isolated in their homes. APBT had always been more than just a gym. For many, it was their sanctuary, their community, their lifeline. Our classes offered far more than exercise; they were a place for laughter, release, and connection.

It struck me how quickly isolation can creep in when circumstances force it upon us. And in that moment, I realised my people needed me to fight harder than ever before. Failure to support my team was never an option. With time slipping through our fingers, self-pity was a luxury we simply could not afford. I had to adjust swiftly. To keep training alive, we transitioned to Zoom almost overnight. Though I've never been particularly tech-savvy, together we stumbled through the initial frustrations, laughing at our glitches, frozen screens, and muffled mics, guiding each other patiently until what once felt intimidating became second nature. Necessity made us quick learners; in no time, we were seasoned pros in the dreaded world of online platforms. It felt as though we had stepped into an entirely new era.

♥

Meanwhile, at the restaurant, in-house dining was shut down immediately. For the first time we truly appreciated the decision we had made months earlier to introduce a takeaway menu. Was it foresight or simply coincidence that our new concept launched just before the lockdown? Either way, it was nothing short of divine timing.

What initially looked like a crushing setback revealed itself to be a blessing in disguise. Our takeaway menu was already running, ready for customers to order. The next step was obvious: an online ordering system. We wasted no time uploading our menu and adding a marketplace feature so customers could order items packaged for convenience. What could have been disastrous became an unexpected opportunity, widening our reach and streamlining our operations. Through it all, leaning on each other made the challenge bearable. Amen to divine timing.

Our dining room, once filled with conversation and clinking glasses, was transformed overnight into a classroom. Tables that had welcomed customers were now covered in laptops, schoolbooks, and half-eaten snacks. It didn't take long for us to realise that teaching was not our strength. Honestly, I take my hat off to teachers. If anyone deserves a pay rise, it's them. I don't know how they do it, day in and day out. Within minutes of sitting down, one of the kids needed a break, a snack, or a rest, and our patience was tested in ways we never imagined.

And yet, in certain moments, having the kids alongside us proved to be a gift. Their innocence brought light to the chaos. Watching them laugh, play, and make the best of a difficult time shifted our focus. Instead of fixating on what we had lost, we began to see the glass as full, not empty. Their joy reminded us to hold onto gratitude, even when everything else felt uncertain. As a united family, we knew that one day this season would become part of our story, the lockdown memories we would retell for years to come.

The children persevered with their schoolwork online and surprised us with how resilient they could be. They helped with real tasks too, answering calls, taking orders, and even mastering coffee-making. And let me tell you, they made a darn good coffee. Sir R, in particular, discovered a knack for frothing milk for cappuccinos and lattes, a skill that far outshone his enthusiasm for homework. Their academic motivation may have wavered, but this COVID-19 chapter gifted them lessons no classroom could teach: resilience, adaptability, and responsibility. Watching their determination and willingness to help, we drew strength from them. In many ways, they carried us through.

Watching Sir R struggle with his schoolwork stirred up a storm inside me. Worry and frustration gnawed at my heart, and questions circled endlessly: Am I doing enough to help him? Am I failing him? I felt like a ship adrift without an anchor, powerless to guide him to safe waters. Master M and I shared anxious glances, both silently asking the same terrifying questions: Is something wrong with our boy? Have we overlooked something vital?

Reaching out to his teacher, I hoped for reassurance and clear direction. Instead, the communication was slow and vague, leaving me more unsettled than before. Each delay, each unanswered query, felt like another dead end in a maze with no map. I couldn't help but wonder: why hadn't these struggles been noticed earlier? Had we missed a crucial window for intervention? Determined to find answers, I contacted a psychologist for an assessment. When the initial feedback suggested possible dyslexia or dysgraphia, my stomach lurched. Fear coursed through me. What would this mean for his future? And yet, beneath the fear, I sensed we were on the verge of uncovering something important.

The day the results arrived, I realised I'd been holding my breath for weeks. Relief and regret hit in the same moment. His high IQ was being smothered not by inability, but by boredom. He wasn't struggling because he couldn't learn, he was struggling because he wasn't being challenged. Relief flooded me; we finally had answers, but it was swiftly followed by the sting of guilt. What if we'd known sooner? What if we'd pushed harder earlier? The weight of those 'what ifs' was heavy, but I knew I couldn't stay there.

Looking at Sir R, I resolved to focus not on what we had missed but on what we could do now. The road ahead would not be easy, but I was determined to be his advocate, his rock, the unruffled guide he needed.

As if life hadn't already thrown enough at me, chaos turned up the volume, as it often did. One evening, utterly drained, I was helping Sir R with a maths problem that had us both stumped, the kids' 'Mum, I'm bored' echoing in the background, when I received a text from the bank about a suspicious transaction on my business debit card. I brushed it aside, telling myself I'd deal with it in the morning.

But the next day, the message gnawed at me. I casually logged in to our online business account, expecting to clear up a minor blip. The homepage loaded and my jaw dropped. Our funds were gone. Vanished. *Where the fuck did they go?* My heart pounded as I clicked frantically through the statements, fingers shaky on the keyboard. Multiple debits appeared, transactions neither I nor any of my partners had authorised. To make matters worse, all four linked cards had been used, even though only one was active. How on earth was this possible?

Fearing the worst, I anxiously wrestled with how to break the news to my business partners, only to have the tension overwhelm me. I abruptly burst into tears. Our account had been hacked. Completely distraught, I reached for the phone and called G. Between the two of us, I am undeniably the one who stresses over everything. Does that surprise you?

G, calm and level-headed as ever, immediately tried to soothe my panic. She began brainstorming solutions, obvious things, yet I couldn't see them in my distress.

'Let's call the bank, block the cards, and fight to get our money back,' she said, calm and reassuring. And just like that, the fog of anxiety began to lift, replaced by a sense of focus I hadn't felt in hours.

After wrapping up my conversation with G, I phoned the bank to explain the situation, the representative's dismissive tone grating through the line. To my dismay, their first response was to shift the blame onto our children, insinuating that they may have used our cards without permission. Their words were not only dismissive, but insulting. Under strict lockdown, our kids hadn't been anywhere. They were all minors, hardly out gallivanting, buying cigarettes from the tobacconist and shoes from Campbelltown, a place we didn't even live near to. The lack of compassion enraged me further.

I insisted the bank go through the statement with me, line by line. Only then did their tone change and the fraud team become involved. The numbers were staggering, an astonishing $10,000 had been stolen from our account. For a struggling small business, this was a devastating blow. While a figure like that might seem insignificant to a large corporation, for us it meant sleepless nights, bills in jeopardy, and our livelihood hanging by a thread. Our accounts were frozen, our cards cancelled, and we waited impatiently for replacements. Yet even with our accounts supposedly secure, more fraudulent withdrawals appeared.

What the actual fuck?! How could this be happening again? Transactions, including cash withdrawals from an ATM, were showing up despite the fact we had no physical cards. The audacity was staggering. Seething, I phoned the bank again, spitting words through clenched teeth, fuelled by frustration and betrayal, my hands shaking as I dialled the police next. Still, the bank's insinuations circled back to us, as though we were the ones at fault. It was as if they spoke another language, one that refused to acknowledge the glaring evidence of fraud.

We were convinced it was an inside job. The bank denied, deflected, and blamed us yet again. Furious, we reported the theft to the police. Persistence eventually paid off: CCTV footage from the ATM proved none of us four business partners were involved. Vindication at last – and damning proof of the bank's negligence. Surprise, surprise.

With the police intervening, we were eventually reimbursed. But by then, our trust was broken. We closed our business account and moved to another bank, disgusted by the treatment we'd received. You hear about these things happening to others but never imagine they'll happen to you. Who was I kidding? My life felt like one big shitstorm.

Eight weeks crawled by, each day dragging longer than the last, until finally restrictions began to ease. That first hint of normality felt magical. By then the kids were desperate to return to school. They were sick of online learning, tired of our constant supervision, and longing for their classmates. And, truth be told, the feeling was mutual. We parents were desperate for breathing space. The endless chorus of:

'Mum, I'm bored.' 'Mum, I'm hungry.' 'Mummm!'

Oufff! I was ready to change my name.

When our restaurant was finally permitted to reopen, the government-imposed limit of just 10 patrons at a time felt like a cruel joke. At first, I questioned whether it was worth it. But then I saw the faces of our customers, eyes lit with gratitude simply to sit, eat, and connect. I realised they weren't only hungry for food; they were starving for human connection. COVID-19 had left so many isolated and lonely. Sharing a meal, even in such limited circumstances, offered warmth and comfort, a reminder that life, though altered, could still be lived together. Our restaurant became more than a business; it became a haven, a place where people could find solace in good food and warm company.

As I watched our patrons find comfort in each other, a lump rose in my throat. It was a bittersweet reminder of how fragile human connection is, and how precious our role was in nurturing it. Every laugh, every smile, every conversation felt like an act of quiet defiance against the isolation that had threatened to consume us. In that moment, I realised our presence, our willingness to listen, to care, and to connect was a gift, not only to our patrons, but to ourselves.

Weeks blurred into months, and COVID-19 went from being a terrifying unknown to an experience we had simply lived through. For many, it became a story to tell. For us, it was both survival and lesson.

❤

At APBT, we adapted to the convenience of online training, and while the women in my fitness classes enjoyed working out from home, I felt an ache. I missed their presence, their hugs, the intensity of our shared sessions. The true value of something often only becomes clear once it's gone.

The hardest loss was visitation with my Mum. Losing that connection was like losing a lifeline. I feared for her safety and wellbeing, trapped inside sterile walls with only the hum of silence for company. Our video calls were precious but painfully short. I'd search her face for glimmers of recognition as her voice, once warm and strong, emerged as barely a whisper. She'd respond with, 'Yes, love' or 'God bless you,' her words separated by long pauses. I'd fill the silences with stories, but what I missed most was touch. The gentle squeeze of her hand. The soft brush of my fingers through her thinning hair. Sometimes my ring would snag, and she'd flinch with a soft 'ouch.' My heart would drop, and I'd murmur, 'Sorry, Mum.' Her reply was always the same: 'It's okay, love.' That quiet forgiveness was a balm.

I'd play Greek music during our calls, watching her eyes flicker with recognition, her lips lifting into the faintest smile. Those moments of connection felt sacred, but they also deepened the ache of distance. I missed sitting beside her in the sunny courtyard, sharing silence in the warmth of the afternoon sun. The heartbreak wasn't only mine. I thought of residents who couldn't understand why their families had stopped visiting, their eyes clouded with uncertainty and confusion. Those images never left me.

When the government finally lifted restrictions, I cried with relief. Alleluia! At last, I could see my mum again. No business hurdle, no homeschooling struggle, had weighed on me the way that separation did. Even the hassle of COVID-19 tests and waiting for clearance was nothing compared to the joy of knowing I could sit beside her again. For once, the government got it right, and I was grateful.

Life began to rebuild. APBT training returned in full swing, and it was pure joy to shelve the laptops and leave Zoom behind. The thump of music, the sound of heavy breathing on driveway runs, and even the f-bombs were like music to my ears. The restaurant slowly steadied itself, returning to full capacity, and our daily rhythm – payroll, waiting tables, cleaning – came back as if it had never left.

For some, lockdown brought a gentler pace, but not for us. If anything, life sped up. We kept the kids active with one-on-one soccer training at the park, giving them both structure and an outlet for their pent-up energy. My dad, meanwhile, surprised us all.

Despite years working in the physically demanding butcher trade, he had never been much of an exerciser. But during lockdown he found a new rhythm in walking around the park each day for over an hour. He'd return with the same line every time, shaking his head: 'There's no such thing as COVID-19, everyone's at the park! No social distancing in Rosebery! It's all bullshit!' It always made me laugh.

Though reluctantly at first, Dad found unexpected joy in the chaos of daily life at home. Having the kids around brightened his days, even if they sometimes drove us all mad. Deep down, we knew we'd miss it when school resumed.

COVID-19 was a defining experience for us; one we'll never forget. No, we didn't face war or famine, but the pandemic was its own kind of battle, a reminder of how precious freedom is and of the privileges of living in a safe country like Australia. The silver lining was learning to adapt, to discover new strengths, and to find gratitude in the smallest of things. My APBT business became even more precious; it gave me purpose and joy when the world felt uncertain.

Above all, we wanted to show our children that even in crisis, unity and love can carry us through. If my mum could endure months confined within the same four walls, facing silence and loneliness with resilience, then what excuse did we have to complain? We had fresh air, freedom to walk, the warmth of the sun, and the sound of laughter at our table. Her strength reminded me, once again, that hardship isn't the end, it's the soil where faith and resilience take root.

CHAPTER 18

The end of an era

It was a bustling Friday night in December 2020 and the festive hum of Sydney's Inner West was pulsing through our restaurant. Christmas parties filled every table, laughter and chatter mingling with the clink of glasses. I was in my element, behind the bar, shaking cocktails, pouring wine, brewing coffee, multitasking to the max. The kitchen pulsed with its familiar rhythm, and the head chef's sharp call of 'Service!' rang out, summoning the team to swoop in to collect plates of culinary brilliance. For a fleeting moment, everything felt just right.

Then it struck. As I poured red wine into stemless glasses, a searing pain shot through me without warning. It felt as though something deep inside me was about to give way, a pressure so intense it stole my breath. Panic surged. I hunched over the bar, toes curling instinctively as if I could hold myself together from the ground up. My face drained of colour. The pain was raw and insistent, like childbirth, only this time I wasn't pregnant.

Through the blur of voices and clinking glasses, Master M noticed. His expression changed in an instant, calm replaced with alarm.

He knew me too well, my stubborn refusal to show weakness, my high tolerance for pain. If I looked stricken, something was seriously wrong. Without a word, he tore off his apron, grabbed his keys and disappeared through the back door. Moments later, his car screeched to a halt at the front entrance. Bless him, he wasn't about to let me stagger out through the laneway in that state.

I eased myself into the passenger seat, clinging to the grab handle as he steered carefully over the speed humps. Even with his caution, each bump sent fresh waves of pain radiating through me. Sitting down dulled the edge slightly, but it was still unbearable. All I could think about was getting home, curling up in bed, and pressing a heat pack against my stomach until morning.

That night dragged on endlessly. I tossed and turned, caught in a cycle of pain and dread, waiting for daylight so I could see the GP. My mind raced with amateur diagnoses: a prolapsed bladder? A uterine collapse? Growing up around doctors, I'd absorbed enough jargon to convince myself I could piece it together, but in truth I was clutching at shadows.

At dawn, I secured the first available appointment with the female GP. I deliberately avoided my usual doctor, the thought of going through something so mortifying with a familiar face was too much. Childbirth strips you of dignity, but still, I had my limits. After explaining my symptoms and enduring a swift internal exam, she offered a cautious verdict: a possible mild prolapse. She ordered further scans to be sure.

By sheer good fortune, I managed to book one for the very next day, practically a miracle in our overcrowded suburb. Determined not to inconvenience anyone, I drove myself and waddled across the car park like a duck, my mother's voice echoing in my head: 'Arrive early. Never keep anyone waiting.' Punctuality was her creed, and I honoured it.

In the waiting lounge I scrolled aimlessly through social media, trying but failing to distract myself. When the sonographer finally called, 'Andrea, you're next,' I leapt to my feet. She led me through to the examination room, where I obediently slipped into the infamous blue paper gown, more tissue than couture, and settled back on the cold table.

As I lay back and pressed my fingertips against my stomach, I felt the thud of my own heartbeat. The sonographer began with the abdominal scan, moving the probe gently across my skin while taking a few snapshots.

'Can you see anything?' I asked lightly, trying to sound casual, as if we were two friends catching up over coffee.

To my surprise, she didn't hide behind the usual silence. She hesitated, then replied, 'I can see something, but I'll confirm once we do the internal scan.'

Oh, brilliant, I thought. Just what I needed, more poking and prodding. My mind instantly spun into worst-case scenarios.

When she reached for the internal probe, I instinctively tensed. She positioned my legs, asking me to relax and breathe – easier said than done. *'You try relaxing with a foreign object where it doesn't belong'*, I wanted to snap. Instead, I swallowed the thought. It struck me, though, how much women endure without complaint. We're practically superheroes, capes optional. I tried to stay still, controlling my breathing as my eyes locked on the screen. Truthfully, it looked like one of my kid's preschool art projects, abstract smudges and shadows that could have been anything. Curiosity got the better of me. 'Can you see anything now?' I asked again.

This time, as she set the probe aside and handed me tissues, her answer was more direct.

'I can definitely see what's causing your pain and pressure. It's not the prolapse your GP suspected. You have significant endometriosis and adenomyosis. It's advanced, which is why it's so visible on the scan. Please follow up with your GP as soon as possible.'

Her words landed like a punch.

Back home, I plunged straight into research. Endometriosis wasn't new to me. I'd battled it after Jnr A's birth, even had it scraped away in hospital a few times. Or so I thought. Clearly, it hadn't been as 'settled' as I believed. Adenomyosis, on the other hand, was unfamiliar territory. Reading about the thickened uterine wall and its symptoms, I realised it explained the crushing pressure I'd been feeling. Slowly, the pieces fell into place.

My GP confirmed the findings and urged me to book in with my gynaecologist. It had been more than a decade since I'd last seen Dr D, after Sir R's birth in 2011. Sitting in the waiting room surrounded by glowing mothers-to-be, I couldn't help but smile. I remembered being in their shoes, rubbing my own belly and dreaming about a new life. This time, though, I felt at peace. I was in a different season now.

When Dr D finally emerged, file in hand, he called my name with a familiar warmth. I stood awkwardly, shuffling towards him with a waddle that wasn't far off that of those expectant mums.

'Just to clarify,' I joked as we walked into his office, 'I'm not pregnant.'

He chuckled, lowering himself into his chair. 'Oh yeah?'

I explained the symptoms while he scanned through my results. He took a sip of coffee, then leaned back.

'So,' he said evenly, 'what are we going to do with you?'

I gave a half-shrug. 'I don't know, Doc, you're the expert.'

He nodded, weighing it up. 'You've already tried the Mirena, and that didn't suit you. The pill wasn't great either. The next option would be an ablation.'

'What's that?' I asked.

'We'd burn away the uterine lining to stop your cycle. That should ease the pressure.' His tone grew more serious. 'You're too young for a hysterectomy.'

Something inside me stirred. Without hesitation, I replied, 'I don't want any more kids, I'm done. Why not just do the hysterectomy?'

He raised an eyebrow. 'That's a bit drastic, don't you think? Let's try the ablation first.'

To be honest, I didn't know how I felt about it. From the minute Dr D mentioned burning the uterine wall, something in me recoiled. My gut urged me to seek a second opinion.

Chatting with my clients before class one evening, I shared the details of my appointment and the options my gynaecologist had laid out. To my surprise, several of them had faced similar health battles. Each one strongly recommended I see their doctor. When I compared the names, one specialist came up again and again. Three different women, same recommendation. I took it as a sign.

Thanks to a last-minute cancellation, I managed to secure an appointment with Dr L, otherwise I would have waited more than four weeks. Before the consultation, I completed blood tests and another round of scans so he'd have the full picture. From the start, I was struck by the efficiency of his practice. Everything ran like clockwork, and that organisation alone gave me hope.

Dr L greeted me with a warm smile. 'Hi Andrea, welcome, what can I do for you?'

I decided to be upfront. 'I'm here for a second opinion. My gynae-cologist suggested an ablation, but I'm not convinced.'

After yet another internal exam (yes, again, for heaven's sake) he gave me his verdict without hesitation.

'Honestly, I don't think ablation is the right path for you. With the level of pain and pressure you're in, adding heat to an already inflamed uterus would probably make it worse. It may stop your periods, but the pain isn't driven by bleeding alone. In your case, since other interventions have failed, removal of the organ might be the only solution.'

I blinked. 'What does that mean?'

'A hysterectomy,' he said simply.

'Oh,' I murmured. Deep down I had suspected this, but hearing it confirmed still landed heavily.

At the receptionist's desk, I hunched over the counter, scrolling through my calendar as if I could magically find spare weeks hidden between soccer training, payroll, and APBT classes.

'How long is recovery?' I asked, dread prickling at my skin.

'You'll need 12 weeks,' she replied gently. 'The first six are strict rest and recovery.'

I laughed darkly, shaking my head. 'Can he just do the surgery when I'm dead? At least then I'll definitely get 12 weeks of rest.'

Her lips twitched between amusement and professionalism. 'I know it's a lot to take in, but this is for you. You need this.'

I sighed, then nodded. 'All right. Book me in for July. I'll make it work somehow.'

Five months. That's how long I had to wrap my head around it. Oddly enough, I wasn't upset. Not even a little. Losing my uterus didn't feel like losing my womanhood; it felt like freedom. A solution.

I was done being trapped in a body that punished me every month. Instead of mourning, I found myself counting down the days.

But as July crept closer, my body betrayed me further. The weight dropped off, kilo by kilo, leaving my face pale and gaunt. The stabbing pain in my abdomen never left me and my energy drained away like sand through an hourglass. I felt myself fading physically and mentally, piece by piece. Work became impossible. I stepped away from the restaurant; standing for even an hour was agony. The gym, once my sanctuary, was no better. I went from leading with fire and sweat to simply standing on the sidelines, calling out cues while others demonstrated. I was present in voice only.

Still, I refused to give up on my tribe. Determined to keep their momentum alive, I spent a solid week preplanning and recording six weeks of sessions. Every workout was tailored with modifications for every level. It felt like deja vu, a return to the COVID-19 lockdown days when we had trained together online. I gave them the option of a break, but they wouldn't hear of it. They wanted to keep going. Their determination moved me. Even in my own struggle, their faith in me, in us, reminded me that resilience is never carried alone.

I thought six weeks of rest would be enough to get me back on my feet, literally. In my mind, I saw myself returning to work and training, relying on verbal cues until my strength returned. After all, my girls knew the routines inside out; they practically had my 'torture book' memorised. I trusted they'd be fine with online sessions until I was back in the studio, leading them again with energy.

❤

While I was preparing for my surgery, Dad was facing his own battle. After nine long months of waiting, he finally received a date for his corneal transplant in May. It felt like such a relief. He would finally get the help he needed and I could be there for him during recovery. Thankfully, his operation didn't clash with mine, which meant I could give him my full support.

Sitting in the hospital waiting room on the day of his surgery, my own body betrayed me. The cramps and stabbing pains were relentless, growing sharper as the morning dragged on. Trying to keep quiet, I excused myself and stepped out to call my gynaecologist. Before I could even explain, another searing pain shot through me, leaving me breathless and sweating. Desperation coloured my voice as I begged her to bring the date forward. The best she could do was four weeks sooner. I seized it instantly. 'Thank you, thank you, thank you,' I kept repeating, clinging to the relief like a lifeline. June. It was happening in June.

When I returned to the waiting area, Dad caught sight of me. My face must have given me away. Gently resting his hand on my knee, he asked, 'Are you alright?'

'Yes, Papa, I'm fine. Just tired,' I lied, forcing a smile. The last thing I wanted was to burden him on his big day.

While Dad was in surgery I took a walk through the city, needing air and space to breathe. My feet eventually led me to St Mary's Cathedral. Inside, surrounded by flickering candles and hushed silence, I sat in a pew and bowed my head. A single tear slid down my cheek as I whispered prayers for both Dad and me. Gazing at the Virgin Mary, I felt the weight of my fear lift, just for a moment. I wiped my eyes and returned to the hospital.

When Dad was wheeled back into his room, groggy from the anaesthetic, he murmured, *'Eisai edw?'* ('You're here?')

'I'm here, Papa,' I whispered, feeding him dinner and tucking him in before kissing his forehead. A small act of care, but one that anchored us both.

The surgeons were pleased with the outcome given how advanced his corneal deterioration had been. Yet in the days that followed, something shifted. Master M and I noticed his behaviour becoming uncharacteristically excitable. He spoke louder, faster, obsessing over scripture, all the telltale signs of a psychotic episode. My heart sank. Not again.

At the follow-up consultation, I raised my concerns with the surgeon's assistant, who admitted she'd also seen a stark change in his demeanour. I explained his history and suggested that the medication he'd been prescribed post op might have triggered this state. After liaising with his GP, they agreed to restart his medication. Within days, Dad returned to himself: steady, calm, and lucid once more. Relief swept through me. With just a month until my own surgery, I was grateful for this mercy.

But my own body was failing fast. Standing for more than five minutes was torture; I leaned on benches and Swiss balls to get through classes, cueing exercises I could no longer demonstrate. Each day was an endurance test, and the only thing keeping me going was the countdown to surgery. The final week nearly broke me. Preparing my body meant cutting out solids days before, and by the morning of my operation, I felt wretched; physically drained and emotionally hollow. All I wanted was for it to be over.

On the way to the hospital, Master M and I stopped at our local church. I wasn't sure the doors would even be open, but they were. Together we climbed the steps, slowly, my body weak but my spirit clinging to faith. Inside, I lit a candle and stood at the back, eyes closed, reciting the Lord's Prayer three times. In that sacred stillness, peace descended. My fear loosened its grip. I felt God's presence, steady and near. For the first time in months, I wasn't anxious. I was ready. Whatever lay ahead, I wasn't walking into it alone.

We arrived at the hospital and, miraculously, found parking right away. Usually, Master M would be getting frustrated, circling the car park while I'd try to calm him down. But today everything seemed to be going smoothly. That is until I reached the reception desk to check in. The staff member's blunt statement caught me off guard: 'Due to COVID-19 restrictions, no one is allowed to come upstairs with you.' Panic began to set in, but Master M's calm nature steadied me. He placed a reassuring hand on my shoulder and said, 'You'll be okay, you've got this.' His words helped ease my nerves, but I couldn't shake off the feeling of uncertainty for what lay ahead.

As the lift doors closed, I waved goodbye to Master M, feeling a wave of emotion wash over me. I changed into my hospital gown and settled onto the bed, waiting for my turn. The clock on the wall seemed to be moving at a glacial pace, and I tried to distract myself by scrolling through social media, but nothing held my attention. I flicked between Facebook and Instagram, feeling restless. I pulled out my book, but the words blurred together on the page, and I ended up tossing it back into my bag. Just as I was starting to drift off to sleep, the curtain swung open and a porter's cheerful voice broke the silence: 'Hi Andrea, are you ready? I'm going to take you down to theatre.'

I nodded, trying to sound calmer than I felt: 'Yep, I'm ready'.

As the porter rolled me down the corridor, the bed's cold rails under my fingers, I suddenly felt overwhelmed and started hyperventilating, the anaesthetic's metallic tang sharp in the air. I pulled the blanket over my face and sobbed uncontrollably. The bed stopped, and I composed myself long enough to pull the blanket down. The anaesthetist approached me with a warm smile and asked, 'How are you going?' His gentle tone was my undoing. I burst into tears again.

'I don't think I'm going to wake up, I don't think my heart can cope,' I sobbed.

He looked at me with kind eyes and said, 'Don't you worry, I'm going to pop the champers in a minute, you're going to have the best sleep, and in a few hours, you'll be awake and all your pain will be gone'. I sniffled, nodded, and turned my head to check the time – 2.30 p.m. Old habit, I suppose. Before I knew it, I was knocked out, G-O-N-E. It must have been one hell of a bottle!

I came to in a groggy haze, the weight of fear lifting in slow waves as my eyes caught the tangle of tubes at my side. I vaguely remember being rolled into the ward after surgery, with no recollection of the recovery room itself. What I do recall, though, is the warmth of seeing my family waiting in the hallway. I heard someone whisper, 'She's here,' and suddenly my kids, Master M, and G gathered around, their gentle voices welcoming me back to consciousness. Master M leaned close, his voice soft with worry he'd held back, later confessing over a shared soy latte that he'd paced the hospital car park, praying silently. Even with heavy eyelids and a foggy head, their presence soothed me. Gratitude washed over me; I wasn't alone.

The post-op pain was brutal. Nurses tried managing it with morphine injections, but my body didn't respond. Three jabs later, I felt barely any relief. The pain was sharp, grinding and unbearable. Tears streamed down my face as I shifted and twisted, desperate to find a position that didn't feel like torture. The catheter only added to the discomfort, making every moment feel more claustrophobic. At one point the agony was so overwhelming that all I wanted was silence; no company, no voices, just space to ride it out.

That first night was a blur of pain and wakefulness. Sleep never came. I tried distracting myself with TV, but that felt meaningless. All I could do was lie there, watching the clock tick towards the next dose of painkillers. My gaze drifted out the window to the trees swaying in the darkness. I prayed for the sun to rise, clinging to the hope that morning light would bring even the smallest hint of relief.

When the sunlight finally filtered through the leaves, it felt like a mercy. Master M arrived, carrying a soy latte that warmed my soul as much as my hands. Soon after, the nurse suggested I try a shower. I hesitated, terrified that moving would tear me apart, but the promise of hot water was too tempting. Sitting under the stream, I felt my body relax for the first time since surgery. Thirty blissful minutes passed, and for a moment, I almost forgot about the pain. But reality returned as soon as I stepped out and the relief slipped away.

I chose to stay in hospital for five days, even though I could have been discharged earlier. I knew Master M was juggling the restaurant, the kids, and Dad, and I couldn't expect him to shoulder my care on top of everything else.

With the chaos of Dad's recent psychotic episode still fresh in my mind, I recognised something I'd never admitted before: I needed to prioritise myself. The hospital became an unlikely sanctuary: quiet, controlled, safe. For once, I allowed myself to put my needs first, and that in itself felt like healing.

Recovery was slow and humbling. I was used to being the caregiver, the strong one, the doer. Now, I was the one being cared for, a role that sat uneasily on my shoulders. Relying on others felt alien to my independent nature. Yet I knew that surrendering was the only way forward. If I ignored my surgeon's orders, I'd undo everything. For the first time in my life, I had to learn how to receive.

Back home, I set myself up in the TV room, camped out in a hired red recliner amidst snack-strewn tables and kids' schoolbooks, remnants of lockdown's chaos. It was far easier than struggling in and out of bed. Everything I needed was within arm's reach: painkillers, tea, books, remotes. I could rest without strain. Every morning I'd switch on the news, only to be greeted by the grim updates: COVID-19 cases rising again.

Just days before, I'd been preparing for surgery. Now, in the haze of recovery, the news broke of another lockdown, the TV's drone cutting through my groggy thoughts. I whispered a prayer, linking the divine mercy I'd felt in church to a plea for global mercy, hoping for strength to endure this new shatter. G carried the stress heavily, worrying about the restaurant, about closures, about survival.

This time, though, we weren't completely unprepared. The online ordering system was still in place, and APBT training had already moved online while I recovered. We had momentum to carry us forward. But as suburbs shut down one by one, it felt like deja vu, the same fear and uncertainty creeping in. By that Saturday, our worst fears had materialised: lockdown, again.

The restaurant staggered under the weight of it. We scrambled to adapt, adding delivery on top of takeaways, but people were spending less. Orders trickled in, though nothing like the surge of the first lockdown. Rent, taxes, superannuation; the bills kept coming, but the cash flow didn't. Even with skeleton staff and tight planning, it felt like we were drowning.

Meanwhile, my recovery crept forward. By six weeks, I could walk short distances again. Even with the 5 km restriction in place, my local clients rallied. They took turns walking with me, encouraging me step by step. Others offered practical help. One selfless client, who I absolutely adore, cooked chicken schnitzel for the kids every

Saturday, knowing how much they loved it and that I couldn't manage it. Their kindness left me undone. I've said it before, but it's worth saying again: my tribe aren't just clients. They're family in every sense. During those weeks, they wrapped me in a kind of love and support I hadn't expected. It touched me deeply, especially when my own blood family didn't always show the same tenderness.

Oddly, lockdown became a strange kind of blessing. It gave me space; space to breathe, to heal, to shut out the noise. The past six months had stripped me bare in both body and spirit. Before surgery, I'd weighed 45 kg, so fragile a strong wind could have carried me away. But little by little, I began to rebuild.

For the first time in years, I stopped worrying about the outside world. My focus narrowed to my home, my children, my tribe, my God. I tuned out the distractions and anchored myself in recovery. Healing became my purpose, my drive. And I realised something profound: being a woman had never been about one organ or one role. My strength, my womanhood, my identity, lived in my resilience, in the lessons of pain, in the courage to keep standing, and in the love passed down by the woman who raised me.

Every new day felt like a new chance. Not to mourn what I'd lost, but to embrace what I'd gained: freedom from pain, a fresh start, and the strength to grow into the woman I was becoming.

CHAPTER 19

Bionic man

I t's one of life's simplest blessings to wake after a peaceful sleep and breathe in the freshness of a new day. That truth felt especially real on that morning in Sydney's Inner West. The distant hum of the Princes Highway stirred as I prepared to take Dad to his cardiac specialist appointment, a sharp reminder that every sunrise is a gift.

Caring for an elderly parent is a quiet, weighty responsibility, one that takes from you physically, but even more so emotionally. When Dad's eyesight began to fail and it was no longer safe for him to drive, he reluctantly handed in his licence. I stepped in to shoulder what he no longer could, but the sadness in his eyes told me this was more than just a practical decision. Handing over a plastic card seemed small in itself, yet it symbolised the loss of his independence.

The scratches on his car no longer mattered. I remember taking his hand and saying softly, 'I'd rather see a few scratches and still have you here.' But the truth ran deeper: losing his licence wasn't just a practical inconvenience. It quietly chipped away at his confidence and distanced him from the social circles that breathe life into one's later years. Watching him learn to depend on me for drives, appointments, groceries, even the smallest errands, has been both humbling and heartbreaking. This is the quiet role reversal that ageing brings, forcing both of us to confront change.

Dad had always been the family's provider, not because he chose it, but because life demanded it, especially with Mum's ongoing health challenges. When he finally retired, he didn't rest. He devoted himself to caring for her, finding purpose in the quiet, unseen acts of love. For a brief and beautiful season, he even began to reclaim a part of himself. He joined a lawn bowls group, made new friends, and stepped just slightly beyond the boundaries of family life. It was a simple joy, but a profound one, especially in our culture where men of his generation rarely seek companionship outside the home.

But life, as it often does, had other plans. His mother had lived with a degenerative eye disease and he inherited it. Now his world is slowly dimming, a circle closing in on him, a bitter echo of the struggles that came before.

In caring for Dad, I took on more than just tasks, I took on his world. The medical appointments, the medication schedules, the meals, the laundry, the weekly shopping runs. One of my most important roles has been driving him to visit Mum at the nursing home. We fell into a quiet rhythm. I would drop him at the entrance, giving him the dignity of walking in alone to be with her while I slipped away to get groceries and clear my head. Later, I returned, often finding a small moment to fit in my own visit. It meant Mum saw a familiar face every single day, and I still saw her at least twice on my own.

It was a delicate balancing act: supporting Dad, staying connected to Mum, and somehow holding together all the fragile threads of our family life before they could unravel.

Over time, a bond has grown between Dad and me, one unlike any other in my life. We are opposites; chalk and cheese. He is calm, measured, stable; I am the wildfire that often disrupts his rhythm. And yet, despite our differences, or perhaps because of them, we have grown close.

That morning, as I prepared to drive him to yet another appointment, I couldn't help but smile at the thought. His heart must be remarkably resilient to have put up with me all these years.

❤

We drove along the Princes Highway, weaving through the morning bustle towards Marrickville. The car was wrapped in our familiar, comfortable silence when suddenly my phone rang, the chime echoing through the Bluetooth speakers. Each of my children and Master M had their own distinct ringtone. This wasn't one of them.

I glanced at the screen while stopped at a red light, and my breath caught. It was my brother-in-law. Calls from him, or anyone on that side of the family, were rare. My finger hovered over the steering wheel button, hesitant, curious, wary. Finally, I pressed.

'Hey...what's up? Is everything okay?' I asked, my voice steady but tinged with weariness. Silence stretched. I drew in a long, shaky breath, bracing myself. A quiet dread settled in my chest. Some calls carry the weight of change before a single word is spoken. I had a sinking feeling this was one of them.

'He's okay,' my brother-in-law said at last, though somehow, the words only sharpened my unease.

'Who's okay? What are you talking about?' My voice came out sharper than I meant, anxiety twisting tighter with every passing second.

'Master M is okay,' he clarified quickly, 'but there's been an accident.'

My heart dropped. The world blurred for a moment. An accident? My mind spun, leaping to the darkest places.

'What happened? Please…just tell me,' I urged, panic coiling tight around my body.

Suddenly, I noticed the impatient honking behind me. I was first at the lights, frozen while the cars stacked up.

Forcing myself into action, I eased off the brake and drifted forward, then veered left, pulling over so I could focus on the call. My hands clung to the wheel, slick with sweat, every muscle in my body tight with fear. *Breathe*, I whispered inside myself, but the air still snagged halfway, refusing to go down. The cars around me felt too close, their horns sharp, their lights flashing like warnings I didn't have time to read. One wrong move and I could cause another accident, before I even reached him.

Finally, in park with the engine idling, I took a deep breath and steadied myself. 'Okay,' I said, 'tell me everything from the beginning. Don't leave anything out.'

There was a pause, just long enough for my mind to race through a thousand scenarios. I could hear the hesitation in his voice, the careful way he chose his words, softening the blow before it landed.

'We were in the middle of a team-bonding exercise,' he began slowly. 'Master M was running, and he slipped. He landed badly on his hip. At first, he tried to get up, but his leg…it was at a strange angle, like it was hanging loose. He tried to put weight on it, but he just collapsed back down.'

My stomach lurched. 'Jesus Christ…what did he break? His leg or his hip?'

'I think it's his hip,' my brother-in-law admitted, 'but I can't be certain.'

'And now? What's happening?' My words tumbled over each other, desperate for reassurance, for any shred of control.

'The ambulance is on its way. Honestly...he actually looks okay,' he said, calm and soothing.

A nervous laugh escaped me, jagged and hollow. 'For fuck's sake, I'm literally on my way to Dad's heart specialist. Maybe I should get him to check mine while I'm there.'

Even in that moment, the strange duality struck me: fear tightening my chest, yet a thin thread of humour surfacing, the only way I could stop myself from spiralling completely.

'I'll finish with Dad, take him home, and then come straight over,' I said firmly. 'I don't want to cancel his appointment at the last minute.'

'No, no,' my brother-in-law reassured me. 'Do what you have to do. Don't stress. Drive safely. I'll stay with him until you arrive.'

His firm voice grounded me just enough to breathe. Master M wasn't alone. As soon as we hung up, I dialled him directly. He picked up after two rings, his voice tight with strain but still carrying that familiar calm I had come to rely on.

'What the fuck happened? Are you okay?' I blurted, my heart racing ahead of my words.

'I'm okay, babe,' he said, though the effort behind his steadiness was clear. 'I slipped. The way I landed...I think I've broken something. If I stay still, the pain's bearable.'

Bearable. The word hung in the air, a fragile mask over the raw agony I could hear in his voice with every shallow breath.

'I'm just around the corner from Dad's cardiac appointment,' I told him quickly. 'As soon as I'm done, I'll come straight over. Do you know which hospital they're taking you to?'

'Probably St George's,' he said. 'But call me once you're on your way. I'll let you know for sure.'

His bravery, even in the middle of pain, undid me. Beneath his steady words, I could hear the truth: he was hurting. And still, he was trying to reassure me. My chest tightened with love and fear all at once, the weight almost too much to bear.

I pressed my foot back on the brake, shifted into drive and indicated to merge, stealing a glance at Dad beside me. My tears were threatening to spill. If they broke free, my vision would blur and I couldn't risk that on the road.

'What's going on?' Dad asked, his tone curious, unaware of the full weight of the conversation I'd just had.

'M's had an accident at work,' I snapped, the words spilling out sharper than I intended.

'Oh shit,' Dad muttered, then fell silent.

Guilt pricked at me instantly. I wasn't angry with him, yet I felt torn, pulled in two directions. Dad, with his vulnerable mobility and failing eyesight, needed me to guide him through this appointment. And every fibre of me was screaming to get to Master M's side.

By the time I stormed into the specialist's surgery, jacket clutched tightly in my hand, frustration bubbled over. I wasn't in the mood for pleasantries. I just wanted this appointment done so I could be somewhere else, where I was needed most.

Sensing my agitation, Dad gently suggested, 'I could get a taxi.'

'No, Papa, it's okay. We won't be long,' I insisted, forcing calm into my voice. 'I'll take you home, and then I'll head straight to him.'

The words sounded confident enough, but inside the guilt pressed down like a weight. Dad didn't deserve the sharp edge of my anxiety.

The specialist greeted Dad warmly, his voice slow and deliberate, as though time itself bent for him in a way it never did for me. I rolled my eyes and huffed, dropping into the chair, impatient with the ordinary rhythm of health checks while my life outside this room felt like it was unravelling.

Questions, scans, notes. Then he asked Dad to hop onto the treadmill. I stared, incredulous. Is this bloke serious? Has he no idea I'm hanging by a thread here! I bit back my frustration, exhaled hard, and let him get on with his job. To my surprise, it was over within 10 minutes. My panic had blown the wait out of proportion, and I realised my energy had been misdirected. Anxiety had written its own story and I had let it.

From there, it was like being a yo-yo, back in the car, dropping Dad at home, then racing across to the hospital. Running on fumes with just a single coffee in my system, I drove with a taut mix of urgency and caution. When I arrived, I slammed the door behind me and sprinted towards the emergency department, clinging to the clear signs that cut through my fog of disorientation. Inside, the waiting room was a swirl of humanity: elderly patients, sick children, people with bandaged limbs and weary faces. Amid the crowd, my brother-in-law stood out, and I hurried to him.

'Come with me. I'll take you to him,' he said, leading me through as the triage nurse unlocked the doors.

And there he was Master M, lying on a stretcher, chatting away with the ambulance officer as if this were some casual meet-up. The green whistle for pain relief dangled in his hand, his smile relaxed, perhaps too relaxed. Relief surged through me, and I went straight to his side, resting my hand lightly on his leg.

'Ouch! Not that leg!' he yelped. I couldn't help but laugh, letting the tension spill out through humour.

'Just checking you weren't faking it,' I teased.

He chuckled, 'I feel fine. Well…thanks to this. Best thing ever.'

The ambulance officer smiled. 'He's a trooper. Barely a complaint. We're just waiting on ED handover before we can move him to a bed. Can't leave until a doctor sees him.'

Master M's mood changed suddenly, indignation flaring in his voice. 'So, you're telling me you're stuck here while other emergencies are waiting for an ambulance? That's bullshit. I'm fine. People out there need you more.' Normally, he wasn't this outspoken, and I suspected the green whistle had dulled the pain and loosened his filter.

The officer offered a sympathetic shrug. 'I know. But that's the system.'

'It's ridiculous!' Master M shot back.

I couldn't argue. The accident had happened around 11 a.m. and now it was nearly 3 p.m. and a paramedic was still tethered to his stretcher. The strain on the hospital was tangible; it was overcrowded, understaffed, stretched to the limit. Looking around, I felt it deep in my soul: this was no place for anyone to heal.

After what felt like an eternity, the handover was finally complete, and the ambulance officer was released from her post. Master M was whisked away for a scan to assess the damage, and I finally allowed myself to exhale.

But the comedy wasn't over yet. When the doctor produced a pair of scissors to cut away his jeans, Master M shot upright, eyes wide with alarm.

'Oh no you don't. Put those away. You're not cutting my favourite jeans.'

The doctor froze, clearly surprised by the intensity of his reaction. 'Alright then,' he said cautiously, 'but if you're in pain, how do you expect us to get them off?'

Dead serious, Master M said, 'It's fine, Doc. I'll just take a big green whistle inhale and hold my breath.'

I couldn't tell if he was joking or completely serious, but the look on his face said it all, this was no act. He was determined to save those jeans. Leaning closer so the doctor wouldn't hear, he whispered, 'Just be gentle...it hurts.'

I held back laughter, half in disbelief, half in admiration. Carefully, I began easing the denim down his leg. Master M hissed a muted, 'F-u-c-k,' through clenched teeth. The fabric was stiff, stubborn against the contours of his hip and thigh, but eventually, I managed.

Then I lifted his foot and froze. His leg hung loosely, unnervingly so, and my stomach turned. Even without medical training, I could see how badly it was distorted.

The scan results came back quickly. The doctor's voice was calm and clinical: 'It's a fracture of the femur. He'll need surgery.'

I blinked, stunned. The femur, the strongest bone in the body. How on earth had he managed to snap it? My mind spiralled, but the doctor's assured tone anchored me, yanking me back to the present and forcing me to focus.

The rest of the day blurred into a whirlwind. Calls from Master M's workplace, updates to family, juggling the kids' schedules; it was chaos. The only saving grace was Jnr A, newly licensed and able to drive Sir R to soccer training. I thanked God for that small mercy; without it, I would have truly crumbled.

❤

In May 2023, reality hit hard. Master M underwent a gruelling four-hour surgery to repair the complex fracture in his femur and hip. The procedure was extensive, pins carefully placed to stabilise the bone. When he woke from anaesthesia, the pain hit him immediately. There was no protective numbness, no gentle easing-in. Just raw, searing agony. Every slight movement sent shocks of pain rippling through his body. The nurses and doctors were incredible, attentive in every way, but even their best care couldn't take away the intensity of what he was feeling.

Then came the expectation that nearly broke him. The very next day, the physio team appeared at his bedside. 'Time to get up and walk.'

His face contorted in disbelief. 'Are you fucking serious? I can't do that. No way, no trolley. I can barely move. How do you expect me to walk?' His voice rose, raw with anger and fear, teetered on the edge of breaking.

I tried to soothe him, but the pain made him sharp with everyone. There were times I wanted to scream, times I almost shook him, anything to make it stop. I even had the fleeting, guilty thought of knocking him out so the moment would pass. But of course, I couldn't. That's not my role. My role was to stand in the storm beside him, strong and present, however rough the winds blew.

I arrived early the next morning, hoping to dodge the usual barrage of calls, 'Where are you?' 'What time are you coming?' No sooner had I stepped into the room, Master M launched into a tirade about his sleepless night, blaming the snoring man in the next bed. I tried to hush him, mindful of the other patient, but he was having none of it.

Great. Just what I needed, a lovely morning dose of grumpiness, I thought.

His complaints quickly shifted to the physiotherapy plan. 'How the fuck am I supposed to get out of bed? I can barely roll onto my side!' His frustration bubbled over, raw and impatient.

'Let's wait until the physio gets here,' I suggested, folding his clean clothes and tucking them aside. 'She might have some tricks to help.'

A few minutes later, the physiotherapist swept in in a bright red T-shirt with a beaming smile, walker in tow. 'Hi M, let's get you out of bed and on your feet,' she said, her confidence almost infectious.

His reply was flat, bitter: 'Good luck.'

I shook my head, stepping back. This wasn't the calm, easygoing man I knew. The anaesthetic had stripped away his usual patience, leaving someone raw-edged and resistant.

The physio gave clear instructions, patient and positive, but every movement drew a sharp yelp from him. After several attempts he sagged back against the pillows, utterly defeated. 'I can't do it. The pain's too much.'

'It's only day one,' she reassured him. 'We'll try again tomorrow. Rest as much as you can.' She left the walker in the corner and slipped out, leaving a heavy silence in her wake.

'You've got to get me out,' he pleaded, desperation threading through his voice.

'How can I if you can't even sit up?' I said gently. 'Give it time.'

He turned towards the window, his brave facade starting to crack.

The following morning, I headed in after finishing my sessions. As much as I wanted to be constantly by his side, I still had to juggle work and parenting responsibilities. My clients kindly offered to cancel classes so I could focus on him, but I couldn't bring myself to take advantage. Those physical activity sessions weren't just for them, they were my anchor too, helping me manage stress and preserve my own mental health.

Walking into the ward with a bag of small surprises in my hand, I braced myself for another day of complaints and discouragement. But what met me stopped me in my tracks. There he was, sitting upright in his chair, eyes sparkling.

'I figured it out!' he announced, grinning from ear to ear. 'I know how to get out of bed!'

The joy on his face was contagious. After 48 hours of watching him flounder, that smile felt like God's quiet reminder that healing was possible. My heart lifted.

'Go on then, how?' I asked, genuinely impressed.

'We took off the bottom footrest. I slid down slowly until my legs lowered, then pushed myself up with the walker. Couldn't twist, so I just...improvised.'

'That's brilliant,' I said, in awe of his stubborn ingenuity.

Then, with a cheeky twinkle in his eye, he added, 'Now, get me a wheelchair and take me downstairs for a cigarette.'

I rolled my eyes but couldn't help laughing. 'Yes sir.'

Recovery was long, gruelling, and painfully slow. Weeks of shuffling on crutches and navigating the wheelchair tested every ounce of his patience. And just as he began bearing weight on his leg, a new challenge emerged: one leg was shorter than the other.

The specialist confirmed it, and while the solution of customised insoles from an orthopaedic podiatrist was relatively straightforward, the adjustment was anything but. The imbalance strained his back, forcing him to lean and twist in unnatural ways. During family walks in the park, to Sir R's soccer games and beyond, the worry often got the better of me, leaving Master M feeling inadequate.

One night, the pain hit with brutal force, jerking him awake in agony. We rushed for help, and the chiropractor recommended a cortisone injection. That single jab turned out to be a lifeline, bringing near-miraculous relief.

Over the following months, Master M's life became a blur of medical appointments, scans, and follow-ups, a whirlwind I struggled to keep pace with. My days became a relentless balancing act: managing his care alongside Dad's appointments, visiting Mum in the nursing home, keeping the house in order, running the restaurant, looking after APBT, and juggling the boys' schedules. Each day bled into the next, a monotonous cycle with barely a moment to breathe. I was utterly spent, running on fumes, yet determined to keep everything afloat.

One evening, G and I shared a quiet, weary hug in the restaurant kitchen, our exhaustion mirrored in each other's eyes a silent vow that we would keep going, together.

Not long after the first cortisone injection had brought him relief, Master M's back flared up again. His right side had been overcompensating for the weakness in his injured leg, and I could see the familiar pattern repeating itself. A second injection was scheduled, but from the moment the needle went in, something felt off. Instead of the swift relief he had experienced before, this time a burning jolt shot through him, as if his nerves were aflame. I rushed him home and dosed him with painkillers, praying they'd settle things down. They didn't. The stabbing nerve pain only grew worse, robbing him of sleep night after night.

After two long weeks, scans finally revealed the full extent of the problem: a three-centimetre discrepancy in the length of his legs, worsened by a limp that grew more pronounced with every step. It was a cruel blow, a reminder of how unforgiving the body could be.

Yet even in the thick of his own suffering, Master M managed to find perspective. He often spoke of my mum, of her years of resilience living with paralysis, the quiet strength she carried.

'I don't know how she's managed so long without complaint,' he said one evening, his voice heavy with admiration. 'I've been struggling just these months, and it's already breaking me.'

But the cracks were beginning to show. His confidence waned as mobility grew harder. Activities that once brought him joy, like kicking a ball around with the boys, were now beyond him. Though he never once cast blame, I could see how deeply the accident had shaken him. His silence about his own despair spoke louder than words.

Nine months after surgery, desperate for a path forward, Master M began exploring medical options for leg lengthening. A consultation with a respected knee surgeon led to a referral to a limb reconstruction specialist. I hadn't even known such a procedure existed.

Workers' compensation approval became the next hurdle. One tense evening, we sat by the phone, waiting, Master M's hand gripping mine as the seconds stretched into what felt like hours. When the voice on the line finally delivered the news that it had been approved, I felt a rush of relief so profound it virtually knocked me off my chair. For Master M, this wasn't just another appointment on the calendar. It was a glimmer of light, a beacon of hope in a season defined by loss, limitation, and relentless pain.

He met with the limb reconstruction specialist, carefully recounting his medical history and the struggles he faced every day. The surgeon spoke with quiet confidence, optimistic that real improvement was possible. But Master M knew that optimism alone wouldn't get him there. The workers' compensation approval was the key to unlocking treatment.

What followed was a wearying process: countless appointments, repeated scans, and finally the dreaded independent surgical review, the last gatekeeper before treatment could begin.

When approval finally came through, we recognised it for what it was: a blessing from God, a turning point in a long, gruelling journey. The surgery ahead was daunting: Master M's femur would need to be re-broken and fitted with a highly specialised lengthening rod. To stimulate new bone growth, he would have to use a magnetic unwinding device three times a day, its cold clicks echoing through our quiet home, gradually extending the rod by tiny fractions of a millimetre each time. It was pioneering, like something out of science fiction, transforming Master M into a modern-day bionic man.

Dr S, the surgeon, carried himself with remarkable calm and precision. He explained what seemed impossibly complex with clarity and delivered with a confidence born of both skill and compassion. His intelligence, humility, and character shone through every interaction. I hold him in the highest regard. In many ways, he handed Master M back his future, and for that, I remain endlessly grateful.

The recovery, however, was anything but straightforward. For over a month, Master M was forbidden to put any weight on his left leg; even the slightest strain could snap the rod. He was completely dependent, and I became his constant support, helping him shower, dress, move around the house, and manage even the simplest tasks. Exhausting as it was, this season of care drew us closer. In tending to his needs, I found myself drawing closer to him than ever before.

I won't romanticise it. I reached my breaking point more than once, mentally, emotionally, and physically drained. Yet every postoperative check-up brought a sliver of fulfilment, the quiet, unspoken reward of watching steady progress unfold. Seeing the rod lengthen, new bone forming day by day, gave us both renewed hope. Slowly, painfully, the treatment was working.

Six weeks later, Master M was finally able to place gentle weight on his healing leg. The familiar thump of weights in the gym felt distant, almost foreign, as he pushed through gruelling physio sessions. It was a small but vital milestone, the moment when faith started to turn into tangible recovery. With every session, he worked to rebuild lost muscle, regain strength, and restore confidence. Weekly physiotherapy paired with hours in the gym became his new routine. It was exhausting, demanding, and sometimes frustrating. Step by step, the man who had once felt broken began to return.

♥

A year after the second procedure in June 2025, Master M went in for what would be his third and final surgery. This time, the doctors removed the rod that had done its job. It was less invasive; this operation was another hurdle in his long journey. Now his focus is on rebuilding, on finding his strength again, piece by piece. Every day of rehabilitation reminds him and me of the distance we've already covered and the long road still waiting ahead.

Those three years after Master M's work accident tested our marriage in ways we never imagined. Pain, exhaustion, and frustration lived with us like uninvited guests. There were days when he snapped, not out of anger towards me, but from a deep, bone-heavy weariness of the soul. I often thought of my mother, how she carried her suffering with such quiet dignity. I tried to offer him that same grace. No, I could never truly feel the pain inside his body. But I could stand beside him in it. And I did.

Ironically, the ordeal that once felt strong enough to break us ended up drawing us closer. For the first time in years, we found comfort in slowing down, just breathing, just being together. Somehow, vulnerability became a strange kind of gift, allowing us to see each other more clearly than before.

We remain profoundly grateful to live in a country where advanced medical care made his treatment possible. Without it, his story could have taken a far darker turn, one marked by permanent disability. But even with everything medicine offered, it wasn't the only thing that carried us. We were held up by the unwavering support of family, friends, colleagues, and even my clients. Their encouragement and love were threads that held us together when we were fraying.

This journey left its marks. Some scars sit on the surface, but none of them represent the end of our story. They stand as reminders of resilience, of survival, of grace discovered in the harshest seasons. And if there's one truth I've learned to hold close, it's that life's challenges are never wasted. They shape us. They refine us. They prepare us to lift others.

And if sharing our story helps even one person to hold on a little longer, to believe that healing is possible, to find hope in a place that once felt hopeless, then I will know I've fulfilled something deeply meaningful.

CHAPTER 20

My heart aches for your touch

Every visit to Mum at the nursing home felt like a gift: quiet, sacred, and more fleeting than I wanted to admit. It was another chance to strengthen our bond and make new memories in the quiet hum of Kensington's care-filled corridors. I reconnected with the woman who shaped me: Mum, the reason I am who I am. I count myself lucky, profoundly lucky to call her my mother.

Some visits were hushed and tender. Mum would be fast asleep, her breathing soft and steady, and I'd just sit there beside her, watching her chest rise and fall, each breath a quiet reminder of her enduring spirit. On those days, she would light up when I played soft music and gave her a manicure or a little facial, her soft spot for dusky pinks and mauves sparking a familiar glow. Reading to her became one of my favourite rituals. She'd curl into her tub chair, wrapped snugly in a cosy blanket, while I sat at the edge of her bed, legs dangling like a child again, book in hand, reading lighthearted fiction or whatever made her smile. Time always felt softer in those moments.

Without fail, every visit began with the Lord's Prayer. Her daily memories may have drifted, but that prayer lived deep in her heart. I would record her saying it, wanting to hold that voice forever. As we finished, I'd pause, and she would always murmur a gentle 'Amen.'

There were days when Mum recognised me right away, her eyes brightening, her voice soft but sure. And then there were days when she looked at me with gentle confusion, mistaking me for the neighbour's granddaughter or even a nurse. Those early moments of confusion hit me hard; it was painful to watch her fail to remember her own daughter. But as I learned to accept the effects of her multiple brain surgeries, I understood these lapses were part of the condition. Her identity would sometimes drift, like mist over water, but my memories of her remained clear, grounded, unshaken.

❤

Once, after one of her hospital stays, Dad and I arrived at the nursing home just as Mum was settling back into bed for her mid-morning rest. I helped prop her up with soft, fluffy pillows and sat close beside her. I teased that she was overdue for a manicure. Before I could say anything more, she leaned in slightly, her voice low and serious.

'Who's the old man behind you?' she whispered.

For a moment, I froze. My breath caught and my heart thudded in my chest. Fear and curiosity washed over me all at once. Was she confused...or was she seeing something I couldn't?

I leaned in closer. 'Who?' I whispered back.

'The man in the red jumper,' she said quietly.

I turned slowly. There was Dad, standing just behind me in his red jumper, a detail I hadn't even noticed before. Relief washed over me, but as I looked at him, I saw something deeper than that brief comfort. His face held a quiet, weary blend of love, sorrow, and exhaustion. Trying to keep the moment light, I said, 'Oh, that's my Dad.'

Mum smiled softly. 'Oh, that's lovely,' she replied.

For a moment, all their years of marriage, all the familiar routines and shared memories, seemed to fall away. The fragility of her mind, the way it slipped in and out of knowing, hit me all over again.

That moment changed me. I made a quiet promise to be fully present with her, to treasure every fragment of connection, no matter how brief. I stopped asking, 'Do you know who I am?' and instead guided our time towards what made her happy: stories of her childhood village in Cyprus, her dress designs, chats about the children, light conversations about work and everyday life.

She adored talking about those village days. Tales of dusty paths, olive groves, and familiar faces became our safe place, wrapping us in the same warmth as her distant memories and past travels. Even when she couldn't offer advice or comfort, just speaking with her soothed me. It steadied my heart and reminded me of the quiet, unwavering simplicity of our love.

♥

In September 2023, Sir R was given the opportunity of a lifetime: training in Spain with his football academy. For a 12-year-old, it was a dream unfolding right in front of him. Yet the excitement carried a quiet ache, because it meant being far from Mum.

I was deeply grateful for the staff at the nursing home. Their kindness and understanding went beyond duty. They arranged regular video calls, updated me on her care, and made sure Mum could still hear our voices. Those calls meant everything to her.

Their thoughtfulness made all the difference. It became the quiet support I needed to move through a moment that held both joy and worry. I wanted to celebrate my son's milestone with my whole heart, yet I also needed to stay close to my mother, whose presence pulls me in a different way.

While we were travelling, I took the chance to spend a few days in Paris with Sir R. On the morning we were heading to Disneyland, a scheduled video call with Mum happened to fall just as we were in the car. I slipped in an earpiece and answered.

'Hi, Mum,' I said softly.

'Hi, love,' she replied, her voice warm and familiar like home.

I told her our plans with childlike excitement. 'We're in Paris, R and I are off to Disneyland!'

Even through the screen, even with the Parisian sky heavy with rain, her face lit up. For a moment, I saw a spark of her old wanderlust, the way she used to come alive at the thought of travel.

'Oh, that's wonderful. Have a good time, love,' she said, smiling.

Before her illness, travel had always been one of Mum's greatest joys, so I made sure to carry her with us in spirit. I sent her updates about everything; the sights, the food, the places we wandered through, hoping she'd feel part of our adventure even from her bed in Kensington.

When we finally returned home, my heart ached with longing to see Master M and Jnr A. Jnr A was deep in HSC exams, my son finishing high school. How quickly the years had slipped through my fingers. But even with all that waiting for me, there was one thing I needed before anything else. I had to see Mum.

We landed late, so I couldn't visit her until the next morning. The anticipation was electric, like a spring in my steps, as I dreamed of her smile.

The next day, after a much-needed sleep, I drove to the nursing home, that same spring still buoying my step. I practically skipped down the corridors and flung open her door with a theatrical flourish, as if stepping into a fairytale.

'Mum, I'm back!' I called, the summer sun warming my face and my excitement spilling over.

Her eyes lit up immediately. 'Hi, love. Welcome back. Look at your tan, you look good!'

I teased, grinning. 'What are you trying to say? Don't I always look good?'

She laughed, the sound warm and familiar, but then it quickly turned into a cough, her body struggling with a small hiccup of breath. Concern washed over me.

'I'm sorry, Mum,' I said softly, leaning closer.

'It's okay, love,' she said, her eyes twinkling as she lazily stretched an arm behind her head, as if she were soaking up the sun herself.

We caught up, and I shared stories of Sir R's adventures in Spain, watching her eyes sparkle with pride. Just then, the resident manager appeared at the doorway.

'Welcome back from your trip, Andrea. I hope you had a great time. I'm not sure if you've seen the email, but there's a facility meeting in a few weeks for all residents' families. Will you be attending?'

'Oh, I hadn't seen it,' I replied, smiling. 'But yes, I'll be there. Thank you.'

Later, at home, I opened the email. The thrill of Paris still clung to me, warm but fading, while a quiet unease settled deep in my gut. The agenda looked routine, just another update about the ongoing management changes. Yet something felt wrong. I couldn't name it, but I felt it all the same. To be safe, I asked my cousin M to come with me. I needed her certain presence, a second set of ears, someone grounded beside me. She agreed without hesitation. Her calm felt like a quiet promise, an unspoken assurance that whatever waited ahead, I would not have to face it alone.

On the day of the meeting, my apprehension only deepened. We arrived early and took seats at the back of the residents' lounge room. The air felt stale, the fluorescent lights harsh, their hum making the sweat on my palms feel louder. Families drifted in, filling the room with low murmurs. At the front, the staff filed into their seats, making a formal panel. Their authority pressed down on the space like a weight. My heart raced.

Then the words fell: the nursing home was closing.

It hit me like a blow to the chest. For a moment, I couldn't breathe. The room erupted with anxious whispers, sharp intakes of breath, muffled sobs of stunned families, one choked cry echoing off the walls. My throat constricted and hot tears burned behind my eyes. Cousin M's hand squeezed mine, her own tears falling freely. Despair hung in the air, thick and suffocating, as if the walls themselves had absorbed our grief. Mum's love for travel, the joy I had carried with me to Spain, now twisted into a sharp pang of guilt for leaving her behind.

The weight of the news settled over me like a heavy fog, shrouding an already uncertain future in deeper shadow. We were given a stark deadline: by March 2024, all our loved ones had to be relocated. Only a few short months remained before the facility's closure in April.

The thought of poring over brochures, touring potential homes, and questioning staff filled me with a sense of dread I could barely shake. Management tried to reassure us, promising help in securing placements for every resident, but their words felt hollow.

My greatest fear was for Mum. Her high-level care needs, especially her PEG tube feeding, made finding a suitable new home feel impossible. I pictured her fragile frame, the clouded look in her eyes, and that gentle smile that still somehow lit up a room.

The thought of uprooting her after more than 12 years in the same home, where she was known, cared for, and comforted, felt unbearably cruel. I could smell the faint blend of disinfectant and fresh laundry lingering in the halls, hear the soft chatter of nurses and bursts of laughter from other residents, and feel the familiar squeeze of her hand in mine as we walked those corridors together. To disrupt that sense of security was like tearing apart the very foundation of her world, and mine.

I threw myself into the search, determined to find a safe, caring place for her. But the reality was harsh: demand was high, vacancies were few, and placements were offered on a first-come, first-served basis. Every family was chasing the same limited opportunities, and the competition felt relentless, almost brutal. The enormity of the task pressed heavily on me, a weight I couldn't shake. But I resolved to keep going. Mum deserved nothing less.

As Christmas approached, the urgency of the situation was even heavier. I couldn't bring myself to move her during the festive season. That time was sacred, filled with love, warmth, and the traditions we held dear. To uproot her then, when stability mattered most, felt unbearable. Instead, I poured my energy into making her days as joyful and comforting as possible, surrounding her with little pleasures and familiar routines to soften the weight of the uncertainty looming over us.

The new year brought one disappointment after another. Every home I visited rejected Mum's application, insisting they didn't have the resources to meet her needs. By the third refusal, my patience had worn thin. Frustration and despair surged through me. How could it be that I, her daughter, the one who had stood by her side through every battle, could not secure a safe place for her?

Each rejection cut deep, a sting that felt intensely personal. The weight of responsibility pressed harder with every 'no,' leaving me breathless, exhausted, and hollowed out. Finally, humbled and desperate, I requested a meeting with Mum's nursing home manager. Sitting in her office, I poured out my frustrations, explaining how unsupported I felt and how quickly time was slipping away. She listened with quiet patience, her expression soft with empathy. Then, without any fuss, she pulled Mum's file towards her and began making calls.

I sat there, shoulders hunched, struggling to hold back my tears. But they came anyway, hot and unrelenting, as I gasped for composure. Meanwhile, she worked calmly, her tone steady, pen scratching across the page as she juggled calls. Every so often, she looked at me, offering a nod or a reassuring smile.

Finally, she ended one call with a warm, 'Thank you so much. See you soon.' Turning to me, she said gently,

'The resident representative from TH in Botany is on her way. If you can wait just five minutes, they have vacancies, and she's available to meet with you today.'

For the first time in weeks, a flicker of hope stirred within me. The crushing weight of fear began to lift, just slightly. Perhaps, just perhaps, there was a way forward. Maybe we could find Mum a new home after all.

My meeting with the resident representative from TH in Botany brought an unexpected sense of calm. She reviewed Mum's medical file carefully, fully acknowledging the complexity of her high-level needs. Her warmth and professionalism immediately reassured me.

After a quick phone call to confirm availability, she told me a bed was ready, pending our decision. Relief washed over me, overwhelming in its intensity. For the first time in months, I felt the weight lift from my shoulders.

A tour of the facility only strengthened my conviction: this was the right place. The environment felt safe, the atmosphere kind, and the sunlit corridors carried echoes of the warmth I remembered from Cyprus. Hope stirred within me, quiet but insistent. I couldn't wait to tell Dad that at last we had found a home where Mum could be cared for with dignity and compassion. A transfer date was set: 1 February 2024.

That date became a bittersweet milestone. It marked the end of one chapter and the beginning of another. Mum had lived at her previous nursing home for more than a decade, and in that time the place had become a second home for all of us. As we prepared to leave, memories crowded in: Christmas lunches and Easter gatherings, birthday candles blown out with laughter, and the quieter moments when illness tested her strength. The scent of disinfectant and fresh laundry hung in the air, as it always had, but that day it carried a sorrowful edge. Even the usual sounds, the rolling of wheelchairs, the soft murmur of conversation, seemed subdued, as if the walls themselves were grieving the departures.

We had built bonds there, not only with the staff but with fellow residents and their families. Shared joys and shared grief had woven us into a kind of extended family. Saying goodbye felt like unravelling a thread that had held us together for years. Tears fell freely; the corridor echoed with sniffles and soft sobs. Each step away from that familiar place tugged painfully at me.

The following week, I visited Mum every day at her new facility, determined to ease her transition. The staff welcomed us warmly, their attentiveness and kindness reaching far beyond the practicalities of care. Watching the way they spoke to her, with gentleness, patience, and respect, brought me quiet comfort. It reassured me that she was in good hands.

I set about making her new room feel like home. Clothes were neatly arranged in the cupboard, photographs and treasured ornaments placed where she could see them. These small touches softened the clinical edges of the space, weaving in a sense of familiarity. I watched her slowly relax. Her eyes would light up at the sight of a familiar object, and her shoulders seemed to sink into the new surroundings.

With each visit, I noticed her growing more at ease. Every small sign of her comfort filled me with quiet gratitude. Mum was safe. She was cared for. And for the first time in a long while, I allowed myself to exhale.

I began to notice a faint wheeze in Mum's chest every time she drew a breath, and unease tugged at me. I went to find the registered nurse, who listened carefully before calling the doctor right away. She reassured me that Mum would be thoroughly examined. Her prompt response steadied me; it reminded me that this place truly cared for her. Still, as I waited, anxiety lingered. Even with confidence in the staff, that fear of the dark remained close.

In the days that followed, Mum's breathing eased, and I finally allowed myself to breathe too. By Wednesday, I'd finished the last touches in her room, the final photo frame hung on the wall, everything in its place. On Thursday, Dad and I visited together, settling her into the comfort of her new surroundings.

On Friday, I was working a shift at the restaurant when I called the nursing home for an update. The staff sounded cheerful. Mum was doing well. They said she'd had her morning bath and was now sitting in her tub chair, joining the other residents for the morning activities. My heart lifted at the image of her there, perhaps even smiling, surrounded by gentle company. They mentioned her back was a little sore and asked if they could put her to bed earlier than usual.

'Of course,' I said without hesitation. 'Whatever keeps her comfortable.'

♥

That evening, Sir R's soccer team was launching their Under 13 season with a presentation night. His eyes sparkled with excitement, and I couldn't stop smiling; pride swelled through me as I watched him buzzing with anticipation.

After the event, we stopped by my cousin's house just up the road. The warm aroma of coffee and sweet pastries drifted through the air, wrapping itself around the laughter and easy chatter in the room. It reminded me of the old village gatherings in Cyprus; simple, heartfelt, and filled with love.

We clustered around the dining table, sharing stories and memories while the soft glow of the lamps cast a gentle light over our faces. Time slipped by unnoticed, marked only by the clink of cups, the scraping of plates, and the tender comfort of togetherness.

As the clock struck midnight, we all jumped to our feet, cheering in the Chinese New Year. The room burst with laughter, joy, hugs, and that beautiful, familiar feeling of belonging. I carried that warmth with me as we headed home, deeply grateful for the blessing of family.

When I finally crawled into bed, exhaustion wrapped itself around me. My body ached from the long day, a dull throb at my temples, soreness in my feet, the kind of tiredness that sinks deep into your bones. I reached for two Panadol, hoping they would soften the pain, and whispered a quiet prayer as I laid my head on the pillow. The mattress welcomed me, soft and warm, my muscles loosening with a deep exhale. As sleep gently pulled me in, I prayed not just for rest for my body, but for peace in my heart.

❤

Somewhere in the depths of that fragile sleep my world was pierced by the shrill ring of my phone at 2.30 a.m. I shot upright, heart pounding wildly against my ribs as I reached for it in the darkness. The screen glowed with the nursing home's number, and in that instant, dread rushed over me cold, sharp, unforgiving.

'H-Hello?' I answered, my voice trembling. A soft, apologetic voice whispered through the phone, 'Hi Andrea...I'm so sorry to call you this hour.'

Panic surged through me. 'What's wrong?' I demanded, my voice trembling.

The words that followed hit me like a sledgehammer. 'We've gone into your mum's room for night observations...unfortunately, there are no signs of life.'

'What?' I screamed, my mind unable to grasp the weight of it.

I put the phone on speaker so Master M could hear, clinging to the fragile hope that this was some terrible nightmare. But the words pierced through my denial with brutal clarity: 'Your mum has just passed away.' The world around me shattered.

'I'm coming...I'm coming now,' I stammered, my voice cracking. In a frenzy, I threw the bedcovers to the floor; they landed with a soft, lifeless thud. I paced the room, back and forth, hyperventilating, my thoughts fragmented and scattered. I collapsed onto the bed, only to spring up moments later, my movements jerky, uncoordinated. Tears streamed down my face, blurring my vision into streaks of sorrow. I turned to Master M, my voice breaking under the weight of despair. 'How...how am I going to tell Dad?'

He drew me into his arms, a calm anchor in my storm. 'Breathe... breathe. Let's go,' he murmured, grounding me when everything inside was spinning out of control. Together, we went to Jnr A's room. Master M knocked softly and opened the door. His voice wavered as he said, 'A...it's Yiayia. She's gone.'

We told him that he needed to be ready, that we would call him when it was time to bring Pappou. I knew this night would carve a scar into his young heart.

Dad, startled by the noise, stepped out of his room. '*Ti egine?*' (What's happened?) he asked, concern already settling into the lines of his face.

I stood there, frozen. The truth sat heavy on my tongue, but I couldn't let it reach him, not yet. I needed to protect him for just a little longer. 'Papa, it's Mum...she's not well. I'm going to the nursing home to see what's happening. I'll call you.'

His trusting reply pierced straight through me. 'Okay, *koukla mou*. Drive safe.'

The streets were dark and silent as I drove, the world outside blurring through my tears. They poured unchecked, landing on my lap like cold rain. My leg shook so hard it made the seat tremble, grief coursing through me in waves that threatened to consume me.

When we arrived at the nursing home, I swiped my card with trembling hands and stepped into the quiet corridor. The residents slept on, unaware of the devastation unfolding around them. My cries echoed faintly along the sterile walls as the RN approached, her eyes heavy with sorrow. Master M walked ahead of me, gently peering into Mum's room first, trying to protect me from the first sight. But then his composure collapsed, and his tears told me everything.

At the doorway, I faltered, unwilling to believe. Yet when I entered, truth engulfed me like a tidal wave. Mum lay there peacefully, her face softened by a faint, serene smile. That sight shattered me. I tried to keep my voice low for the sake of the resident beside her, but the grief broke through anyway.

'Mum, I'm here,' I whispered, my knees giving way as I sank beside her bed. I reached for her hand; it was cold. I pressed my forehead into the sheets. 'Mummy mou,' as if calling her name might tether her back to me.

Then came the hardest call of my life. Dialling Dad's number felt like pulling the pin on a grenade. My hand trembled as the line connected.

'Papa...it's Mum.' My voice cracked, the words splintering into sobs. 'She's resting in peace now. She's not suffering anymore.'

The silence that followed was broken only by his sobs; deep, raw, and guttural, each one cutting through me like shards of glass. His grief echoed in my bones. I swallowed hard and forced out the words, though they tasted hollow on my tongue.

'Dad...get ready. A will bring you soon.'

After the call ended, I sank onto the bench outside her room. My body felt numb and my mind was spinning. Every breath felt heavy, as if grief itself pressed upon my chest. Then I heard Dad's footsteps in the corridor. Slow. Unsteady. Each one weighted with dread. When he reached me, I took his trembling hand and gently led him into her room. We walked in together, fingers intertwined, both of us already broken. At her bedside, he let go of my hand

and moved towards Mum, unstable, as though every step cost him something. His hands shook as he touched her cheek.

'She's smiling,' he whispered, his voice barely holding together.

And then it came, the rawest sound I have ever heard. A cry ripped from the deepest part of his soul, so fierce it felt as though the walls should crack, the windows should shatter, the heavens should answer by returning her. But they didn't. The cry echoed down the corridor, a haunting testament to love and loss, lingering in the quiet space she left behind.

Jnr A lingered outside, frozen, unable to step inside and face the reality that his yiayia was gone.

Inside the room, Dad gathered what little strength he had left to make the calls no one should ever have to make. His voice trembled as he told my sister, then one sibling after another, the unthinkable, each call tearing the wound open all over again.

I took a deep breath before calling Mum's sisters, trying hard to keep my voice calm even as the words broke apart. Master M reached out to our cousins, his tone firm but shaking underneath. One by one, our family began to arrive at the nursing home. Their faces were pale, their eyes wide, every expression lined with disbelief and a grief none of us were ready for.

The stillness of Mum's body became unbearable. We stepped outside to wait for the transport team, our grief heavy in the air. Master M and my cousin found hollow comfort in one cigarette after another, smoke curling into the night. In desperation, I reached into my bag for the packet I had hidden from Dad. My hands shook as I lit one.

'I'm sorry, Dad. I'm smoking in front of you, don't you dare say anything,' I muttered, my voice part defiance, part shattered. But he said nothing. He just sat there, vacant-eyed, too submerged in sorrow to notice or to care.

When the van finally arrived, my heart beat against my ribs as the team came forward with stretcher and body bag. Their calm movements made it undeniable: this wasn't a dream I could wake from. This was real.

We stood in the corridor while they prepared her, spared the sight but not the sound of zips and movement. Moments later, they wheeled her past us. My hand reached out instinctively, trembling as it met the cold, unfamiliar material of the bag that now held the woman who had given me life.

The lift felt like a tomb. The doors closed, and with them, the last thin thread of denial snapped. A cry tore from somewhere deep inside me; raw, primal.

'My Mum...my Mum!'

The sound echoed through the sterile hallway like a wound opening. Jnr A rushed to my side, tears in his eyes, yet his voice stayed steady with love.

'Mum, you're strong because Yiayia was strong. Breathe, Mum – please.'

His words, so small, steadied me enough to remain standing as I watched the van disappear into the rain, carrying my mother away.

♥

20 February 2024 – her final farewell. The day of her funeral is etched into me like a scar. I used to think black was the darkest colour a person could wear, but even that felt too faint compared to the emptiness inside my heart. The heavens themselves seemed to grieve with us. Rain poured down relentlessly, drumming against the

pavements like a sorrowful hymn, while the wind howled as though creation mourned with us.

She left us on her own terms, a final act of quiet defiance, one last reminder of her unyielding spirit. Even in death, she refused to be diminished. And as the storm raged around us, I felt as though the universe was acknowledging her strength. Each drop of rain seemed like a benediction, a final touch from her hand, a reminder that love does not end, but flows on.

Yet grief has a way of sharpening itself into anger. I remember looking around and wondering, Where were all these people when she needed them? Why did they suddenly gather now, drifting in like shadows summoned by death? Was it respect, or guilt masquerading as it? The hypocrisy stung, fuelling the ache in my chest.

The storm intensified. Thunder tore the sky apart while lightning carved the horizon into harsh, blinding flashes. The ground at the cemetery grew unstable beneath the downpour, and we were urged to proceed quickly when her coffin arrived. The turmoil of the heavens mirrored the storm within us, raw, chaotic, unrelenting.

When the boys carried Mum's coffin to its final resting place, something changed. The rain eased, as if heaven paused to grant us a breath of mercy. The priest's voice rose above the quiet; gentle, calm and resolute as he spoke the final prayers. And then came the final act: her coffin was lowered into the earth.

I bent down to toss my white rose into the grave, but grief stole the strength from my legs. I buckled, the world tilting, and Master M caught me before I could fall. His arms became a lifeline as I clung to him, shaking.

'Mum...it's not goodbye,' I whispered through my sobs. 'It's see you later. I love you. I promise I'll take care of Dad. Rest now.'

The words felt like both a vow and a surrender. Tears streamed down my face as I stared into the open grave, my heart screaming in silence, refusing to let her go, yet knowing I had no choice. In that moment, fragile and undone, I felt something change inside me. I carried both her love and her legacy within me.

As I finally released the white rose and watched it fall onto her coffin, a roar of thunder cracked through the sky. Lightning followed sharp, blinding splitting the darkness as though the heavens themselves were crying out. For a heartbeat, the world felt alive with grief, echoing ours. Then, just as suddenly, the storm gave way to a strange, unsettling calm. In that silence, I felt her presence; my mother, even in death, still searching for a way to reach me.

In the weeks that followed, I found myself suddenly afraid of the dark. Sleep eluded me, shadows stretched long into the night, and my mind refused to rest. Eventually, I sought comfort from the priest who had led her funeral. His presence felt like a warm hand on a trembling heart. His words came softly, like a balm rubbed onto a raw wound.

'I understand your fear of the dark and of death,' he said gently. 'But remember, life itself is a cycle. It is natural to seek light while you sleep. It is believed that a spirit remains on earth for forty days before ascending to heaven. Your need for light suggests your mother is with you. Do not be afraid. She is in a place of safety and peace.'

Until that moment, death had always been my deepest dread. The thought of being buried beneath the earth, trapped in eternal darkness, swallowed by the very soil that once nurtured life, felt suffocating. But the priest's voice softened the terror that had lived in me for so long.

'Do not see it that way,' he continued. 'At death, the spirit departs, and only the body returns to its origin. We arrive as dust, and we return as dust.'

His words settled into me like a warm summer breeze, easing the weight that had been pressing against me for weeks. For the first time, I began to see death not as a final ending but as a transition, a return to where we all began. And slowly, peace began to find me. I accepted that my mother's time had come, and with that acceptance came a quiet surrender. I could sleep again, no longer frozen by the fear of darkness.

But grief changed me in ways I never could have anticipated. After my mother's passing, I felt like a stranger inside my own skin. The ache was constant, echoing through my bones like the chill of winter. And yet, somewhere in that ache, a truth began to reveal itself: my longing for her had been rooted in my own need. I wanted her here for me, not for her peace. It was her time to rest, and my love had to loosen its grip and let her go.

Even now, in the quiet moments, I sometimes catch the faint trace of her perfume drifting through the room soft, familiar, like a whispered reminder that she is still nearby. Her love continues to shape me, steadying me, guiding me forward even when the path feels uncertain. When the shadows close in, I cling to those small fragments of her, and in their warmth, I find the courage to take the next step...one heartbeat at a time.

I see now that my mother's purpose was woven into every lesson she ever gave me, to teach me patience, to deepen my trust in God, and to help me stand firmly in faith through loneliness and hardship. She awakened the tenderness inside me, the same tenderness I now pour into my children.

Though our relationship wasn't traditional, her love, constant, unwavering, and unconditional, created a bond unlike any other. Her legacy lives in me. It breathes through the way I parent, the way I love, and the resilience she planted deep inside my spirit.

The Fifth Commandment has never felt more alive: 'Honour your father and your mother, that your days may be long in the land which the Lord your God is giving you.' Those words have guided me like a compass, shaping not only the way I honour my parents but also the way I treat others. It has become a value stitched into the fabric of who I am: compassion, kindness, and a willingness to serve with sincerity.

Mum, you will always live in my heart. Without you, the world feels a little emptier, and each breath carries a quiet heaviness. I miss your voice, your touch, the warmth of your presence. Visit me in my dreams, please. Lend me the strength of your warrior spirit, so I can continue walking this road with courage and love.

Still becoming

I once believed healing meant forgetting. That one day the ache would disappear, the memories would soften, and the weight I've carried for as long as I can remember would finally lift. But healing, I've learned, doesn't erase. It teaches you how to hold what remains.

My mother is no longer here in the way I once needed her to be. I no longer hold her hand, whisper prayers beside her, or feel the quiet steadiness of her presence in the room. What I do carry is something deeper – something that never left.

I carry her strength when life asks more of me than I think I can give. I carry her faith when doubt creeps in. I carry her resilience when my body, my heart, or my spirit feels tired. She lives in my posture, in my stubbornness, in my refusal to give up when things feel impossible. She lives in the way I love my children – fiercely, protectively, sometimes imperfectly, but always with everything I have. I see her in my hands, in my expressions, in the way I show up when it would be easier to give up.

For a long time, I grieved the childhood I didn't have. The softness I missed. The version of a mother I never fully knew. That grief still visits me from time to time. It always will. But it no longer defines me. What defines me now is survival with meaning.

I now understand her choices in ways I couldn't before. I understand her fight. I understand why she held on, why she persisted, why she chose life again and again – even when it came at a cost. And now, as a mother myself, I carry that understanding with respect and admiration.

This story is not about tragedy. It is about love that refused to leave. It is about faith that held firm in the darkest hours. It is about becoming someone you never planned to be, and discovering strength you didn't know existed.

I am still becoming. I am becoming softer where I once had to be hard. Stronger where I once felt small. More grounded in who I am, and less apologetic for who I am not.

If there is one thing I know for certain, it is this: nothing was wasted. Not the pain. Not the waiting. Not the unanswered questions. God was present in all of it, even when I couldn't see Him – especially then.

This book holds my past, but it does not keep me there. It stands as proof that love survives loss, that faith endures suffering, and that even through the deepest shatter, something beautiful can still emerge.

This is not the end of my story. It is where the telling pauses, but the becoming continues.

ACKNOWLEDGEMENTS

I would like to pause and acknowledge the people who stood beside me when the storm clouds rolled in – and who reminded me that even through thunder, I was still allowed to shine.

To my incredible business mentor, Skye H – thank you for believing in this story and for connecting me with the extraordinary Jennifer L. Jen, your patience chapter by chapter, your guidance through pacing and emotional arcs, and your honest, thoughtful critique shaped this manuscript in ways I could never have done alone. You held my hand when I doubted myself and reminded me I was capable when I couldn't yet see it. For that, I am forever grateful.

To Sophie and Emerald, a truly dynamic duo – thank you for walking alongside me during the editing process. Your feedback was insightful, your encouragement unwavering, and your attention to detail transformed these pages into something I am deeply proud of. The countless emails, the back-and-forth refinements, the added sparkle – I see it all, and I appreciate you more than words can say.

To the remarkable team at Hembury Books – thank you for welcoming me into your publishing home. I stepped into this world unsure and inexperienced, and you met me with professionalism, patience and heart. Jessica, Sinead and Ariba, you helped turn what once felt like a distant dream into a tangible reality. And to Alison, thank you for crossing every T, dotting every I, and ensuring everything was polished and ready for this moment.

And finally, to my family – my foundation, my strength, my why. Thank you for the nights you gave me space to write, for the dinners delayed, for the laundry left waiting, and for loving me through every emotional wave this book required.

To my husband and my children, I am nothing without you beside me. Your belief in me carried me through. I am the luckiest woman in the world to call you mine.

With all my love and gratitude

Andrea